livelifeaberdeenshire.org.uk/libraries

THIS COUNTRY BUSINESS

THIS COUNTRY BUSINESS

Tales from the Dales

Max Hardcastle

WINDSOR
PARAGON

First published 1995
by Little, Brown and Company
This Large Print edition published 2012
by AudioGO Ltd
by arrangement with
Little, Brown Book Group

Hardcover   ISBN: 978 1 4458 2707 0
Softcover   ISBN: 978 1 4458 2708 7

LP

This book is dedicated to all those men who served
in the Merchant Navy 1939–1945

British Library Cataloguing in Publication Data available

Printed and bound in Great Britain by
MPG Books Group Limited

CHAPTER ONE

'Hello, hello—anybody here?' It was a woman's voice, loud and strident and with more than a touch of pique in it.

Now, when one is painting the penis of a life-size bronze of Apollo with a mixture of sal-ammoniac, vinegar and common salt, the last thing one wants is to be interrupted by an irate woman—for it is a delicate job. A job that requires concentration and a steady hand.

Laying my brush and jam jar aside, I pushed my spectacles up my nose and peered through the dust-streaked window of the apple house.

She saw me. 'Are these your damned dogs?'

They were my dogs, two of the bonniest English Springers in the Yorkshire Dales.

'Yes, madam,' I replied, rather meekly, as one is apt to do in such circumstances.

'Well, they've just eaten my friggin' dinner.'

I thought it best to put on a bold front, and went out into the yard to meet her.

'I'm sorry,' I smiled.

'I was painting on the fell, and when I looked around these damned dogs were into my lunch box—scoffed the lot.'

The dogs did look guilty, edging away from the woman's fierce glare. They crawled under the barn and looked out at us with soft brown eyes.

The artist—for she was undoubtedly one, having paintbox, easel, folding stool and folio case draped about her person—was tall and thin. She was wearing sensible brogues, knee breeches and a worn and patched tweed jacket. At her throat was a blue silk scarf pierced with a fine cameo brooch, and on her head one of those enormous, black floppy-brimmed hats that were much favoured by the intelligentsia in the nineteen thirties. I have tried unsuccessfully over the years to buy such a hat.

Her face was thin, with an unhealthy yellowness, her eyes a very cold grey. She was, I estimated, well into her sixties.

'I must apologise for the dogs. They are well cared for but greedy animals. Would you allow us to make amends? We live simply, but I'm sure my wife could rustle you up something.'

'It was nothing fancy. Just cheese and bread.'

She began to divest herself of her trappings, laying them carefully on the apple house steps. Refusing my invitation to sit in the kitchen whilst sandwiches were being prepared for her, she wandered across to the orchard and started making a fuss of the goat.

Vicky is adept at sandwich making, and soon a neat round onion stood beside a pile of rough cut homebaked bread liberally interlayered with best Wensleydale cheese.

'Think that's enough?' she asked.

'The old girl's as thin as a lat, but sometimes that type can eat like a horse.'

A slice of curd tart was laid on top of the pile.

'Good God man, are you out to feed the five thousand? That'll keep me for two days.'

'Yes, well, we felt you'd been inconvenienced.'

She broke off the corner of a sandwich and strutted back to the apple house.

'Look here, couldn't help noticing what you were

2

doing—mind if I have a look?'

I followed her into the cool, dingy apple house. We stood in silence, she chewing vigorously, before the statue of Apollo. Very slowly she began to walk around it, her sandwich clutched to her chest, her steel-heeled brogues clicking on the cobbled floor.

'It's magnificent—really magnificent. Is it signed?'

'No, but it's nineteenth century French school.'

She wiped a crumb of cheese from the corner of her mouth with an immensely long index finger, then wagged the finger at Apollo.

'I think it's earlier. No matter, it's a fine piece. But tell me, how did he acquire such gleaming genitals when the rest of the splendid fellow is so richly patinated?'

'My fault I'm afraid. For safety I laid him down in the van. Unfortunately I had a Chesterfield in at the same time, and it broke loose from its moorings. Every time I braked or accelerated it passed over that part of the poor chap's anatomy, making it shine like a brass button in a chimney sweep's navel. Shame, he was all so nicely patinated.'

'What are you doing it with?' she asked, picking up the paintbrush. When I told her, she gave a loud 'Bah,' and called me a silly man.

'What you need is some copper acitate on there—nothing like it for bringing up that nice green.'

The sandwiches were stuck into the crook of Apollo's arm, the artist's gear safely stowed in the barn, and off in the van to Lalbeck we went, in search of copper acitate.

Like many middle-class women of mature years, she felt free to question constantly, but she did it in such a charmingly guileless way, and in such a beautifully modulated voice, that I felt no pain in bearing my soul.

Yes, the antique shop on the green was ours. Yes, I did come originally from the West Riding. We had two children, Sally and Peter, a goat and a pony, and we found the Dales people friendly.

By the time Mr Jones had found us some copper acitate she knew all about me, my family and my business, and I knew but little about her.

'Stir it well,' she advised, as I carefully tapped the blue-green powder into my mixture. She retrieved her sandwiches from the beautifully formed arm of Apollo, and seated herself on a straw bale.

'Did you pay a lot for it?' she asked, as I gently applied the new mixture to the glistening parts.

'Not mine. Bought it in for a friend, Otto Denk. Have you heard of him?'

'No. I lead a very secluded life, really. I get myself off my bottom two or three times a year and take off on a little painting trip.'

'Been in the Dales before?'

'Yes, we spent our honeymoon here, before the war.'

'You'll have noticed many changes, then.'

'Yes—and that many things are unchanged.'

She took out a small, silver pocket knife, and began to peel the onion, balancing the sandwiches on her thin knees. 'What you really need is to speed up the process—it's the drying action that does it. Has your wife a hair dryer?'

Vicky has, so soon I had an extension lead stretched across the yard and was playing a stream of hot air on to Apollo's genitals.

It worked very well indeed; three applications

and three dryings later there was a noticeable and gratifying dullness taking over. This is great, I thought, tomorrow I can get it up to Oriental Otto's and get paid. The rich hotel owner had been on the phone four times that week asking when I was going to deliver his statue. Otto could get very petulant, and the last thing I wanted was for him to take the huff and find someone else to buy on commission for him. The brown envelopes containing bank-fresh notes were most welcome, especially in the depths of winter when on some days the shop bell does not ring even once.

'These are good,' the woman said, cramming a sandwich into her mouth and chewing expressively. She had speared a quadrant of onion on her knife and she wagged it at me as she chewed. 'You know,' she went on when the bulge in her sallow cheeks had been reduced by lumpy swallowing, 'I've been quite ignorant. Here I am engaged with you in an intimate activity, eating your food, and you don't even know my name.'

As she stood up and brushed the crumbs from her breeches and held out a skeletal hand Fiery Frank's van burst into the yard, scattering the ducks.

She immediately turned from me and squinted out at the van, obviously taken by the scrawly paint—red and white signwriting that had run on its rusty sides.

'What a stunning effect,' she mumbled, 'could be from the hand of Picasso himself.'

When Fiery jumped from the cab, and rubbing his hands approached us with his renowned worldwide grin, our artist was visibly stirred. When he came into the apple house, slapped Apollo's thigh and turning to face her asked: 'And who is this fascinating little minx?' she was beside herself.

Her tongue searching around her yellow teeth, her once dull eyes now glistening with interest, she walked slowly around the little Lancastrian dealer.

'She's an artist,' I explained.

'So am I—in a way,' Fiery replied, with a wink.

'I must paint this man,' she said glancing briefly at me. 'I must paint this man.'

I carried a bale of straw out into the yard and on her instructions set it alongside the goat house. She sat Fiery on it and teased his neckerchief into a more flamboyant arrangement and turned the fob of his watch chain so it didn't catch the sun. With flicks of her comb she gave his hair a wild and unkempt look.

She narrowed her eyes and tilted her head. 'Perfect. But I'll never get that mouth right—and that waistcoat, such a bright scarlet, I'll have to tone that down.'

She worked in watercolours, heightening them with gouache, and she worked at an incredible speed.

By the time the children rushed home from school for lunch she had finished Fiery and was seated on the green, her hat tilted against the sun, sketching our house and shop.

She refused to sell the portrait, stating baldly that on principle she never sold anything. I would dearly have liked it for she had caught the ebullient little man perfectly. The humorous line of his generous mouth looking as if it were poised to break into one of his infectious grins, the mischievous twinkle in his eyes; his cockiness, the way he held his head.

It was reminiscent of the gypsy portraits by

Augustus John, unfussy and with strong, dramatic lines. Fiery was well pleased with it. He stood it on the apple house steps and, shoving his thumbs deep into his waistcoat pockets, grinned at it.

'She's no mug is she? I like it, guv, I do like it.'

All thoughts of business were put aside as we traipsed out on to the green to watch her at work. She had acquired quite a crowd of watchers: Rabbit Joe, old Mr Hall, Charlie from the pub, Baz our village Jack-of-all-trades and master of most.

She was washing a pen-and-ink sketch with colour, swift deft strokes transforming the flatness; giving it depth and texture. We watched in silence, a semi-circle of rustic connoisseurs.

When she had finished she lifted it from the easel and held it at arm's length. Cocking her head, she stared at it, giving an occasional tiny grunt.

Baz was the first to speak. 'Look,' he said, 'she's even got yer cat in.'

We craned forward, and then with a chorus of 'ayes', and a ripple of nodding heads we confirmed that she had indeed got, 'the most beautiful cat in the world', in.

To my delight she handed the sketch over her shoulder to me. 'There you are, a little reminder of me. I've had a lovely afternoon.' She started to pack away her things, refusing offers of help with a wave of her hand. 'What time is the next bus up the Dale? I'm booked into Stone House Hotel.'

We shook our heads in unison. 'No more buses today, Missus,' Rabbit told her in a lugubrious voice.

Spontaneity is not a usual trait in an antique dealer of many years standing, but my idea found immediate favour, if not with Baz, then with the rest of the crowd. If our well-muscled handyman would give me a hand with Apollo, we would take it up to Otto's and then deliver our artist to the Stone House on the way back.

I do not know the specific gravity of bronze but as I grunted and puffed out of the apple house with Apollo's perfect legs in my arms, I resolved that one day I would look it up.

Baz is strong, very strong—and he can lift. I have seen him walk along the ridge of a barn, a stone flag weighing over a hundredweight under each arm, but even he sweated and groaned as he shuffled along with the Greek God's splendid head cradled in his hands.

'Haven't these buggers heard of aluminium?' he asked, as we slid the statue carefully along the van floor.

Our artist peered at Apollo's dull and green creased genitals, and gave a smile of approval. 'Do you know something?' she laughed, 'all you men here have probably never noticed something about your very own anatomies. The left testicle always hangs slightly lower than the right one.'

Rabbit scratched his head. Baz thrust his hands into his pockets, then withdrew them quickly. Old Mr Hall looked flabbergasted, Charlie from the pub slightly embarrassed; and Fiery laughed a deep, chest-heaving, laugh.

'It's true. It's the first thing I always look for in any representation of the male nude, be it statuary or drawing. If that's not right, nothing else is—believe me, I studied at the Slade.'

There we stood, five men, examining a male statue and being lectured on the intricacies of our own bodies by a woman. She was supremely

8

confident. But being of a doubting nature—a common trait in my trade—I resolved to make it the subject of a little investigation, along with the specific gravity of bronze.

I wedged Apollo carefully, packing rolled blankets under his buttocks and arms, for I had no wish to injure or indeed brighten any other part of his splendid body.

Otto was getting restless and we were low in funds again; the brown envelope was badly needed.

Baz was subjected to the same intense questioning that I had been on the trip to Lalbeck. I had to interrupt our artist quite brusquely as we swept into Otto's drive, to point out the coachhouse which housed the Deusenberg and the Rolls Royce.

Otto came out to greet us, his old English Mastiff at his side.

'Welcome. Where is my beautiful Greek god?' he called in his throaty, broken accent. The dog bounded towards us, causing Baz and me to recoil, but our artist showed no fear. She knelt, and taking its huge head in her hands, kissed its wrinkled forehead. 'Cerberus knows,' Otto laughed.

We stood Apollo on a blanket and dragged him across the marble floor to the conservatory.

'A fitting place for the god of light and beauty,' Otto chuckled as we shuffled him alongside the grand piano.

'Very fitting,' the lady added, 'for he was also the god of music you know.'

Otto took her hands in his. 'You, my dear lady, are—let me see—a musician? No, an artist.'

'Bang on,' she laughed, 'but paint-stained fingers are a bit of a give away.'

Baz pulled at my sweater. 'Come on, let's be off.

9

I've a darts match tonight.'

But we could not be off until I had the little brown envelope. That was not produced until Otto and the artist had laughed and joked together, admired the view from the terrace, and made arrangements for her to go the following day to—as Otto put it—'paint to her heart's content'.

We dropped her off at the Stone House after hurriedly piling her things in the magnificent foyer and shaking the thin hand.

Life, the philosophers tell us, is a journey of discovery, but search as I did I could not find, amongst our large collection of books, anything about bronze other than that it was an amalgam of tin and copper.

Perhaps I should have persevered more, but a stone-built Dales farmhouse is a chilly place to potter about in dressed solely in a bathrobe; even in September.

I lay in bed and looked at the sketch of our house and shop, smiling as I remembered the wreck it had been when we bought it two years ago and how Baz had thrust his unshaven face through the window and asked if we wanted a hand.

Pushing my head back into the pillows I closed my eyes. They had been two marvellous years, and today had not been bad either. An interesting character, a sketch of our house, a little brown envelope from Otto—and one of life's great truths revealed.

Vicky was shuffling things on the top of the dressing table.

'Psst,' she whispered, testing to see if I was still awake, 'have you seen my handmirror?'

CHAPTER TWO

Long John hates using the telephone. It is therefore a course of action he only takes when absolutely forced to. It is understandable, for the nearest phone is two miles from his isolated farm, in the middle of the triangular green at Harts Leap. This is a tiny hamlet of two farms and three cottages; and in one of those cottages lives Ada, the newsiest woman in the Dale. When anyone enters the phone box her mongrel dog invariably feels the need for a walk, and Ada invariably takes him across the green so he can cock his leg against the brave red box. There are people who maintain that she salts the dog's food so it consumes large quantities of water but the infrequency with which the phone box is used lends no credence to such a tale.

Her presence is tolerated by all but the adolescents, for in the nature of things they have more secrets than others. In fact most welcome her attendance for she always has some small change about her person and acts as a very reliable checker of facts.

When Long John bellowed down the phone that he would pop in and see us on Thursday after the sale of store lambs in Lalbeck, I could hear Ada tap on the glass, then her whispered voice, 'T'sale is on Wednesday John, not Thursday.'

And so late on Wednesday afternoon Long John's van clattered into the yard. He had done well at the lamb sales, but he was still not a happy man, for once again he had fallen into his pine-stripping tank.

11

'I've made me mind up—it's goin',' he said, folding his arms and leaning his long frame against the barn. 'When that little fella comes over from Lancashire again tell him it is for sale. Cheap.'

'John,' I said gently, 'do you think it's wise to resort to the bottle before you start stripping? I mean the old Swaledale Lightning tends to blunt one's judgement.'

He glared at me. 'Wise! What's wise got to do wi' it? If you went out and stripped pine all day in that cold miserable hole, you'd want a little libation to keep yer going.'

That I thought was true, for the enormous tank was housed in a dingy, stone-floored barn, its windows sheeted over with tin. No ray of warming sun ever penetrated that clammy, dismal building.

'You've finally decided?'

'Aye. Last year I fell in six times, year before that four, an' so far this year—what is it now, September?'

'Yes.'

'I've fallen in seven. Things is definitely gettin' worse—it'll have to go.'

'It's a big tank, John.'

'Aye, it'll suit yon little fella—he's been after one for some time.'

He turned his head and spat expertly into the beck.

'What's it worth, you reckon?'

'Hard to say. It's so big, it'll take some moving.'

'Aye, it's a good tank. See what you can get for it.'

Half sliding into the van he searched under a pile of straw and old rope, and bringing out a bottle of Swaledale Lightning he held it out with a grin.

12

'See what yer can do.' And with that he dragged his long legs into the van, slammed the door and drove off.

Swaledale Lightning varies enormously in quality. A period of rain washes down acidy peat from the tops, and we have a decidedly brown liquor with a creosote-like bouquet. A mash goes really well, the water it's boiled in as clear as crystal, and we have a spirit that rivals vodka in its clarity and beats methylated spirits for potency. We never drink it. It brightens copper, and is most effective in cleaning lichen from the stone flag path, but since my first and only brain numbing, disorientating, and distressing mouthful of liquid fire I innocently took from a tin cup, most of it goes down the drain.

But this looked a good bottle, clear as crystal, with no sediment to speak of; and there are men in the Dale who would look askance at the tragic waste of it. So I tucked it into the little niche in the apple house wall where I keep my Stockholm tar and Jeyes fluid.

In my role as honest broker, I rang Fiery Frank and asked him how much he would give for a splendid and capacious stripping tank. He was enthusiastic, but full of questions: how big was the tank? how thick the metal? was there any corrosion?

Memory plays tricks with us. I had seen the tank many times and I knew it would easily accommodate two wardrobes and a couple of chests of drawers with the odd door or two stuck down the sides—but for the thickness of metal, and the corrosion.

'I know I'm buying a pig in a poke here, but offer him fifty quid,' Fiery said finally.

13

Honest brokerage, as I found out, necessitates a certain amount of travel. Up the rough track to Long John's I went; three times in all, as the price was upped from fifty to sixty. Then John finally stated, somewhat petulantly, that he would give it away for sixty-five. Fiery agreed it was a good buy, then after a long pause on the phone added that he would have it, if I would give him a hand. No way would the tank fit into my van. 'We'll have to cut it in two,' Long John groaned. Fiery reluctantly agreed, and the cattle dealer set off to borrow some oxy-acetylene cutting gear whilst Fiery and I drained the tank and sieved through the sludge.

We found nothing of value; many chicken bones, an assortment of handles, bits of moulding and the top half of a set of false teeth.

Long John rinsed the teeth under the tap and inspected them carefully.

'None the worse, they aren't,' he said, wrapping them in his handkerchief. 'She'll be glad to get these back.'

Diligent questioning failed to reveal who *she* was, but we all knew the bachelor had of late advertised for a wife, and had entertained several prospective ones up at the lonely farm. The giant tank, with its walkway of scaffolding planks, was always on the agenda of any tour of the farm, so we smiled to ourselves and drew our own conclusions.

The tank was measured and neat chalk lines drawn down its sides. Long John lit the cutter from his cigarette and, peering at the hard blue flame, adjusted knurled knobs until it almost disappeared, the resultant hiss sending his geese squawking off up the ghyll. He squatted on a milking stool, his goggled eyes intent as glowing metal shrank from

14

the flame and dropped in red gobbets about his feet to sizzle amongst the cobbles.

He was quick and accurate and soon the tank settled gently in the middle as the sides were cut through.

'I'll have a cig, then I'll cut through the bottom.' He winked at me and gently poked a finger into Fiery's waistcoat. 'Think them Lancashire men'll be able to weld it up watertight?'

Fiery Frank thought so. 'Anyway,' he added, 'watta's a bit thicker on't right side of the Pennines.' He had borrowed Ted's trailer to move the tank; a long, low, green and black homemade job, with artillery spoked wheels and wood sides pulpy with age.

Long John's smoke breaks are not hurried affairs. A pot of brackish tea, two or three cigarettes, a discourse on the hill subsidy or the relative merits of Marans and Light Sussex; they last at least half an hour.

I left him and Fiery in the dingy barn and walked through his farmyard and up the ghyll.

Polly, his Dales pony, lifted her head from the sparse pasture and ambled towards me. She was getting old, and in the harsh environment of the upper Dale, age is a burden that is borne very visibly.

Her bottom lip hung loose, her coat was matted and lacklustre, mane and tail were unkempt. Her pelvic bones were thrust up like those of an old milk beast, and as she picked her way over the rough ground her lameness was very noticeable. I brushed the tangled forelock away from her sad brown eyes and stroked her white blaze and whiskery muzzle. She had had a hard life earning her keep jagging

15

hay on to the fell tops, bringing new-born lambs down in panniers and dragging manure out to be scaled over Long John's precipitous bit of in-bye land.

The leaves of the silver birches which clustered up the side of the ghyll were already turning. That brilliant pointillist, Autumn, was already dabbing light brown, beige and taupe amongst the sage greens and the soft greys. Thistles stood out from the close cropped grass, withered and black, and every leaf on the patches of nettles was edged with ochre. The elders were curling their leaves and taking on a pink blush, bunches of jet black berries hanging on bent stalks like sleeping bats.

The breeze that whispered down off the tops was fresh and had that tinge of dankness about it which chills the cheek and warns us that winter is just wiping his feet before he marches into the Dale.

It would be a hard winter for the pony; probably her last.

'Aye, she's knackered,' Long John said emphatically, flicking his cigarette end to sizzle out in the tank bottom. 'She's rising eighteen. She's just gone down this back end.' There was a catch in his voice as he saw the pony limp into the yard, its head drooping, its unshod hooves slithering on the cobbles.

'Come on, let's be at it.' John picked up the cutting torch and, climbing into the tank, clicked the lighter. 'You two get some planks sorted out and back the trailer up.'

Fiery and I pushed the trailer up to the barn door and chocked the wheels. The tank would overhang each side, and as the trailer woodwork was none too sound, we decided to reinforce it. We

16

were nailing on the second batten when there was an ear-piercing shriek from the barn followed by a heartfelt, groaned obscenity, several loud gasps and the clatter of metal on metal.

Fiery's hammer went flying as Long John burst through the barn door and leaping over the trailer made giant and erratic hops down the yard, smoke pouring from his left boot. Every hop brought a half yelled, half gasped exclamation.

'Hell! Bloody! Fire! Jesus Bloody Christ!'

He plunged the smoking boot into the horse trough, and raising his eyes to heaven he let his jaw drop open and lowered himself to sit gently on the cold stone.

'Hell's bells,' he said quietly and with great feeling, 'set me bloody boot on fire.'

There is something farcical about a burn. Trap a finger, cut it, pierce it with a needle or a nail and we get sympathy and a show of concern. But sustain a burn of equal magnitude and all we get is some trite and unfeeling comment and a grin. ('Is it heavy?' they smile, as we drop the hot baking tin.)

We ran to Long John and, unable to resist a grin and guffaw, asked if he was all right. He withdrew his dripping boot and gingerly prised the sole from the upper, revealing a ring of charred sock and a startlingly pink piece of foot.

'Hell's bells. I got to thinking about poor old Polly and me torch wandered.'

'Polly, is that the woman the teeth belong to?' Fiery asked innocently.

'Stuff off,' Long John mumbled into his beard as he gently touched the area of startling pink.

The first half of the tank traversed the Pennines without incident. The second came adrift in the lea

17

of Buckden Pike, and was manhandled back on to the trailer by a troop of venture scouts delighted to be confronted with a real-life initiative test.

Before he'd left I had pressured Fiery into parting with the sixty-five pounds for Long John. When he had reluctantly counted the money out on to the kitchen table, I held out my hand expectantly and smiled, for after all I had wasted the best part of two afternoons helping him.

'Bit tight at the minute, guv'. But I'll see you all right,' he said.

It transpired that the 'seeing all right' was to be a load of logs. He had done a house clearance, and in the back garden had been a shed crammed with seasoned logs.

'Mainly ash,' he had confided happily as I pressed the unwanted bottle of Swaledale Lightning into his hands. 'When I bring the trailer back I'll fill it. There'll be the best part of a ton of good dry logs—mainly ash.'

We all know the jingle about ash—wet or green, fire fit for a queen—so I waited confidently and happily for his return, and bribed the children into cleaning a corner of the lean-to ready to receive them. Logs that are dry deserve to be kept dry.

Visitors always arrive when you are in a mess—it's a law of nature. The junk from the lean-to was stacked against the apple house, and the kitchen table and floor were covered with the remnants of a house clearance when the Snows called.

Dr and Mrs Snow had told us when we bought Topic from them: 'Put her to a good stallion and you'll have no trouble selling the foal.' They were right. The young filly, coal black and without a touch of white about her apart from her tiny star, was an absolute beauty and attracted many a would-be buyer.

Long John wanted to buy her; Apple Tom, the gypsy, wanted to buy her, and so did half a dozen others. She was an affectionate and intelligent pony, and we were determined she would go to a good home—so we varied the asking price and told blatant lies.

To Long John, who would be kind to the pony but work her hard, we harped on about her impeccable pedigree and asked a price that made the bachelor cough. To Apple Tom, who would break her into the shafts and sell her on at Appleby Fair to end up God knows where, we said she was sold.

'To a man from Abu Dhabi,' we lied. 'He's coming for her in a month or two.' It is a good ruse, Abu Dhabi; nobody questions you further in case you ask them where it is.

The Snows had looked at Starlight before, and had been taken with her, but their yard was full and we had asked a heavy price. But, as I pointed out to Vicky as I swung the kettle into the fire, this time they had brought their horse box, and that was a good sign.

I trotted Starlight around the yard for them and brought her to rest with her forefeet on the banking, showing off her strong forequarters and well-boned legs.

'She's too dear,' Dr Snow said, somewhat cheerfully.

'She's beautiful,' his wife added, coming to stroke her.

I like a bit of bargaining; pipe drawing well, a good wall to lean on, the daily happenings of the

19

village being played out in the tail of one's eye. But the Snows didn't.

'Throw in a dozen fresh eggs and we'll have her,' the good Doctor joked.

'You can come and see her whenever you like,' Mrs Snow said, bending to wipe a tear from Sally's eye. Peter put on a brave face and coaxed the filly up the ramp into the horse box, pushing his head against her and whispering a farewell as he tied her up.

We stood in the yard and watched them drive off, our sadness at losing the bright and lovable pony tempered by the fact that we would still have contact with her, and that she was going to the best possible home.

As the horse box disappeared behind the chestnut trees on the Lalbeck road, Fiery's van appeared round the bend by the maypole field, Ted's trailer behind it. It was sheeted over, the green tarpaulin flapping wildly.

'Here come the logs,' I cried, rubbing my hands together.

Fiery drove into the yard with a flourish, and grinned broadly.

'One bringer-in is worth two takers-out,' he shouted as he jumped from the cab.

The children ran and unfastening the tarpaulin ropes threw it back. We all stared into the trailer in disbelief. The pulpy floorboards were gone completely, one solitary log was jammed across one corner. I took it out and turned it in my hands, inspecting it carefully.

'Yes, Fiery, it's undoubtedly ash—and dry, and well seasoned.'

Fiery leaned over the trailer and clicked his

20

tongue.

'Honestly guv', there was the best part of a ton of logs in there when I set off.'

I carried the log into the kitchen and put it on top of the delft rack.

'That's for Christmas Eve; anybody burn that log before then and I'll kill 'em.'

Fiery showed all the penitence of a snake oil salesman when confronted with a tenacious wart he'd failed to cure.

'Honest, it wor full to the top. Best logs in England, sheeted 'em up well I did. Thought—this bloke's helped me enormously, so I'll keep these logs good an' dry for him.'

He had seated himself, as usual, on the milking stool, his short legs thrust together in front of him, his Norfolk jacket buttoned high, Paisley neckerchief carelessly tossed over his shoulder.

Sally put her arm around him and archly slipped her hand down his coat and taking his gold hunter out of the pocket of his scarlet waistcoat she began to wind it up. Fiery watched her and happily clicked his tooled leather cowboy boots together. The watch was a repeater and its tinny little chimes never failed to bring a smile to the child's face.

'Tank all right?' I asked him.

'Fine guv', up and functioning.'

Vicky noticed it when Fiery put his watch away. 'What on earth have you done to your waistcoat, Frank?'

The bright waistcoat was Fiery's pride and joy, his trademark, his talisman. He sponged and pressed it himself, and regularly checked the security of its much coveted hunt buttons, for they were from a most prestigious pack.

21

Vicky pulled the Norfolk jacket fully open, revealing a sorry state of affairs. The lower half of the waistcoat was bleached a sickly beige, a sinuous line of sepia demarcating the pristine from the violated.

Fiery pressed his generous lips together, stopped clicking his boots and pushing his open hands between his knees he lowered his head.

'Do you know anybody who wants to buy a pine-stripping tank?' he asked in a subdued voice.

CHAPTER THREE

I don't know who said the first duty of a wine was to be red, but I am more than inclined to agree with him. Our wine buying has to be carefully undertaken, for reasons of economy and lack of knowledge.

It was, then, with some sadness that we received the news that Mr Johnson was to retire. He's a good advertisement for the trade of wine merchant—thin and sprightly, with a sharp mind at seventy years of age. Since leaving school he's been associated with the wine trade, starting as a delivery boy, then in mature years having the good sense to fall in love with the boss's daughter and marry her. He's never really expanded the business; true the wines of the antipodes and the New World now sit cheek by jowl with the products of the revered European vineyards, but the lovely shop still retains its genteel mustiness. The façade is tiny. A Georgian arch built in with door and window, the latter carrying several panes of union glass; a tiny upper window with protruding sill, a swinging jib crane rusting quietly by its side.

The interior is delightful. A cool, dimly lit cavern floored with stone flags and shelved to its whitewashed ceiling. The thick mahogany counter is wedged across one corner, and the brass till is angled to catch the light from the window. Behind the counter there is a trap door to the cellar. A hefty contraption, its worn and splintered wood framed in steel and a huge ring-pull set into one edge.

When it's raised Mr Johnson clips a rope barrier in place to protect the unwary and we are treated to a glimpse down the worn steps.

Mr Johnson descends in search of a special bottle. He doesn't switch on the cellar light until his bald head is level with the floor of the shop. If we press ourselves against the till and crane our necks we are rewarded with a wonderful sight; row upon row of dust-covered bottles nestling in their cradles, peeling whitewash laced with cobwebs, a damp floor cobbled like a stable, with a central drainage channel.

His footsteps recede, another light is clicked on. We can hear hrmphs and coughs. He doesn't hurry; he lifts a bottle or two from the cradles, gently turning them in his hands. He climbs the steps and wipes the dust from the bottle, then his hands, smiles, and shows it to us. He whispers the price almost inaudibly, as if money is an unwelcome intrusion. How can you put a price on that 1906 Madeira which has lain in the end bin since he first donned the long fringed smock and pushed the delivery bike out of its shed?

The big till no longer feels the jab of his thin

23

fingers, no longer gives the cheery jangle that hints of many ingenious levers and mechanisms and shoots elegant flags into its window space; clean black numerals, large and understood by all. He's electrified now, a sharply angled slab of plastic peeps and whirrs and ejects a paltry, badly printed ticket we screw into our pocket.

Mr Johnson will write out a receipt if we request one. These we fold and put in our wallets, for they are worthy of our respect. Wine merchants since 1840 we are told, but the premises are much older than that. They have been a slaughterhouse, hence the drainage channel. 'They used to kill down there and sell up here,' he'd told us. 'Have a look down the side when you go out—there's a small door and a ramp they used to drag the beasts down.'

It's much better as a wine shop. No bleatings of frantic beasts, cursings of herders and slaughterers, no stench of blood and entrails, just quiet gentle mustiness.

'And it is all to go,' the Colonel has told us. 'Pity after all these years. Knows what he's at, Mr Johnson.'

We noted the 'Mr'. All other tradesmen are Jones or Brown, but the Mr is due to the wine merchant, his deep knowledge—like his elegant receipts—commands respect.

I had seen the Colonel's Bentley come back from Lalbeck, the boot lid tied down over the protruding crates. Completely missing the import of the thing, I'd idly mused over a mental calculation as I unloaded the van. How many bottles of vintage port can you get into the boot of a Bentley R1?

There's one thing I became aware of the next day: it's a sufficient number to make Dolly's legs

24

ache carrying them down the cellar.

'Fussy as hell he is,' she complained, 'won't do here—too draughty—won't do there—too damp. You'd think it was the damned elixir of life he's storing down there.'

'It is,' I told her, and went to waylay the Colonel. 'You know something we don't?' I asked, fully anticipating being told we were on the brink of World War Three. It was then he informed me of Mr Johnson's forthcoming retirement. We had had a good summer. The overdraft had been whittled down a bit, the shop was well stocked and Vicky's egg money filled the lidless teapot to its brim.

'How about investing in a little wine?' I had judged my moment carefully. After skilfully washing up, I'd plumped the cushions in her Windsor chair, flung her shoes into the corner and eased warm slippers on to her feet.

Vicky pulled her sewing bag on to her knee and gave me a quizzical look. 'How can you invest in wine? You end up drinking it.' There were many who disagreed with her, and I told her so. She threaded her needle. 'The kids want new shoes and I need . . .'

I pressed a finger to her lips and knelt before her. 'Man cannot live by bread alone—we work hard, we deserve some of the better things in life.'

'There are plenty of things I'd rather spend money on.'

'Just a bit,' I wheedled, 'a few bottles. Mr Johnson has reduced all the prices—bargains galore.'

'All right,' she finally agreed, flinging a holey sock into the fire, 'whatever you spend on wine, I spend on new clothes for the kids.'

25

It was a hard bargain, but an irrefutably fair one, so I was painstaking in my selection. Claret is a must: it's not just the fruity mellowness of a good one, it's also the name.

'Have a glass of claret. Pass me the claret jug, please,' and what springs to mind—Regency rakes, three-bottles-a-night men; elegant society ladies, polished mahogany, sporting conversations. I put a dozen bottles into the wicker basket.

'Well, that's shoes all round,' Vicky commented dryly.

Port was a new coat for Sally; Madeira a blazer and two shirts for Peter; Rioja socked, handkerchiefed and underclothed the lot of us.

It was Morton's fork all over again. Tempting wines at tempting prices, the joy of selection and purchase balanced by the horrifying prospect of squandering an equal amount of money in the clothes shops of Harrogate.

Wine, fast cars, pretty women, well patinated old oak; all have their seductive powers and in that beautiful shop, that calm epicentre of civilisation, I was seduced—and the stack of bottles grew alarmingly. Mr Johnson packed them into boxes. Fine, thin-sided wood boxes stencilled with magical names.

'May as well take these,' he said. 'We've been keeping them for years. They'll be collector's items some day, there's some good names there.'

Vicky raised an eyebrow and nudged me. 'If he's closing the shop, what about the fixtures and things. We could sell the old till—and that counter, and what about the collection of things he has on that shelf?'

Mr Johnson was willing to sell the till and

26

counter, but the articles on the high shelf he was keeping. It was understandable; the wine cradles, funnels and corking machines he had collected over the years he had a special feeling for. They were milestones in a long and loving journey.

He'd worked the wine corker down in the dingy cellar, lit then by hissing gas jets, when he had started as a boy. Even in those days the occasional horse-drawn brougham had drawn up outside, its occupant bowed into the shop to make their selection. The exciting ride up to the big house on the pony cart, helping the cellarman to carry the bottles in under the watchful eye of the butler.

'The wine racks any good?' he asked. I rubbed my chin thoughtfully. They were in oak, the wood that seems to have an affinity with wine. Cut down, they would suit a restaurant or a guest house with pretensions.

'Yes,' I replied after some reflection. The thought of potential profit, off-setting the cost of the wine, pleased me.

'What about the cellar—anything down there?'

'Better have a look.' The trap door creaked open, the wiry wine merchant clicked on the light then skipped back up the steps as the door bell jangled. 'You nip down and have a look around whilst I attend to this gentleman.'

I handed Vicky down the worn stairs. It was cool and dank in the cellar, and before our eyes could become accustomed to the gloom I flicked on the second light.

The roof was vaulted, formed from large stones and whitewashed to a thickness that blurred the work of the mason. In the walls several pockets had candles set in them, the accumulated grease of years flowing into tiny stalactites brown with age.

The bins were formed from thick pine, some empty, some harbouring no more than half a dozen bottles. A high desk rested against the wall, a cobweb-draped gas fitting above it. In one bin was a pile of wicker baskets, a little wormy but sound enough. Cluttering the cobbled ramps, down which had been forced the luckless beasts, were several barrels of varying sizes—oak, banded with iron, and sound as a bell.

'The barrels, the baskets and the desk,' Vicky smiled.

'Don't you think we could do anything with the bins?'

'No—take too long to dismantle. Stick to what's portable and saleable.'

She was right, so when Mr Johnson clattered down the steps that's what I told him. 'Barrels, baskets and desk.'

'You haven't been in here?' he grinned, and pushing open a vaulted door he led us into a side tunnel. The floor was now flagged, patched here and there with concrete, the vaulted ceiling of brick barely clearing my head. A shaft of light shone from the end of the tunnel, where two beams rose, parallel and huge, to a grating in the roof. 'Know where we are now?' asked Mr Johnson.

'Under Love Lane?'

'That's right. All the barrelage came up from Lalbeck station on a special dray. It used to take two strong men with ropes to get the barrels down here. Not only Madeira and such; we used to get barrels of whisky in those days. I remember once the dray shed a barrel of whisky cracking against the wall, and before we could get up there with ought to catch it in every kid in Lalbeck was there.' He held his hand out a yard from the floor. 'There were kids this big staggering around the town as drunk as lords.'

He tapped a long oak bench that had an iron tramway above it. 'My first job was on here, filling bottles and corking 'em. Spent hours here; used to go out when I'd finished and couldn't keep my eyes open—it was so bright outside, old Winterton would only let you bottle by candlelight. "Soft and gentle wi' wine," he used to say, "soft light and gentle hands."'

Vicky kicked gently at the ranks of stone bottles that stood under the bench. 'What about these, Mr Johnson?'

'Aye they can go—everything's to go.'

They were gallon and two-gallon bottles, the names of old Lalbeck grocers around their fat shoulders. 'Lapwater', 'Shuttleworth', and the delightful 'Lamb and Daughter', all warning us that the bottles remained their property; an edict we felt we could safely ignore after half a century.

The door bell announced another customer, and Mr Johnson hurried off. We welcomed being left alone again, for it gave us a chance to work out some prices. We view sales together, discuss our bids late into the night, revise them over breakfast, modify them whilst milking the goat and finalise them as Vicky hands the flask of tea into the van.

We wrote out a list and priced each item. Mr Johnson thought them acceptable, raising his eyes only over the stone bottles—he'd thought they were worthless. The shop was closing when Saturday's trading was over, so we agreed to collect the stuff Sunday morning. 'I'll need help with the barrels,' I told Mr Johnson.

'Don't fret, I can manage 'em—been shoving 'em around all me life—be here at nine, I have to get away because I'm reading the lesson,' he answered with a twinkle in his eye.

Saturday was a day I would prefer to forget. A perfectly good October day, starting with a nip in the air and getting out into pale sunshine with just enough breeze to send the odd dried beech leaf clicking down through the branches. But a day of outgoings of the kind that make a shopkeeper groan.

A bill for the van and one for the electric, Gwen in the shop all day, and the entire family off to buy clothes.

Vicky and Sally were in their element; so much to spend, so many shops. Peter and I trudged after them, sat on uncomfortable chairs, breathed the fetid air of shop after shop, carried the parcels and had opinions dragged out of us that we were completely unqualified to give. 'Is this too loud? does this match that? is this too much?—what do you think?' We said yes and no, and that it was all right; and as the day dragged on I'm afraid I grew a little tetchy.

Equanimity restored by a visit to the best teashop in England for a drop of broken orange pekoe and a plate of fat rascals, we returned to the fray.

'Just the shoes now,' Vicky confessed with a weak smile as she pushed the bags on to my arms.

I quite like the smell of shoe shops but their chairs are invariably uncomfortable, and there is always a wealth of mirrors. Not only do we feel dishevelled and footweary, we see ourselves dishevelled and footweary, from every possible angle, and in an unflattering light.

I slumped in the chair, a dejected heap, parcels stuck around me like limpets on the hull of an old ship, and watched the circle of shoes under consideration grow like a fairy ring.

There must be a scale of acceptability of shops: wine at the very apex, shoe in the very pits. Vicky and Sally would reverse that order. Their faces shine with eagerness and zeal; the right fit, the right shape, the right colour—price is of little consideration today.

Peter and I mumbled approval when the three-quarter heels in black were paraded for our benefit. I reached out and lazily retrieved the box. 'Good God—how much?' And that for two pieces of flimsy leather stitched over a sole no thicker than a kipper's skin. I could have two pairs of workboots for that; a decade of wellingtons.

But it is Vicky's day and it is long overdue. For two years we have ploughed every penny we could spare back into the business.

We've made do and mended long enough; we're 'splashing out,' as Rabbit is apt to do when he's had a little inside information at the flapper track in Stockborough.

It was getting dark when we finally sought out the van, tired, burdened like packmules and as hungry as jackals.

Peter ran ahead and pulled the plastic bag from the wiper blade—I'd got a parking ticket.

I poured the tawny port into the pewter wine funnel and watched it spread a rubiginous fan against the side of the decanter. Tawny is a wine for reflection, an autumnal wine, mellow with a gentle fragrance; a soother away of aches and cares. This

31

one had leached away its colour, then matured to perfection in that cool cellar at Lalbeck.

The stock fed and locked up for the night, a pile of logs in the hearth, 'the most beautiful cat in the world' perched on the milking stool, the sounds of the village muted by a heavy mist, the dogs snoring under the table—and the tawny, mellow and seductive. Such nights pass quickly.

I've barely got the Gainsborough portrait out of the attic, hardly had time to brush the cobwebs from the Ming vase before Vicky is nudging my legs with her knee. 'Come on, up to bed, you've the wine shop to clear in the morning.'

*　　　*　　　*

Mr Johnson was a little depressed. Neat and brown-smocked he turned the key in the lock as Lalbeck church clock struck nine.

I loaded the heavy old till then together we carried out the counter and slid it into the van. All the racks were now bare of bottles, his collection of wine antiques had disappeared, and there was an air of sadness about the place.

The cellar seemed colder than before, colder and damper. Mr Johnson may have lost a little of his agility, but he was still a wiry man, manhandling the desk up the stairs by himself whilst I carted baskets and stone bottles.

'We'll have the side door open for the barrels,' he declared, drawing the huge blacksmithed bolts. We pushed the barrels up the cobbled ramp together, letting them clatter and yaw into the waste patch alongside the shop. Mr Johnson grabbed a rope that hung alongside the door, and

32

hauling himself up the ramp, he beckoned me to follow him. We pushed our way through chest-high weeds, now browning and brittle, to the bottom of the tiny yard where stood two pigsties.

'Look in there.' I did as I was told. Both sties were piled high with empty bottles. Mr Johnson leaned over the wall. 'I wouldn't like to think how much money they represent. They have been there since the war. You know I showed you the grating at the end of the tunnel?' I nodded. 'Well, there was an ARP bloke who found out how to get the grating up from the outside. Every night he was on duty he used to nip down and filch a couple of bottles, and fling the empties in here. Me and the father-in-law rooted through them one day. And do you know, that fella developed a very fine palate over the years.'

He leaned over the wall and picked up a bottle. 'These on top were 1935 Cabernet Sauvignon—God knows what they would fetch today.' He flung the bottle back on to the heap. 'Collector's stuff.' He sighed and shook his head. 'It's a sad day.'

'Couldn't you have sold it as a going concern?'

'No! These last few years it's hardly made owt. I'd have kept on, but the missus isn't well. I'll still go around giving me talks, keep drawing a cork or two.'

'Bit of good stuff tucked away?'

He laughed. 'You could say that. Come on, let's get these barrels shoved on.' Lalbeck clock was striking twelve as he locked the door and climbed into the van, a chinking cardboard box under his arm. 'Here,' he said, pulling a bottle from it, 'red Bordeaux, Château Haut Brion 1970. Just two left—we'll have one apiece.'

I know when Rabbit wants something; there is a certain way he slumps against the wall and stares at his boots. I was right, for as soon as I jumped out of the cab I received a big grin, a hurried query about my health, and then a request to borrow my footpump.

'Give me a lift with this first, Rabbit,' I said, throwing open the rear doors.

'It's the bottling bench.'

'That's it—bottled its last.'

'Shame, terrible shame.'

We carried the bench under the barn and then I took the bottle of wine I had been given and set it on the apple house steps whilst I searched for the footpump.

Rabbit picked it up, and cradling it in his big hands he stared at the label. 'Château Haut Brion—red Bordeaux—an' a good year. Won't have reached its peak yet; ought to be put by for a year or two.'

'You seem to know your stuff, Rabbit.'

He took the footpump from me, gave me a cursory nod and shuffled off home.

I waited until Ted had chivied the last cow into the Alma, then went and leaned alongside him on the gate.

'Ted, was Rabbit ever in the ARP?'

'Aye, funny enough it wor the only thing he stuck at. Tried his hand at all sorts when the war started—fire service, LDV, firewatching, but he really took to that ARP job.'

34

CHAPTER FOUR

'We'll make something special,' Vicky said, as she took the big casserole dish out of the cupboard. I hung the milk can on its hook and nodded my agreement. It was Sunday, and Lalbeck church bells could be clearly heard, for it was a cold, sharp morning.

'We're having duck,' I said, suddenly remembering the plump Muscovy drake I'd plucked and dressed the previous night.

'Yes we are—but in a special way.'

I left it at that, and went out to sort the furniture in the barn, for a new buyer was doing the rounds.

'Chucky' Cockerill had started calling upon us every Sunday morning. His massive American pick-up—flamboyantly painted with red and yellow flames tailing from the wheel arches, and equipped with enough spotlights to illuminate the average airport—was a real load carrier, and Chucky had a wallet to match.

His arrival—announced by a horn blast which was supposed to simulate the crowing of a cock— was welcomed by all the dealers in the Dale. He bought pine, shipping gear, architectural items, and, as his gold embossed card told us—memorabilia. I like the evocative and loosely defined words the trade adopts; serendipities, bygones, memorabilia. And I liked Chucky, for he was not too discerning, and he paid cash. He also mopped up the space-consuming junk that Fiery turned his nose up at, buying old horse ploughs, turnip choppers and, to our undying relief, mangles.

There is something about massive Victorian mangles that makes us lay aside the sledge hammer. That ingenious train of cast iron gears that run like silk, those heavy white rollers of sycamore, the ornate casting of the frames. We are reluctant to scrap them—but what on earth can we do with them?

The Crown Eagle, made to last; the squeezer of a million gallons of soapy water, the Monday morning exercise machine of three generations of housewives, weighed a ton. Even Chucky, a mountain of a man with a barrel chest and biceps as thick as telegraph poles, grunted and wheezed as we slewed the wringer up a scaffold plank and on to his pick-up.

The other nice thing about these large American vehicles is the height of the bonnet. It is perfect for leaning on as Chucky takes out his wallet and counts out the dirty and limp fivers.

'See yer next week,' he called, giving a cheerful blast of the horn—or to be accurate, horns; for there is one of those enormous red-mouthed atrocities at each side of his cab. The bonnet, each door, and the tailgate are painted with a crowing cock of indeterminate breed, heavily spurred, magnificently combed, and with a piercing eye.

Chucky had had a good morning, for roped alongside the wringer was a cast iron bath on lion-paw feet, several Bradford winguard chimney pots, and a Victorian hip bath with a rust-perforated bottom.

A little Sunday morning cash-in-hand trade can, if we are not careful, be forgotten when we fill our daybook; and we are as careful as can be expected.

Sunday morning is a good day for us and, apart

from Chucky, we do not let business intrude. It is the day I am completely and wholly a smallholder; mucking out, hoof trimming and grooming fill the hours not spent leaning over the wall talking to Ted. Vicky and the children join me, and we harness Topic to the coup cart to do some little job we could do quicker and more easily with the wheelbarrow. The pony and cart become the fulcrum of our activities—a mobile base; repository for tools, oven sticks for the fire, an interesting stone or piece of fungi for the children's nature corner.

The traditional Sunday lunch we dispensed with years ago—it is far too time consuming, and there are better things for Vicky to do. But today she is kitchen bound. The table is littered with utensils we haven't used for years and her Mother's dog-eared recipe book is leaning against the salt jar.

We have got our kitchen just about how we want it. The black-leaded Yorkshire range, fore-runner of those wildly expensive and aesthetically unpleasing efficient cubes favoured by the wealthy, is functioning well now that Baz has replaced the damper and riveted a patch on the oven bottom.

The deep fender, bright from its emery papering, is just the right height to support slippered feet, and I swear that the two broad arm Windsors get more comfortable by the year.

There is a friendly clutter on the mantelpiece; two odd candlesticks; a pot dog; the lidless lustre teapot Vicky keeps her egg money in; several pewter tankards; a photograph of the dogs; many small interesting things the children have found; and an inlaid clock that is correct twice a day.

The pine kitchen table has lost a castor but, as

37

it's going nowhere, it sits steady and uncomplaining on the remaining three and a block of elm.

Our dresser is better favoured, perhaps because it cost us so much money. It has had its bracket foot skilfully repaired, and its top and delft rack carry our carefully arranged treasures. There is no clutter here. Three pewter chargers, a fine tureen with lid and ladle, our ruby-fonted oil lamp and a Prattware jug. The black and white Wemyss pig that used to sit happily beside the tureen now languishes in a drawer, awaiting the gluing back of its left ear.

Hooky rugs with their vivid colours and simple geometric patterns cover the floor, stop the cold striking up from the stone flags, and find great favour with the cat and dogs. The wallpaper—sprigs of flowers on cream—needn't have taken so much choosing, for we can hardly see it for photographs and prints. Indeed, in the children's corner it cannot be seen at all, for the paintings, charts and clippings overlap each other like tiles on a roof.

A square, deep sink, flanked by generous draining boards, is fed by a capricious tap. It is large and brass, and when the pressure is good it flings droplets of water in graceful arcs to wet your chest and arms.

As well as the coal oven we have an electric cooker. Used in summer, completely idle in winter, it is an unloved thing, difficult to clean and completely useless for Yorkshire puddings. In winter we place a tin over its despised rings and turn to the fire; to the griddle pan and blackened kettle and to the oven where—as an eminent French cook once said—'miracles are to be seen.'

If not a miracle, the first cassoulet Vicky had made brought gasps of admiration as it was drawn from the oven and the lid lifted. So time consuming a dish must be for a special occasion, and it was—Canary Mary was coming to dinner.

Once a month she comes to lunch, self-invited, but welcome. Her little notelet pushed through the letter box, delivered by a network of acquaintances, telling us of the appointed day always pleases us and excites the children. She still refuses to use the telephone, shaking her head sadly when anybody asks her why. The churlishness and intractability of the GPO hurt her deeply when they insisted upon restoring to vulgar red the telephone box she had painted yellow. And so she communicates by notelets, neatly written and concise.

But this time we had done the inviting, for Canary Mary, in spite of her big, sunny, outgoing nature, and her undisputed position as Queen of the Fleamarkets, was a lonely woman. True she has ports of call the length and breadth of the Dale. She'll sit a whole rainy afternoon in drunken Sam's kitchen with his cat Sheba on her knee, and she will pester Long John into taking her with him to some distant cattle sale. But as she told us with a shrug of her shoulders, 'It's the nights, them long winter nights—they get me down.'

'They are long winters in the Dale,' Vicky had agreed and after we had discussed it together we hatched a plan to have her over at least one night a month. Initially we decided to start in November, but she had looked so sad when Sam's sale was over, huddled in her little car watching the other dealers load up, their friendly calls across the saleroom yard: 'See you tomorrow—are you going for a drink?—I'll be down to look at that clock.'

I had walked across, tapped on the windscreen

39

and pointed a finger at her.

'Vicky says you've to come to dinner tomorrow, at seven thirty sharp—and bring Piccalilli.'

*   *   *

Canary Mary is always punctual. Her seemingly chaotic existence has a core of routine that is inflexible; an early riser, a despiser of housework and all that is allied to it, she allots one hour per day to domestic chores and three to her cats, her rabbit and her dog. This is why it takes her a month to bottom her pantry and her cellar is never whitewashed.

A hundred shades of green is easily eclipsed by fifty of yellow. From her saffron shoes to the lemon rose in her hair, she was aglow with hues of her favourite colour. A large woman, but not without some shape to her, she carried the sleeveless cadmium yellow, ankle-length gown with its full pleated skirt and broad-stitched waistband superbly. A deeply plunging neckline was saved from the dramatic by a tasteful froth of citrine lace gathered above an agate brooch, from which sprang a folded sash that lay elegantly over her right shoulder to swing friskily a handspan above her buttocks.

Her arms, from wrist to elbow, were alive with bangles, and her eight fingers carried twice that number of rings. The amber necklace—the one she would not set foot outside the house without—clicked against the agate brooch as she straightened her back and, smiling, extended a hand to me. Amber earrings winked from under her golden curls and a handbag, that matched to perfection the broad brogue shoes, was thrust at me.

'Hold that, pet,' she breathed, and reaching under the seat she withdrew a bottle of wine and a small parcel.

She does not hurry herself, our Mary. Calling Piccalilli, her ginger sheep cur, from the back seat, she piled the wine and parcel on top of the handbag, then began a thorough self-inspection. Firstly in the wing mirror, which resulted in a licked finger being drawn across an eyebrow, then a toes to bosom scrutiny which resulted in a flick of some invisible thing from the frothy lace. Several rings were rotated on their fingers, the brooch centralised, the sash primped and patted, the handbag retrieved and swung into the crook of her arm causing a jangle of bangles.

The hand was extended again, this time more elegantly. I was smiled at again, this time more warmly, and we began our well observed walk to the front door, followed by Piccalilli.

I could see Dolly at her kitchen window, and I knew the scathing comment she would direct at her sleeping husband.

'There she goes—all on in case of fire.'

All on or not, she created a stir as she waltzed into the kitchen, kissed the children and took Vicky by the hands.

'You are so kind to an old woman,' she sighed.

'Old woman?' Vicky and I exclaimed. She smiled again, and when I gave her a glass of sherry and told her not to be ridiculous and that she was in the prime of life, she gave that delicious little bubbly laugh of hers.

'I've never done a cassoulet before, so don't judge it too harshly,' Vicky warned.

41

Mary waved her hand.

'Everything you produce is superb, my dear,' she joked as she pulled the children to her, half-bullying them in folds of yellow and glittering bangles.

Piccalilli dived under the table, squirming on his belly and, stabbing a paw at the spaniels, tried to entice them into a game. Failing, he lay down alongside them and went to sleep.

I was not altogether happy with the idea of a cassoulet. A prime English duck, free range and grain fed, demands a certain respect. Stuffed with apple and onion wedges, roasted until there is just a tinge of redness left deep in the breast, brought to the table glazed and surrounded by roast parsnips, garnished with watercress and wafer-thin lemon fringed with chopped parsley, was what I had in mind. But there it was in small pieces, buried deep in the big casserole, layered with *sauté* lamb, pork chunks—and sausages. It did not sound right. Even when I had the intricacies of the dish explained to me, the forming of a crust, pushing it in, baking until another formed, it still did not sound right.

But when it came from the oven it looked right and it smelled right—a heavenly, warm, mouth-watering smell that brought the children hurrying to the table unbidden.

It was a success. We all said so, and raising our glasses we toasted a courageous Vicky, for it is not a dish for the fainthearted cook. It is an autumn dish; a dish to be eaten with friends when a good fire crackles in the grate and a dank mist rolls down from the fell, when dogs are asleep under the table and a beautiful cat half closes its eyes and yawns as it toasts itself in front of the fire.

The children were being spoiled, and they knew

it. Peter gave a half smile as he unscrewed the cap off the lemonade bottle for the third time, and Sally coyly eyed the little parcel Mary had in her lap. It was for her and her brother—but *what* was it? This power that adults have—to forbid, to tantalise, to reward, to make deliriously happy.

Mary's gift for the children was well wrapped, layer after layer of yellow tissue followed the gold ribbon to the floor.

'Careful now,' Mary warned, 'it's quite delicate.'

Delighted squeals from the children greeted the little tin-plate gramophone as it was drawn from the last layer of tissue. It played the tunes of three nursery rhymes, and the favourite one, 'Ring-a-ring-a-roses', tinkled away time and time again. It was a generous gesture, for Mary knew quite well what this little 1930s gem would have fetched at auction.

Peter busied himself with the intricate mechanism, whilst Sally lay on her stomach, head propped in her hands, and happily kicked her new shoes into the carpet.

Mary sang, 'Little Bo Peep,' in a trembling falsetto, and was rewarded with a chocolate, which she shared with the sleepy cat.

Piccalilli opened one tired eye and, deciding he was too warm and too comfortable for jealousy, closed it again and began to snore.

We pulled our chairs up to the fire and inevitably the talk turned to antiques. What the Ring was doing, the killing they had made at the last sale, would Jack the Pat join them?

Mary did not suffer from the actions of the Ring as we did, and, it was rumoured in some quarters, she had a soft spot for Fatty Batty. We had to admit that Fatty was the best of the bunch. He looked after his ailing mother and did not appear to be as greedy as the others. He would chat pleasantly, enquire how we were doing and be congenial company until the 'good gear' started to come under the hammer. Then he retracted back into the clique, stern faced and hard.

'I've no friends in a saleroom,' Mary said, 'I just put my head down and bid away. I've a living to make.' And a living she did make. She knew fabrics, jewellery and more tricks of the trade than anyone else. She still carried 'Made in Taiwan' stickers in her purse, which she surreptitiously put on the bottom of any piece of porcelain she fancied on viewing day and she could stick a hair on to a bowl in such a clever way that even the old hands passed it over with a dismissive 'It's cracked'.

Her contacts spread across the north, but many times she had elicited sympathy as she sat surrounded by junk at some fleamarket.

'Poor woman, hardly sold anything all day—let's buy a bit of something from her.'

Mary would give her wan smile, thank them profusely and with a yellow shoe gently push her yellow handbag further under her chair, for it contained the pair of silver gilt grape scissors she had bought for nothing before the market opened to the public.

'One more tune, then it's 'jamas,' Vicky told the children as she poured us a second cup of coffee. Sally flew to Mary, climbed on her knee and trickled the amber beads through her fingers, and Peter found a book he just had to show to his Aunty Mary. These delaying tactics, well practised and accompanied by charming ways, worked once

44

again; it was nearly ten o'clock before they were washed, changed, kissed and bundled up the stairs.

In a reckless moment, instantly regretted, I told Vicky, 'Leave the washing-up—I'll do it in the morning.'

It was a still night, the mist had rolled down the valley, leaving a bright starlit sky and an ivory moon. An owl called from the blighted elm behind the Colonel's, and from the river bank, still enveloped in grey, came the bubbling musical call of wild geese.

The dogs bounded about the village green, yelping excitedly. Piccalilli, faster and more agile than the ageing spaniels, led them in a wild chase, leaping the washfold, tearing up the track in the field and disappearing behind Ted's farm. We listened as their yelping grew fainter, then disappeared.

'Hope they're all right,' Mary sighed, 'Piccalilli goes crackers sometimes.'

'They'll be OK,' Vicky assured her. 'Ours always come home.'

And so they did, ten minutes later, tongues lolling and chests heaving; but they were alone, Piccalilli was nowhere to be seen.

I left Vicky and Mary standing on the green, climbed the wall behind Ted's and began to whistle. At the top of Moor Lane a single slow moving light disappeared, then reappeared as it worked its way down towards the maypole field. I whistled on as loudly as I could, but no dog appeared.

'We had better search for him,' I called as I jumped down and ran towards the Lalbeck road. Vicky and Mary followed me, calling out the dog's name.

45

The single light was bobbing past Tinker's pond. It was a cyclist going quite fast, his head bent over the handlebars, pale legs flashing. He swung past me, grunted as he changed gear to negotiate the bend to the top of the green, and, rising on his pedals, disappeared around the bend.

There was a squeal of brakes, the sound of tyres skidding on gravel, a shouted oath, and the yelp of a dog, followed by a thud.

Vicky and Mary were bending over the huddled body of a small man.

'Are you all right?' Mary asked, kneeling and cradling his head in her arms. He groaned, a low, long drawn-out groan of pain. Very carefully I lifted him to his feet. He felt his arms, rolled his shoulders and moved his weight gingerly from one foot to the other.

'Nothing broken,' he gasped.

'Come on, let's get him inside.' I silently motioned Vicky to pick up his bicycle as Mary and I carried him into the kitchen, followed by a very subdued Piccalilli.

'Poor, poor man,' Mary crooned, 'it was my stupid dog. I do apologise.'

The little man looked up into her eyes and smiled a toothless smile. 'Don't worry, nothing broken. Just a bruise or two.'

'Sit there,' Mary commanded, pointing to a Windsor chair.

The man did as he was ordered and gave his thin legs over to Mary as she gently lifted them on to the milking stool.

'Now, get me warm water, a cloth and some Dettol.' Vicky rushed to the kettle, and I fetched a bottle of Swaledale Lightning from the pantry—a slightly peaty bottle that did not look unlike Dettol.

Mary bathed his grazed knees and elbow very gently, carefully wiping the runs of water from his legs and arm.

'Whatever were you doing out on a bicycle at this time of night?' she asked.

'Well, you see,' he answered, wincing a little as the Swaledale Lightning was dabbed on. 'It's me birthday. I'm sixty today, and I had this idea.' He groaned, and stretched the leg Mary was holding. 'I had just had me tea and thought—I'm sixty today, why not get the old bike out an' do sixty miles. Just to prove like, that I'm still fit, I can still do it.'

Mary dropped her swab. 'You don't look sixty.'

'I don't when I've me teeth in,' he answered with a grin. 'By the way, me name's Cyril.' Mary offered a wet hand and introductions all round followed, with Mary once more apologising for the dog.

'Hope I didn't hurt him.' Cyril raised himself in the chair, and peered under the table where the ginger sheep cur had curled up alongside our dogs and gone to sleep.

'He's OK,' I told him, and went out to look at the bicycle.

The front wheel was twisted badly, the lamp was shattered and the handlebars askew. The bike was unrideable, but not too badly damaged.

Vicky brewed a pot of tea, but it was a very solicitous Mary who took care of Cyril's needs. 'No milk, two sugars; here you are, you poor man.' Cyril basked in the attention. He laid back in his chair, the mug of tea held to his chest, stretched both legs and looked about the room with bright grey eyes.

'Very interesting, very interesting. This is Ramsthwaite, isn't it? Used to ride through here years ago—a good pub if I remember rightly.'

'You remember rightly,' I told him.

'Think they'd put me up for the night?' The bright eyes peered steadily into mine from under bushy grey brows.

'Sure they would.'

Mary screwed her hands together, stabbed in her handbag for the tiniest of handkerchiefs and dabbed her nose gently. The rose had become dislodged from her hair and I caught it as it fell on to her sash. She took it from me with a smile, then she smiled at the pot dog on the shelf and said rather nervously: 'Nonsense, I won't hear of you staying at the pub. The wounds will need dressing again. You are coming home with me.'

Cyril seemed very happy. He drained his mug, and slowly lowered it into the hearth with his undamaged arm. 'Can't argue with that, can I?'

It took a long time to get bicycle, dog, and Cyril into the 2CV. The hood had to be lowered, then a headscarf for Mary and a cap for Cyril had to be found. A car rug was tucked around the bruised knees, and Piccalilli tied to the seat belt anchorage in case he suddenly got the urge to take off on another night time chase.

'Is there a Missus Cyril?' I asked absent-mindedly as the little car drove away. Vicky shrugged her shoulders and made a pensive mouth.

*   *   *

Mary was not at Sam's monthly sale in the Church Hall, and she did not do the antiques fair at Middlethwaite. She had not missed a sale for years; twelve according to Fatty Batty, and the annual fair

48

at Middlethwaite had always been a lucrative one for her.

We had seen Cyril speed through the village three or four times in the week following his accident. The bike had obviously been quickly repaired, and he now sported a bright yellow jersey. He waved cheerily, but never stopped.

'Something's going on,' Vicky said gleefully. It took a full five minutes for her to convince me that we should pay Mary a visit. After all, she had found some good stuff in the past, and the name of our game is contacts.

'That's it,' I exclaimed, clapping my hands together. 'We have to keep in touch with our contacts.'

The car was missing, but the bicycle—shiny new wheel and shiny new lamp—was in the outhouse. We looked at each other, grinned, wrote a note, and pushed it through the letter box.

We were not the only ones to notice the difference in our friend. Drunken Sam asked, 'What the hell's gotten into her?'

Fatty Batty rolled his eyes, and sang something about romance being in the air.

Baz stomped into the shop and asked outright, 'Is it right that she's got a fella at last?'

We admitted we had suspicions. The bike in the outhouse, the yellow jersey, the absence from the sales.

As Ted said, 'Summat's up.'

They were seen picknicking on the moor top on a cold day, walking hand in hand through the ruins of Jervaulx, and taking tea in the Copper Kettle. Rumour reached fever pitch when Cyril was spotted early one morning in jogging suit and trainers

49

turning out of the cadmium yellow gate followed by a happy Piccalilli. But all was confirmed to us when we received one of Mary's little notes.

It said: Cyril and I are on the lookout for a tandem—a yellow one, if possible.

CHAPTER FIVE

Dick was seventy-nine years old, and he was beside himself.

'Sether, just come an' look at this fire,' he said, gleefully pulling me along the passage and into the kitchen. It was a fire worth looking at on that grey cold morning. The fire grate was piled high with glowing coals, cheery flames licked at the blackened reckan, then leapt up a broad fire back that was festooned with a trembling growth of soot.

'Right fire, eh?'

I had to agree. The kitchen was stifling hot, and Dick's marmalade cat had forsaken the hearth to lie in the window-sill, its front paws twitching as it half closed its eyes and lazily watched us.

'Pull up a chair, an' we'll sit a bit,' Dick said, taking the poker from its stand and rattling it between the ribs.

'I'm damned near eighty, an' this is t'first coal I've bought in me life. It's reight stuff, isn't it. I haven't had as much fun since I had electric put in twenty year sin.'

Dick's cottage is wonderful. It's cosy and cluttered, it smells of cat and dog and home baking, and apart from the three naked light bulbs that hang from the rough hewn beams and the new

50

plastic coal hod that now sits on the hearth, it hasn't changed since his mother died fifty years ago.

The furniture is too large for the rooms. A huge Scotch chest and a linen press dominate the kitchen. Crammed between them is a chaise longue on which the dog sleeps, a spoon-back lady's chair favoured by the cat, and a lovely scroll-arm carver where Dick now sat and smiled at the wonder of coal.

'Logs is all right. I haven't fully gone off 'em—I'll still burn some now and again—but this coal is reight stuff.' He pushed the poker deep into the fire and, levering against the top bar, broke through the glowing crust.

I pushed the spoon-back chair further away from the hearth. 'It's a good fire, Dick, that'll cook your dinner.'

'Cook! Cook! You've seen nowt like it, me spuds is done in no time.' He wagged the poker at the oven. 'There's a rabbit pie in there now nearly done—and,' his free hand stabbed at my knee and his rheumy eyes blazed, '—I haven't opened the damper yet.'

We sat in silence for a while, both of us gazing into the roaring fire. Then Dick muttered very quietly, 'Only thing is—it's mucky. Why do yer think that is?'

'Mucky?'

'Aye, look at this.' He wiped his hand on the edge of the mantelpiece and peered at his finger ends. 'Mucky as 'ell—why is that? Never got this mucky when I used logs.'

'Must be the ash.'

'Aye. Well, ash or no, I'm stickin' wi' coal. It's reight stuff.'

I would like to buy Dick's cottage and leave it as it is. Well, I'd leave the light bulbs—all three of them—but I'd throw out the plastic coal hod and then lock the door.

The walls are covered with religious tracts, the floors with hooky rugs, and every flat surface with the acquisitions of three generations. The Wallers of Dovehills Farm have never been ones for throwing things away.

The oil lamps still sit on the Scotch chest, there is a horse harness hanging from the trap house walls, and in the kitchen table there is a drawer full of worn-down pocket knives.

We had been surprised when Dick had sent a message with Baz that there were things he 'wanted shut of'.

The big dairy—pleasantly cool after the hot kitchen, with its whitewashed walls, a wet looking floor and huge slop stone—had once been the most important room in the farmhouse, for the Wallers had always been great cheese makers. It was still neat and well kept, even though it was a quarter of a century since the last cheese had been made in there.

The scrubbed shelves were full of chesfords of oak and tin, elm sinkers stacked beside them. Two backcans and a giant cheese kettle stood on a stone bench, and under the window was a cast-iron cheese press, a carved stone head hanging from its rack arm, serving as a weight.

'I'll sell t'lot except t'stone head—come on, gi' us yer best price.'

The chesfords were wormed, but not too badly; the backcans, like new.

'Cheese press to go, Dick?'

52

'Aye, gurt awkward thing.'

'I'm surprised you're selling this stuff. Your family had a good name for cheese.'

'Aye, things change—I'm making this into a coal place. I can get a winter's load in here. There's a lot to consider when you goes over to coal. It isn't cheap—by hell it isn't cheap—but it's reight stuff.'

*   *   *

We laid all the cheese-making equipment out in the back yard and drew a bucket full of hot water from the boiler. The scrubbing brush had hardly been laid on the first chesford before Ted's head appeared over the wall.

'I know who them's is.'

'Aye, they're mine.'

'No—who you've getten 'em off—old Dick.'

There was a long pause, during which Ted improved his footing and found a more comfortable placing for his left elbow.

'By, they'll have made some cheese; an' good cheese. They were known for it up at Dovehills. There's two things wi' cheese yer know.'

I didn't know, but as Vicky took the scrubbing brush from my hand I felt I was shortly going to. It was Ted's stance, his far away, knowledgeable look, and the way he scrubbed his unshaven chin.

'The two things yer needs is herby land and knowledge.'

'I've got the herby land.'

'Aye, well, suppose you have. Mind you, it doesn't make good cheese, this time o'the year. We used to call it hay cheese. You see . . .' The left elbow was still not happy, it moved along to the

53

next topping, then three large fingers were held up. I stared at them expectantly. 'There's grass cheese—off the first bite, early spring. There's fog cheese—after hay time; an' there's hay cheese—back end an' winter, when the beasts are being foddered.'

'Which is best?'

'Grass cheese is best, hay cheese t'worst; but you can still make good cheese all year—if yer know how.'

'Did you used to make it?'

His fingers tapped on the wall as his eyes looked steadily into mine. 'Wish I had a pound for every chesford I've turned out—I'd be a rich man.'

'You are a rich man.'

He gave a brief laugh, and lifted his cap off his forehead. 'If yer fancy making a bit, I'll keep yer straight.'

We did fancy making a bit, so instead of feeding the surplus goat's milk back to the stock we kept it in a kit in the dairy. In five days we had saved nearly four gallons. It looked a pathetically small amount to start cheese making, and when I told Ted he had another scrub at his chin, then smiled.

'Tell yer what, I'll bring a coupla gallon round and we'll go halves, 'cos it'll be just about right for Christmas.'

There were problems: the size of the cheese kettle, and its weight when filled with eight gallons of milk. How were we going to heat it up?

'You'll have to make a fire in the yard, it's the only way,' Ted told us cheerfully, 'an' don't worry about the rennet—it's ready when you are.'

It took quite a while for us to get ready. I tried various ways of suspending the cheese kettle, but

54

none were stable enough.

Peter had a bright idea. 'We've stacks of old bed irons, Dad; stick one end in the apple house wall, build some bricks up to support the other end.'

'That's all very well, son, but when it gets up to temperature we have to get it off the fire quickly.'

'That's easy.'

'Easy?'

'Yes, instead of taking the kettle from the fire, we take the fire from the kettle.'

'This is a brilliant idea, my boy,' I told him as we stacked wood on the sheet of corrugated iron. We had attached it to the van by a length of wire rope, and the minute the milk was up to temperature all I had to do was leap in and pull the fire from under the kettle.

I peeled a willow stick and stirred gently as Vicky dunked the thermometer in and out, screwing her eyes up to catch the thin column of mercury.

'Too hot and yer kill it,' we had been warned by Ted, who had disappeared into his kitchen to prepare the rennet. He had winked and held up a cautioning finger when I asked him if he was making it from keslops, which is the dried stomach of a calf. 'One of me little secrets,' he told me.

Sally was stationed in Ted's kitchen, ready to rush round with the rennet when we got the milk to temperature. I eased the van forward, pulling the fire from the kettle, and blew the horn. Sally wrinkled her nose as she walked quickly and stiff-legged into the yard, a small enamelled saucepan held at arm's length.

'Ugh, it smells awful,' she said, pulling a face. The rennet did smell awful, but we poured it in and stirred away.

55

In half an hour we had a custardy mass; in three quarters, rubbery curds. All was going well. We broke up the curds as instructed from over the wall, and built a small fire to gently re-heat them. Ten minutes and this was raked away and the whey poured off.

I broke up the warm curds with my hands and packed it into two chesfords.

'We'll have one white and one blue,' our expert announced.

'How do we do that?' Again there was a wink and a raised finger.

Peter cranked the cheese press up, and we put the first chesford under it. Grey whey spurted through the holes and gathered to trickle from the press base. It was soon discovered by the ducks, who fought and squabbled to get their greedy beaks into it.

Cheese making is a messy if satisfying process. 'Christian food,' Benn Gunn called it, and when the two cheeses stood on the draining board, Ted drew the sign of the cross on both of them before we wrapped them in linen.

'Traditional,' he smiled, 'a cross has allus been put on Christmas cheese in this Dale.'

'Which one will be blue?' I asked him.

'We'll see. In a week or so I'll have a look at 'em, and make the softest a blue un'. Meantime you keep turning them every day.'

We put them in the dairy, and we dutifully turned them every day. They weighed a little less than four pounds each; a nice weight for a cheese. Too small and they dry out quickly, too large and it takes a long time and a lot of care to get them evenly textured.

56

'Fine weather coming—the cheeses are running.'

Mr Hall grinned when he saw them. 'Don't get a draught on 'em or you'll be making nowt but old peg.'

Ted was most put out when we told him.

'How the hell does he know? I've never made old peg in me life. I've eaten plenty, mind. They used to nearly give it away—that an' ramp cheese.'

'Wild garlic?'

'Aye, it makes milk as sour as buggery. They say that the old cheese factors who used to go buying round the farms used to give the bairns brass to go out into the fields and knock all the ramps down.'

'Will this be OK? Being half cow half goat milk.'

'Better than owt you can buy,' he grunted, and then nodded towards the village shop.

*   *   *

'Sunday? But I'll miss Chucky.'

'Just once won't harm.' Vicky poured a steaming arc of water into the vacuum flask, 'We've been invited to lunch and we're going.' There was that tone in her voice which means she has dug her heels in and will not be moved. It is useless to argue, so I just moaned a little, knowing full well that if we had to socialise we couldn't do better than Canary Mary.

I lingered as long as I dared, going back to make sure the goat was well tethered and the pony had water. Lalbeck church struck half eleven, and I looked at my watch then up the Moor road. He was usually here before twelve.

'Could we wait a little?'

'No,' chorused Vicky and the children. They

57

were already in the van, and getting impatient. I took the dogs because Mary's lounge is always warm and stuffy, and behind her cottage there is a good walk down to the river.

The dogs would be my passport to half an hour of fresh air and freedom from women's gossip. I had impressed upon Vicky the need to get away early.

'Sunday is my busiest day. I don't know why you said we'd come,' I grumbled.

'Stop moaning. We never go anywhere. It's ages since we went out together, and all I get is moan, moan, moan.'

I slumped over the wheel and made a mumpy mouth like Ted does, and suffered a non-stop lecture that began about punctuality, rambled on a bit about socialising in general and ended, as we pulled up in front of Mary's, about clean shoes.

Determined not to enjoy myself I waved to Mary then sloped off down to the outhouse where Cyril was oiling his bicycle. He was enjoying himself. One of those flashy and expensive Russian cigarettes hung from his mouth and on an upturned box stood a bottle of brown ale and two half pint glasses.

Piccalilli raised an inquisitive head then flopped down on his bed.

'Sit down, take the weight off,' Cyril laughed as he pushed a stool towards me. 'She doesn't like me smoking in the house so I decided to make this place into a little den—so to speak. Not that I smoke a lot, probably five a day. You want one?'

'No thanks, Cyril. The pipe is my weakness, and I get a bit of stick about that too.'

'Not complaining mind. She's a grand lass. She's asked you about a tandem?'

'Yes. I'll bear it in mind.'

'I'd like to get her out a bit, get some weight off her. Not much.' He leaned forward and, pouring me a glass of beer, grinned wickedly. 'I've allus liked big 'uns.'

'She's a fine woman.'

'Aye. Reckon I got lucky when he fetched me off me bike.' He nodded towards the sheep dog.

'How's the legs?'

'Like new. That stuff she put on worked wonders. She says a chap up the Dale makes it—an' you can drink it.'

'Wouldn't advise it,' I said, raising my eyes. 'Best kept for external use.'

Cyril had installed a pot-bellied stove and a bench, above which were neat ranks of spanners and screwdrivers. From the ceiling hung several wheels and a bike frame freshly sprayed a daffodil yellow.

'I see you're getting into the company livery, Cyril.'

'If it makes her happy. It's harmless enough.'

Mary's stock of bric-a-brac was now neatly housed on new shelving, but the many pots of paint in varying shades of yellow still cluttered the wide window-sill.

Cyril drained his glass and squatted on the box. 'She lets me paint her stuff now. I've just done a pair of shoes and a handbag for her.'

'She cuts a dash, Cyril.'

'Aye, she does. An' there'll be two of us shortly when I get that bike done. She's bought me a yellow jersey. You find us that tandem an' we will cut a dash—the pair of us.'

Sally skipped down the garden path and stood a

59

little nervously in the doorway. Her blue eyes were alive with merriment, and her tiny pink tongue lolled from side to side before she rose on her toes, grinned broadly, and announced in a piping voice, 'It's ready. Aunty Mary says you've to come.'

Very few people are able to talk clearly and acceptably with a full mouth. Children are castigated for doing it; adults, even in a close family environment, are actively discouraged from doing it, but it is a minor art, and one which Mary has perfected. As she talks incessantly, laughs frequently, has many coy and attractive speech mannerisms, it has become a necessity. The thread of a tale can be lost, the spice of some gossip, the very juice of a rumour, can, she feels, be diminished by a pause.

Cyril stood at the head of the table, carving, Mary sat at the bottom, talking. Her two cats, Amber and Topaz, sat on her lap, Piccalilli at her feet. Always one for a good fire, Mary had Cyril stack the grate with logs until the chimney fairly roared. She was wearing a lemon yellow jacket with mustard trousers, and in her hair was the plastic rose she had worn the night Cyril had been fetched off his bike.

It was a conventional meal, well cooked and adequate. The children were allowed to dispense with it quickly, for on Mary's golden pine dresser stood an enormous glass bowl of trifle.

They had been eyeing it surreptitiously, and their Aunty Mary knew full well the magnetism a good trifle exerted on young minds, especially one showing an inch and a half of custard.

'Go on, help yourselves.' Chairs were abandoned rapidly, dishes grabbed, and the silver serving spoon subjected to a good-natured tug of war.

Mary had two new pictures on her wall. They were large and identical prints of Van Gogh's sunflowers, and they hung side by side.

'I just love them,' Mary sighed when I asked about them. 'Some days, when I've been to a sale and I come in frozen stiff, I make a cup of cocoa and just stand in front of them. I can feel the sunshine in my face.'

Cyril beamed and refused the trifle. He was in a really good mood. He fondled Piccalilli's ears, cleared the table, then sat cross-legged on the leather pouffe and told us of his days working in the gold mines of South Africa.

Mary had heard the stories before, but she sat on the chaise longue, Sally on her knee, and smiled and nodded her head happily.

Cyril looked younger somehow. His eyes sparkled as he told of trips to the veldt, the herds of animals he had seen, the orange groves he'd visited.

'Put into Cape Town during the war and I thought—this is the place for me. Soon as I was demobbed, back I went, and stayed there twenty years.'

He seemed to fit in the room very well. Slightly built, lightly tanned, with sparse sandy hair and a ready smile. The dog liked him, the cats seemed tolerant, and Canary Mary was besotted with him.

It was Cyril this and Cyril that: Was he warm enough? Comfortable? Did he want more coffee? Her eyes rarely left him. Perhaps we would all look younger if we were bathed in adoration, the focus of attention in a warm sunny room that had been furnished and draped with the utmost care, and had two copies of Van Gogh's sunflowers on the wall.

61

Cyril had been a widower for many years, and he had, as they say, a good bit put by. The taste for exotic cigarettes seemed to be his only vice; his virtues many. Mary told us about them. How he brought her tea in bed every morning, gardened furiously, was not averse to a little 'drinkies', and worried over her health. He had cycling trophies galore, and he was very, very tidy.

'My years in the Merchant Navy,' Cyril explained, 'you had to be—a locker as big as a rabbit hutch and one drawer, that's all we had.'

Mary's head was tilted to one side, her arms around Sally. She gently rocked the child, whose head had fallen sleepily on to her shoulder. Peter wanted more tales of Africa, but Cyril sprang to his feet. 'Later my boy. Let's get the dogs out and down to the river, it's a grand afternoon.'

Sally stayed behind with Mary and Vicky, but Peter was only too eager to join us. He had a slight problem: did he call his Aunt Mary's boyfriend Uncle Cyril? I didn't know, so I asked.

'No, I'll not have Uncle, it makes me feel old,' Cyril laughed.

It was a lovely afternoon, cold and still. Across the meadow a veining of black branches reached through a gauze of mist into a steely blue sky. The pallid sun had no warmth in it, and had left a grey frost in the lee of the tussocky grass.

When we leaned over the bridge our breath plumed in front of us, and below us the water slid away, brown, oily, and silent, bearing here and there a crumpled leaf. A fretwork of ice, thin and delicate, fringed the banking, and a dark green ivy had wrapped itself tightly around the trunk of willow and beech and caught the wintry light on its

62

waxy leaves.

Peter ran ahead with the dogs, leaving Cyril and me to watch the river. He took out one of his exotic cigarettes and absent-mindedly offered the packet to me. He shook the match out with exaggerated wagging of his arm, then carefully inserted it back into the box.

'Me an' Mary is as right as a box of birds.'

That's what I told Vicky as we drove home.

'They're as right as a box of birds—and didn't Cyril look younger,' I added, as I remembered the brilliant smile he'd given me on the bridge.

Vicky pulled the scarf up around her ears. 'Of course he did, he had his teeth in.'

I had to admit it had not been a bad Sunday. It was one of those days I will remember. That long walk with Cyril, Mary's love spilling out over him, enveloping him in a dozen ways. The buttoning of his overcoat, the pinched cheek, the smile, the constant concern for his warmth and comfort.

'Yes,' I said, as I slapped Topic's round rump, 'it hasn't been a bad day, and I suppose Chucky will be here next Sunday.'

* * *

It is rare for any member of the Ring to call on us, but Thursday morning I hurried into the shop to find Elly standing by the door, looking rather self-conscious.

'Morning Elly, nice to see you.'

'Morning.'

'Can I help you in any way?'

'Did Chucky come last Sunday?'

'No, I missed him.'

There was a definite lowering of the Ellwood brow, and a thrusting of hands deep into the pockets.

'The sod,' he hissed.

'Something amiss.'

'I'll say there is—he came round all of us: me, Batty, George, all of us, he only missed you and Jack the Pat.'

He shuffled his feet and looked around the shop briefly.

'Some bloody con trick. Been buying junk for weeks and paying cash. Sunday he bought all the better stuff and paid by cheque—an' they've all bloody bounced.'

'Oh dear,' I said with some feeling, for it looked like Chucky had done the entire Ring.

We keep a journal. It's a bit of a cheat really, because we only write pleasant things in it. I had written quite a screed about the Sunday visit to Canary Mary's, ending up with the words 'a splendid day'.

I couldn't resist a little chuckle as I crossed 'splendid' out, and wrote in 'brilliant'.

CHAPTER SIX

I nearly didn't go to the sale at Foxly Hall. One of the big London auction houses had been and taken all the good stuff south, and a local firm was to sell the residue; mainly carpets, kitchen equipment and the outside effects. It was a raw kind of day, a cold drizzle covered hat and coat with beads of moisture, the heavy sky was oppressive, and it never really got light.

Get a good fire going in the workshop and repair the writing slope, or go to the sale. Vicky made the decision for me. 'Of course you go,' she cried, 'you've been moping about for days now.'

She was right. I had had a stinking cold and had been out of sorts; hugging the fire, then taking off into the shop to sit huddled behind the counter, sniffing and moaning before seeking out the fire again, and pulling my dressing gown around my shoulders.

'It'll do you good. Get well wrapped up and I'll make you two flasks of tea.' It's all very well for people to pull on your lapels and stuff a scarf around your chest whilst telling you that you're a bad patient, but if you are normally a healthy being who rarely ails you're bound to be—you've had no practice.

Vicky, I felt, did not agree with the logic.

'Just go,' she said, rather brusquely.

Foxly Hall sits on a high mound in a crook in the river: mid Victorian, with high pitched roofs of Welsh blue slate, it is an imposing house, a bit of an architectural hotchpotch, but its setting is superb and it commands some stunning views. When the architect first stood on the site he must have looked around and decided he had to build something special on such a favoured spot.

It is a tall house with pleasing stonework, well proportioned windows and very ornate barge boards. On its southern side is a massive turret, which is surmounted by a wrought iron gallery, now unsafe, but which must have afforded some of the best views in the county. We are told that on a clear day, York Minster, some forty miles away, could be seen.

The terraced gardens surrounding the house were well kept, and had a wealth of stone balustrading and flights of low pitched steps. The architect had made sure that every point of the compass would provide a good view, even to the extent of siting the coach house and stables a quarter of a mile from the house and well below it.

The river had been diverted, and an area of marsh land dredged and turned into a lake, three acres in extent and sporting a whimsical boathouse which was a miniature of the main house, down to the last detail.

There is a nonsense of a Japanese bridge spanning the outlet of the lake and, half buried in the woods, a mock ruin, ivy-covered and well supplied with stone seats. But tucked away on a rock shelf over the river is an absolute gem.

It is an Edwardian smoking room. Built some fifty years after the house, it is pure Strawberry Hill Gothic, with thin lancet windows, crocheted spires and much fancy stonework. Hideous gargoyles jut from all of its six corners and over the door is a beautifully carved stone basilisk, that fabulous half-reptile, half-bird, that could kill with its breath.

'Hell of a place,' Fatty Batty said, rubbing his pink hands and blowing on them.

'There's nothing much for me,' I told him.

'Nothing much for anybody.'

The auctioneers had marked off an area for parking in one of the paddocks, but Fatty, rich and arrogant and disdaining to be lumped with the herd, had driven his Mercedes up to the house. No one said anything to him—he was too big a buyer; but when Canary Mary tried the same thing she was stopped and bossily waved back to park with the rest of us.

'Mean sods,' she panted, heaving her bags on to a stone balustrade. 'Fancy living here. Big cold hole.'

'How's Cyril?'

'He's fine—bless him. I've left him doing his bike. What a day. I hope they get on with it.'

They did get on with it. We wandered from room to room after the auctioneer and his clerk, pushing through the knot of people who clustered round every door. The lots were knocked down quickly, for there were only two or three things left in each room: a fender, an overmantel, some curtains. There was no feeling of a 'big house' sale. It was cold and gloomy, and the prices were not frightening. Everything looked shabby, curtains moth-eaten, carpets holed and threadbare.

Mary held out a piece of yellow peril, a solid cake sprinkled with caraway seeds.

'Excuse fingers,' she said softly.

'Did you know him?'

'Who?'

'The old boy who lived here.'

'I know a bit about him. Apparently he was a queer old stick. You see her over there? She was his housekeeper.'

A crooked little finger indicated a big, broad-shouldered woman standing by the fireplace. She was very straight-backed, and wearing an ankle-length, grey dress with a white, starched collar; from her waist hung a very ornate chatelaine, that rarely found badge of office of the housekeeper. Her iron-grey hair was pulled back severely from a high and smooth forehead, and on her nose rested a pair of pince nez; her hands were clasped in front of her, and held a blue notebook which she looked at from time to time.

I bent towards Mary and whispered in her ear, 'A formidable looking woman'.

'They say she ruled the old man. He was a retired bishop you know; came from a good family.'

'There's been money here—real money. Look at that chandelier.'

In the hallway hung a fine cut-glass, five-branched chandelier with heavy faceted pendant drops and a knopped and deeply cut domed corona. It was a beauty. Even on that dull day it caught what little light there was, and as the pendants turned slowly in the draught from the door it sparkled and looked alive.

'Wouldn't like to clean it,' Mary sighed.

'What will it fetch?'

She leaned close to me and gave a little conspiratorial smile.

'Fatty's after it—made his mind up, it's going to be his. You know his father used to work for the bishop?'

'I didn't.'

'He was his secretary—left under a cloud.' Mary's eyes rolled, and she drew in her prim mouth. She held her head back and her eyes looked steadily into mine; then her mouth widened and twisted expressively. There was more; and she was teasing.

'Come on, Mary.'

'It was only a rumour,' she said, drawing out the words, letting them tumble slowly from a laughing mouth.

'Well?'

'Promise not to tell.'

'Cross my heart.'

She turned her back to the housekeeper, and her be-ringed hands seized my lapels.

'This goes no further—right?'

'Right.'

'Apparently Fatty's dad was a bit of a laddo. One for the ladies. He and old frosty face over there had a wild affair.' She leaned closer and half turned her head, brushing her hair against my chin.

'There was a child.'

'Not Fatty.'

'No—a girl.'

'Where is she now?'

'I've said enough.'

'Mary!'

I grasped her arm, but she wriggled free and giggling like a schoolgirl hurried off down the hall to where they were auctioning piles of faded curtains.

It was bitterly cold in the house, I pulled up my collar and shivered. There was nothing of interest for me until they got to the gun room. Oak-panelled with built-in cabinets and a broad marble fireplace, its ceiling yellow with nicotine, it had been cleared of all its furniture with the exception of an octagonal table on which lay several gun cases. Their labels bore some superb names: Purdey, Holland and Holland, Pape of Newcastle. But they were all empty.

'Where have they gone?' I asked Fatty as I raised the lid on a brass bound Purdey box.

'London boys must have taken them,' he replied curtly.

'Why take the guns and leave the boxes? Surely

69

they would fetch more together.'

He shrugged and hurried out into the hall. I bought all the boxes with the exception of one for a single rook rifle by Joseph Lang.

A small crowd gathered under the chandelier; the housekeeper slid into the library doorway, and pushed her straight back against it. Fatty peered around, buttoned his sheepskin coat and, thrusting his hands into his pockets, backed himself into an alcove. They were going to sell the chandelier.

The auctioneer had bids on his books and opened at £1000. 'It's electrified,' he warned, 'and it's heavy. The purchaser ought to have professional help to remove it.' He looked at Fatty, who raised one eyebrow.

'One thousand one hundred pounds, I have £1100.' He glanced up at the glittering fronds of glass. 'Lovely piece. 'Gainst you on the books, £1200.'

Fatty raised his eyebrow again, and kept on raising it until the price reached £2300. The auctioneer was about to bring his cane down into the palm of his hand when a voice came from the library door. It was the housekeeper. In a very clear and well modulated voice she said, '£2,400 pounds.'

Fatty's face was like thunder. There was no raising of an eyebrow now—he nodded his bids viciously. And they rose steadily until they reached £3600. There was complete silence as the auctioneer looked at Fatty. Fatty shook his head and scowled. There was the slap of cane on palm. 'Yours, madam.'

The housekeeper had the thinnest of smiles on her parchment-like face as she advanced into the hall. She addressed the auctioneer, but she was looking at Fatty. 'Leave it where it is.'

Turning sharply she marched away, the chatelaine slapping on a thin thigh.

Above the rustle of conversation that sprang up the auctioneer announced that the sale of the house contents was completed, and that there were several items in the coach house and stables if we would follow him.

Fatty's Mercedes roared past us down the drive, and out on to the Lalbeck road.

'Not a happy man,' Mary sniffed.

'Come on, who's his half-sister?' I asked, putting my arm around her waist and giving her a hug.

'I've said too much already.'

'And all the favours I've done for you.'

'You'll have to do a few more before you get that out of me.'

Ranked in front of the coach house were rows of garden tools, wheelbarrows, fencing posts— all the outside gleanings of a large house. As the auctioneer disposed of cloches and plant pots I wandered into the stables.

The ample loose boxes were stacked with junk. Empty packing cases were thrown on top of rotting furniture, bottomless buckets and old bicycle frames. Some of the furniture had been quality stuff, but it was all beyond repair. Perhaps a set of period handles might be found, but years of dampness had done their work on wood and fabric.

I leaned over a loose box and stared at the sprung veneer and worm-riddled carcass of a Georgian commode.

'There's nowt in here,' came a cheerful voice from the doorway.

'There's been some good stuff.'

'Aye, but time has taken its toll.'

He came and leaned alongside me; a tall man, fresh-faced, slightly stooped, with weather reddened hands.

'There was only one decent piece in here, and I've taken it next door.' He jerked a thumb towards the coach house. 'It's one of them fancy gold chairs wi' arms. Upholstery's gone like, but the frame seemed sound.'

'You work here?'

'Gardener—for another week that is. Then it's the dole, after forty-five years.'

'I'm sorry.'

'He's left me mi' cottage for the rest of mi' life— wasn't a bad old stick, the bish.'

'Place for sale?'

'No, the housekeeper's copped the lot. She's having a right clear out. Folk and stuff.'

'Can you tell me why the London lot took the guns and left the cases?'

'They didn't.' He lowered his chin on to his hands and made clucking noises with his tongue. 'There's a funny tale there.' We stood in silence; my feet were like blocks of ice and my head felt like it was in a tightening band of iron. My cold was coming out again. I stamped my feet and rubbed my hands together.

'Funny tale eh?'

'It was before my time.' He was obviously not one to be hurried, but the empty gun cases intrigued me.

'The guns would be worth a lot more in the original boxes,' I said quietly.

'Them guns is no more.'

'What, the Purdeys, and Holland and Hollands?'

'Aye, all gone.' He made more clicking noises then gave me a sideways glance. 'That chair in there was one of a set of six originally. They used to be in the smoking room, set round a card table. Way back, sixty, seventy year ago in the bishop's father's time, they used to have big house parties here, mainly when Thirsk or Ripon races were on. An' in that smoking room t'gentry used to get down to a bit o' gamblin'—big money stuff. Now t'bishop's uncle were a bit of a card, got himself in over deep like, an' it wor rumoured he'd started cheatin' a bit. Nowt were ever proved. But he went down on to that queer bridge one night an' shot 'issen. Bishop's father had all the guns taken out o' t'gun room, smashed up and thrown in t'lake. So that's where yer Purdeys an' such is; t'bottom o' t'lake. There's never been a gun nor a pack o'cards in that house to this day.'

'A tragedy,' I said, thinking of the guns.

'Aye, nowt were ever proved—it might have been just talk.'

The chair was a fauteuil, a copy of a French eighteenth-century one, well made and gilded, but in a parlous state. The red plush covering was moth-eaten, one arm was completely broken off and laid on the seat, and the back was splayed out at a wild angle. Repaired it would fetch good money, so I hastened back to the gardener who was still leaning over the loose box, a blue haze of pipe smoke about his head.

'What happened to the other five?'

'Burned 'em,' came the laconic reply.

Quality shotguns smashed up, fauteuils burned, it was a head-shaking day—but there would be plenty to tell Vicky when I got home.

73

'You look terrible.' Canary Mary pulled a ream of tissue from her bag and thrust it into my hand. 'You ought to get off home—into bed with Dr Whisky.'

'Can't, I'm after that chair,' I said, nodding at the fauteuil.

'Get your stuff, pay up and get home. I'll bid for you.'

I did not take much persuading—a warm bed and a warming tot called to me like the sirens of old called to lovelorn sailors.

The big house was locked. A scrawled note pinned to the door told me that the auctioneer's clerk was now set up in the smoking room.

Wrapped in a multi-coloured scarf and with a travelling rug around his shoulders, the clerk shivered and chattered his teeth as his pen scrambled up the column of figures.

The room was bare apart from the clerk's table and stool. Under the tall windows were elaborate cast-iron radiators smothered in decoration; orange blossom leaves vied with each other over every square inch of their silvered surface. Streaks of dampness discoloured the stonework and the mosaic floor was cracked and uneven.

I stood shivering and waiting for my bill, picturing the six gold fauteuils, Edwardian dandies in evening dress, draping themselves in the window seats. The idle chatter of the rich; a hunter for sale for a thousand guineas, the latest ball, tomorrow's favourite for the two o'clock. And the card table, brushed baize; the pack still unbroken, the box of ivory gaming counters—and a desperate man, mouth dry and palms wet as he awaited the call to the table, the cigar smoke pricking his eyes, the

74

undrunk port clutched to his starched chest. A decisive night, an all or nothing night, the highest stakes a man could play for. The numbing chill of the accusation, a heated denial. That last walk, head erect, oblivious to everything but the crushing shame: the shot . . .

'Your bill, sir. The stuff is still up in the house. She'll let you in.'

The housekeeper ignored my greeting and, taking the bill from my hand, led me to the gun room.

'There,' she half smiled as she pointed to the stack of gun cases.

As I staggered down the step the door slammed behind me and I turned to see her shoot the bolt. She was not wearing the chatelaine—she was the mistress now.

*   *   *

I quite enjoyed the first day in bed. My nose was sore and every bone in my body ached, but as I lay in the middle of the warm bed, medicine to hand, happiness spread over me. The noises of the village, the jangle of the shop bell, Vicky's step on the stairs, the laughter and shouts of the children. They all, for some inexplicable reason, brought a smile to my face.

I was quite spoiled. I had boiled eggs with soldiers, lean slivers of Thievin' Jack's roast ham, and half a pheasant with a liberal glass of wine, and 'the most beautiful cat in the world' jumped on the bed to lick my fingers. Ted came to see me, and so did Baz. They are both poor visitors of the sick. Ted nearly broke my foot as he sat on the bed, and

Baz, pouring himself a generous glass of whisky, bellowed in my ear: 'What the hell are you doing in bed? Folk die in bed.'

He went and sat in Widgeon's old chair, and putting his feet on the window-sill stared across the green at The Ship.

Ted did not let me down; he had an infallible cure. 'Boil a big onion, smother it in butter and black pepper. When you've eaten it rub goose grease on yer chest and wind one of t'wife's old stockings round yer neck. You'll sweat like a pig in a haystack, but you'll be as right as rain tomorra.' I thanked him unenthusiastically.

When Charlie opened the door of The Ship and switched the sign on Baz jumped up.

'Sorry, but we'll have to be off—it's domino night.'

'I'll tell yer missus to put an onion on,' Ted called over his shoulder as they thumped down the stairs.

The second day I felt much better and I had better visitors, for Canary Mary and Cyril came. I could hear them whispering on the stairs, a bang and a scrape then Mary threw open the door and Cyril marched in carrying the fauteuil.

'Got it for you,' Mary shouted gleefully. Cyril plonked the chair down and sat in it. 'Well, aren't you going to say something?' Mary asked, after she had given me a wet kiss on the forehead. I looked from her to Cyril then to the chair, and then it tumbled. Cyril had repaired it.

I smiled, thanked him profusely and inwardly groaned, for that quality of chair demanded expert attention.

'He's done the arm and the back and he's made ever such a good job, has my Cyril.'

76

Cyril beamed a toothy beam, crossed his legs and patted the chair arms. 'Good as new—just needs re-upholstering.'

'That's where I come in,' chanted Mary. She pulled a length of cream watered silk from her bag and draped it along the arm of the chair. 'Perfect.'

I must admit it looked good, but it did present a problem. The faded plush of the fauteuil was original, of that I had no doubt, but it wasn't a period chair, it was an Edwardian copy.

A stuffy nose and general tiredness are not conducive to problem solving so I smiled, thanked her and said, 'Perfect.'

Some women are in their element in the kitchen, some in the sick room. Mary scrutinised the medicine bottles, smiled at the whisky, straightened the Durham quilt and opened the window. She felt the soil in the pot plant, adjusted a picture, then plumped up my pillows.

'Warm enough?—Comfy?' she asked in that tone of voice one uses to very small children and men in their dotage. 'Keep warm, that's the thing—and eat. Are you eating?'

'I'd eat better if I had the answer to a gnawing question.'

'What's that, luv?' she asked innocently.

'Fatty's sister,' I whispered, 'who is it?'

Mary pointed a stern finger at me. 'Never mind that. I shouldn't have told you.'

She sat in the Windsor chair, her yellow handbag on her knee, and happily clacked her yellow shoes together. 'Tell him our news, Cyril.'

'Eh?' Cyril looked puzzled.

'The bike.'

'Oh, aye, we've got a tandem.'

Mary put her head back and gave me a long look from half-closed eyes.

'That gardener up at the sale. I got talking to him. Well, it was him who carried the chair out for me, and he said there was an old tandem under a pile of junk in the stables. He had it all to clear out so I bought it for a tenner.'

'Frame's like new,' Cyril put in excitedly.

'We're stripping it down now. Cyril's going to paint it.'

'What colour?' I asked, firmly pressing my tongue into my cheek.

*   *   *

If we can, after a bout of 'flu, put ourselves on 'light duties' for a day or two, so much the better. I carried the fauteuil down into the warm kitchen and had a good look at it. Cyril had done a workmanlike job, and to my relief he had used period glue.

The chair was made in beech, with quality gilding, and our Edwardian cabinetmaker had no need to bow his head to his predecessors of a hundred and fifty years—he was equally as good, and it was a finely made chair. The arms and legs could have been a bit more restrained, but no doubt as he laboured over his commission the Victorians, with their love of curves and comfort, looked over his shoulder and guided his arm.

There was hardly any rake to the back; it was a very upright and correct chair, well sprung, with its short shepherd's crook arms at an easy height, and an altogether solid feel to it. A chair one could sit in for a long period; not slumped, but upright and attentive, a good chair for the gaming table.

78

I told Vicky the tale of the bishop's uncle. 'He could have been sat in that very chair,' she said in a subdued voice.

'Nothing was ever proved. One of the card school accused him, he just got up, walked out and shot himself.'

'Poor man.'

The problem of re-upholstering the chair was a thorny one. I suspect a genuine Louis the Fifteenth one would have originally been done in silk or a worked brocade, but when our chair had been fashioned at the turn of the century there had been no slavish copying of early continental practices. A rich red velvet had been the choice.

Did we do the chair in Mary's silk or stay true to the period? It was like many of that great fictional detective's problems: a two pipe one.

'Red velvet,' I announced, jumping out of the Windsor and taking the phone off the wall.

The little seamstress in Lalbeck would do the chair for us if we stripped it to the frame and retained the old coverings so we could use them as patterns.

It is a dirty job stripping old furniture. The years of dust that has seeped into the fabric and webbings is very fine, it tickles the nose and makes the face itch.

Vicky attacked the arms and the back whilst I prised the dome-headed tacks out of the seat. A horse hair mat was laid over the springs, and it was thick with grey dust. I removed it gently, carrying it to the door and shaking it gingerly at arm's length.

When I got back into the kitchen Vicky was kneeling on the floor, her face screwed up as her fingers fished under the fabric.

'There's something in here,' she gasped.

Very slowly she drew out a playing card, creased and discoloured but still recognisable.

It was the ace of spades—the death card.

CHAPTER SEVEN

She was reputed to have been the cleanest woman in the Dale. Hannah Blenkiron, widowed for many years, had kept the Copper Kettle in Lalbeck, and had built up an enviable reputation. Her baking was second to none, her jam making only slightly inferior to Mucky Marion's, but her tearooms were supreme in the Dale.

'Just as they should be', was a phrase often heard in that cosy retreat. A low, beamed ceiling, large, stone fireplace, Georgian snap top tables covered with pristine cloths, cutlery that shone, and a warm friendly atmosphere that caused many to linger and have another buttered scone.

The kitchen staff changed quite frequently, for Hannah was a stickler for hygiene and any lapse brought a fierceness to her tongue that made them wince and leave. But her two waitresses, black frocked with little lace pinnies and tiara-like caps, had been with her for years.

They were sisters, not twins, but as alike as two peas in a pod. They were efficient, and even on a market day lunchtime when things got really hectic, they never hurried their pace but worked away steadily, not forgetting the hot water for table four, or that Mrs Smythe-Robinson took milk with her coffee and not cream.

Not only was the tearoom just as it should be, it was also a little gold mine. Hannah lived with her two corgis over the tearoom, but she retained one small room downstairs that opened out on the tiny walled back garden, and here she would take her rest. One of the sisters would, in a quiet moment, take her a tray with her favourite silver teapot and thinly buttered toast. She had a special tea, a blend that was never served to customers and was known as 'Hannah's Special'.

Hannah's tea was delivered along with the other supplies for the business, but was always whisked away to the rest room where it was locked in a cupboard and transferred, as required, into Hannah's silver tea caddy.

When Hannah died the business was soon sold. The two sisters, nearing retirement age and deciding they could work for no one else, took the little bequests Hannah had made to them and opened a bed and breakfast place in Richmond. One sister had the silver teapot, the other the caddy.

'Who did she favour most?' Rosie asked, with a stern look at her sister as they unwrapped their parcels on to the counter.

'We just want them valuing, they're definitely not for sale.'

I always think silver is better for the using; it acquires a patination by being handled and jostled amongst its fellows that gives it a warm charm. Silver can look too sharp, too pristine.

Neither the teapot nor the caddy were pristine; they had both been well used. The caddy was the finer piece; by a good London maker and quite early—Queen Anne in fact. The teapot, although

81

much later, had obviously seen more use; it too was by a London firm, and from the reign of George the Third. A hundred years separated the two pieces, but they both bore the same armorial device, a leaping fish pierced with an arrow.

'You know about the crest?'

The sisters shook their heads. After a nervous glance at her sister, Sophie traced a finger over her caddy.

'Hannah was very touchy about it. Over the years several people asked her about it, but she always clammed up.'

'The strange thing is, ladies, that the two pieces—although both showing an amount of wear relative to their age—have had these crests put on them at a much later date. Probably forty or fifty years ago; you see they are relatively sharp, especially the one on the caddy.'

Both sisters peered closely at the crests and ran enquiring fingers over them.

'You've no idea?' I asked again, and once more they shook their heads.

'We just want to know how much they are worth. They're not for sale.'

Anything that has been messed about with is difficult to value. To the purist, any alteration or addition—with the exception of an old and sympathetic repair—renders a piece unacceptable. They shake their heads, sigh and cast it aside; but to some the piece is actually enhanced.

Victorian carve-ups, which many superb pieces of restoration furniture suffered under the chisels of keen amateurs, is a case in point. Few are well done; all had been better left alone. And this I felt was the case with the teapot and caddy. A little emery paper followed by a good buffing with jeweller's rouge could have made the crests look contemporaneous, but I would still have preferred a simple empty cartouche.

We dealers are in a cleft stick when we are asked to value anything. Sweet little old dears with rosy cheeks and soft twinkling eyes become balls of hatred, spitting fire and vengeance if we give a valuation that is below their expectations. Cast-iron assurances that the piece is not for sale, repeated to the point of tedium, melt miraculously upon receipt of an unexpectedly high valuation.

'It's just for insurance purposes. Our Ada's lass is having it if anything happens to me.'

We believe them until next time we view Drunken Sam's; then there it is, the oil lamp; polished and lotted, the star of the sale.

'It's a difficult one, ladies. They are both nice pieces devalued a bit by wear and the crests, but easily worth £100 each.'

'But my caddy's older than *that*,' protested Sophie, as she gave a depreciative look at her sister's teapot.

'Yes, but it's a good shape—the melon shape, esteemed by all collectors.'

Rosie smiled and began wrapping her teapot in tissue paper.

'What do we owe you?' Sophie snapped.

'Put something in the charity box.'

Rosie waited until Sophie had fiddled in her purse for coins, then she folded a pound note and with an impish grin patted it into the tin.

The two women were still waiting for the Richmond bus when Ted's tractor drew up in front of the shop. There are disadvantages in living next

83

door to the world's leading authority on all things, and there are advantages.

'Where did Hannah, of tearoom fame, come from?'

'Now, you've got me there. Her husband was a Blenkiron from Fosset's End; fine, well set up fella. She was in the Land Army during the war, married Blenk' in forty-six or forty-seven, but where she come from I've no idea. She was supposed to be the cleanest woman in the Dale; a bugger for fettlin'.'

'So I'm told.'

'I've just been trimming sheep's feet. Cold job. Wind's in the east, not a good sign. It's cold enough in that bottom land to make a snipe shiver.'

'Coffee?'

'Why not?'

He followed me into the kitchen and spread his hands to the fire. 'What I've really come for is about the straw. You want half a load?'

'Yes, that'll do me.'

'Are you all right for this aft'?'

'Yes.'

'Right, I've borrowed our Billy's wagon. We'll go halves on the diesel, it's a fair way—out on the Wolds,' he warned.

'Right enough.'

'Tell you what, I'll have a look at that cheese whilst I'm here.'

Vicky had put the cheeses on a high shelf in the dairy, and draped them with muslin. Ted lifted them down, turned them slowly in his hands and pressed his thumbs into them.

'This'en. We'll mek this'en blue.' He took the worn, horn-handled knife, the one he uses for sheep's feet, from his pocket, and jabbed it to full

84

blade depth all over the cheese. 'Reckon that'll do it,' he said proudly.

I like riding in the cab of a wagon. They always have such good heaters, and being high up we have views which are denied the car-borne. The long wall of the estate does not block our view of the ruined abbey; we see the deer alert and elegant at the wood's edge; and the hump-backed bridge at Middlethwaite affords us—as Ted curses and searches for the missed gear—a delightful glimpse into the gamekeeper's back garden.

Labradors peering wistfully from their pens, poultry coups, the stiff breeze turning the ginger fur of a fox that hangs from the porch, fantail pigeons strutting on the roofs of the ferret hutches.

Ted leans forward as he drives, feeding the big wheel through his hands. 'This fella we're going to see—bit of a character.' His arm jagged at the long gear lever then flew back to the wheel. 'Aye. Nice enough fella. Good to deal wi'—but,' he stole a quick glance at me, 'he's delusions of grandeur.'

'Sounds interesting.'

'Oh aye, it's interesting, but it can be a bit awkward. Yer see he thinks he's a lord. Goes on about it. He's got reams and reams o' papers and documents which he says proves he's a lord. Whatever you do, don't mention lords, aristocrats, royalty—owt like that. 'Cos once he gets goin' nowt stops him.'

'Right Ted; avoid it like the plague.'

'That's it—bit o' diplomacy.'

He wound the window down and shouted a most objectionable word at some poor old man in a small car who mistakenly thought he had a right to half the road.

85

It was a big farm and very well kept. The gate swung sweetly on its hinges, hedges were laid neat and the surrounding fields were well ploughed, leaving very small headlands.

'This fella,' Ted said, momentarily taking his hand from the wheel and pointing at a red brick Georgian house, 'is one hell of a farmer. A lot of folk think he's as daft as a brush, because of the lord thing, but you look around—everything is as it should be.'

We pulled into a fold yard where under pantiled roofs huge Hereford cattle breathed smoky breath into the afternoon air. They stood hock-deep in yellow straw and eyed us balefully.

'Look at 'em,' Ted enthused, 'did you ever see such beasts?' We leaned on the railings and watched them as they slowly ploughed through the straw towards us, wet muzzles thrust out, unblinking oily eyes staring at us, tails swishing.

A bullock pushed up to us and bathed us in his marsh smelling breath as Ted slapped its fat neck.

'Right stuff. He milks Dairy Shorthorns and fattens Herefords—an' if you go darn there,' he swung an arm out, 'there's breeds of pigs you haven't seen for years. Gloucester Old Spots and Tamworths.'

'Has he any poultry?'

'Buff Orpingtons—won't keep owt else.'

The bullocks started lowing, and with much rustling of straw trotted to the far end of the fold yard.

A squat, thick-set man in tapered breeches and leggings, followed by two golden retrievers, walked into the yard.

His face was as round as an apple, gently

86

smiling, with periwinkle blue eyes and a flamboyant moustache that swept in two arcs to join his sideburns. He was wearing a waistcoat of Newmarket check, a shirt of Tuscan red that was too much of a match for his complexion, and a Norfolk jacket. At his throat was a white silk cravat with a diamond pin, and on his head a wide-brimmed hat, stained and worn, but still with a stylish wave in its brim. Tucked high under one arm was a gold-topped cane and in his right eye a monocle.

'Good afternoon gentlemen,' he called, unshipping the cane and resting his hands on it, 'come for the straw I presume.'

'That's right,' Ted replied, 'an' how are you keepin' milord?'

'Milord' grinned broadly, told us he was tolerably well, and bade us follow him. We followed at a distance, not through deference, but because he set such a pace. The burnished leggings fairly twinkled on his short legs as they took him rapidly across the fold yard, through an orchard peppered with Buff Orpingtons, over a superb lawn and through a gate, into the stockyard.

'Ted,' I panted, 'what's with this milord stuff? I thought he was a—'

'Shush. We keep him humoured and he'll knock a tanner a bale off.'

Milord stopped in front of a huge stack of straw and prodded it with his cane. 'Here you are gentlemen, good stuff, jolly good stuff. Load your vehicle, then come across to the manor—right?'

'Right,' Ted and I answered brightly.

Loading straw is not one of my favourite jobs. I haven't got the hands, the arms, or the back for it.

The binder twine bites into your hands, the straw raises a brutal looking rash on the inside of your arms, and by the time you have got the third course of bales on to the wagon your back is advising you to stop. Ted, on the other hand, is built for such work. His hands are leather, his arms tough and impregnable, and his spinal cord is tempered steel. He works like a machine, steady and unhurried, never seeming to tire.

'Let's have a breather, Ted,' I pleaded.

'Hell, we've nobbut gotten started.'

'It's half loaded.'

'Aye, but I want to be back afore dark. It's to get off at yon end don't forget. Ar' Billy wants t'wagon in t'mornin'.'

Prickly lengths of straw had worked their way down my collar and down the front of my shirt and stuck to my sweaty body. We had not been sat more than two minutes by any clock in England when Ted got to his feet and doffed his jacket.

'Come on, let's get at it.'

But before we could get at it, a woman walked through the lawn gate with a tray. She was a large woman, white haired and she limped badly.

'Master's sent you this,' she said, holding out the tray, on which were two pint mugs of tea and two slices of apple pie.

'Thank him most kindly,' Ted said, taking the larger slice of pie. It was the best mug of tea I've ever had, and the pie was delicious.

'Been better wi' a slice o' Wensleydale,' Ted complained affably.

I unbuttoned my shirt and, letting the cold air cool my body, I swung my legs and happily picked pieces of straw off my sticky chest.

'Tha'll git a chill,' I was warned with a frown.

'I think I'm going to die anyway,' I said, as I climbed back into the wagon.

'I've done two wagon loads a day an' still milked when I got home.'

'Ted, I'm an antique dealer, not a work-horse.'

'Antique dealer? Did I hear you say you were an antique dealer?' I looked down into the periwinkle blue eyes of milord.

'Yes, believe it or not.'

'Come with me.' He marched off towards the house at a very brisk pace.

'Oi!' Ted yelled after us, 'I'm not doing this on me own.'

Milord turned and waved his cane at Ted. 'Don't worry, old chap. I'll send one of my men to give you a hand.' Then turning to me, he smiled, screwed his monocle into his left eye, and said encouragingly, 'Come along, old bean, I need your advice.'

We tore through a kitchen, large and modern, across a parquet floored hall, up a flight of rather grand stairs and into his oak-panelled study.

I sank happily into a deep-buttoned, leather chair. He opened a walnut *secretaire abattant* and took out a bottle of whisky. 'The sun must be over the yardarm somewhere on this troubled globe of ours,' he said, pouring two large measures. 'Now, what I want to know is this. What is pewter doing these days?'

'Fairly steady,' I replied cautiously.

He downed his drink, let the monocle fall from his eye, and beckoned me to follow him. Another fast walk down a corridor was followed by a skip up wooden steps into the attic.

It was packed with the jumble of generations.

89

A superb Victorian rocking horse, nostrils flaring, eyes agleam, laboured under a load of period coats and dresses. Brass-studded trunks, their lids ajar, afforded me a thrilling peep at the discarded treasures of the rich: a fine, tin plate battleship, a doll that just had to be a Simon and Halbig, a one-eyed teddy bear—was that a button in his ear?

There was an order in the jumble, just as there appeared to be an order in every aspect of this man's life. Toys and clothes gave way to kitchen artefacts: a scrubbed churn, stacks of Georgian copper pans, a graduated set of fish kettles. There was then a nest of chairs, some country Hepplewhite amongst them, and an oak table of breathtaking proportions; laid out on it was an equally breathtaking array of pewter.

'The basest of metals,' he grinned, as I stood staring at it. 'Now just give me a rough estimate of its value. You see,' he walked to one of the skylights and opened it slightly, 'I'm into silver myself. Thought I might flog this lot off and buy something really nice.' His eyes sparkled. 'Well, what's it worth?'

'A great deal of money,' I said slowly, and in a subdued voice. He tore the lid from a cardboard box and brought from his waistcoat pocket one of those lovely fat fountain pens.

'I'll make a list, you shout out the values.'

There were eight broad-rimmed chargers, all I estimated to be over twenty inches in diameter; and they were early ones, with London touch marks. There were two stacks of pewter plates, thirty-seven at the first count, thirty-eight at the second. 'What do you reckon—a fiver apiece?' he chirruped.

I found a set of six Irish haystack measures, and

90

arranged them in order of size. It was a perfectly graduated set, from half a gallon down to half a noggin. With no damage to speak of, save a dented rim or two, they would make a thousand pounds on a good day.

There were four large wine ewers and the funnels to match them; three sets of candle sticks, a bit continental looking, but very choice, and lidded tankards in profusion.

When I had finished, 'milord' took his cardboard tally to the skylight and, with deep concentration and only the slightest movement of his lips, added up the prices I'd given him.

'£5500, near enough,' he cried, striking a sweeping line under the total.

'The basest of metals,' I mumbled.

Ted was sitting at the kitchen table with the white-haired woman, in front of them a large, brown teapot. 'Loaded an' roped on,' he announced loudly, trying to make me feel guilty.

I sat, and thrusting out my legs, flexed my aching back muscles. 'I've not been idle,' I protested. 'Milord' stood in front of the Aga, his legs planted firmly apart, his thumbs in his waistcoat pocket. He looked a happy man as he took his tea and stirred it gently and smiled at the white-haired woman.

'Want you to get up in the attic and pack that pewter ready for the saleroom.' He sipped his tea, rose on his heels and grinned at us. 'I can feel a nice piece of silver buying coming on.'

'Not more silver,' the woman said in a tired voice.

'Yes, my dear—more silver. It's the mark of an old and aristocratic family—the quantity, and the quality—of their silver.'

She gave him a long, steady look as her tongue searched around her bottom teeth, her elbows on the table, her hands holding her teacup in front of her. 'You're crackers, you know that, don't you?'

He laughed, showing strong yellow teeth and made an elaborate show of clamping the monocle to his eye. 'Come on chaps, I'll make out your receipt, I've no doubt you're dying to part with your lucre.'

He led the way jauntily across the hall and through double-panelled doors into a well proportioned room that was light and airy and sparsely furnished. The broad varnished floorboards were bare except in front of the white marbled fireplace, where a tiger-skin rug lay.

In one corner was a large partner's desk, and behind it a Queen Anne wing armchair. A sarcophagus shaped wine cooler and two oak hall chairs were the only other furnishings.

The fat fountain pen came out again, and a receipt pad slapped on to the desk.

'Can you give us two?' Ted asked, 'yer see, we're sharing this load, milord.'

'No problem, old bean.'

I looked at my receipt; it was signed 'Fishbolt', and at the top of it was the crest I had seen on Sophie and Rosie's silver—a leaping fish pierced with an arrow. It was obviously a rebus on the name Fishbolt: bolt, arrow.

'Interesting crest,' I said to milord.

Ted groaned and rolled his eyes; the man behind the desk grinned broadly, leapt to his feet and with brisk jerky movements screwed the top on the pen and plunged it into his pocket. 'Follow me.'

It was a large room, warm and comfortable, with

a merry fire crackling in the grate, heavy drapes on tall and barred windows, a thick carpet spread with several rugs, big dark ancestral portraits in alcoves each side of the chimney piece; and set around the wall between the windows and the doors, cabinets which reached from floor to ceiling. Every one was crammed with silver.

In a Queen Anne wing chair, the match to the one behind the desk, sat the white-haired woman knitting. Our host walked into the centre of the room and held out his arms.

'Now, where to begin.' Ted groaned again, loud enough for the woman to hear him. She bobbed around the wing of the chair and gave us a wide grin.

'Fishbolt! An ancient name—and a proud one.' The thumbs were back in the pockets, the monocle dangling, the red face happy and intent. 'There was a Fishbolt standing alongside Harold at Hastings on that fateful day, there was a Fishbolt at Crecy and Agincourt. One stood by Charles the First and faced the taunts of the regicides, one stormed the Heights of Abraham and gave all for his beloved commander. There was a Fishbolt in the farmhouse of Hougoumont, and Lord Archibold had his horse shot from under him in the charge of the Heavy Brigade. My grandfather, Freddie Fishbolt, chased the Boers from the doorsteps of Ladysmith, and our ancient blood has seeped into the mud of the Somme.'

He walked up to a cabinet and took out a silver punchbowl. He stared at his reflection in its concave bottom for a moment, then shot us a fierce glance. 'And there was a Fishbolt on the beach at Dunkirk—me.'

The white head appeared again: 'He was a lance-corporal with a mobile bath unit.'

'No matter, no matter,' he replied hurriedly, and with a trace of pique in his voice, 'we've always served in whatever capacity we could.' He held the punchbowl in front of me, slightly tilted. 'See the crest—it's on every piece of silver in this house—and that, sir, is quite a bit of silver.'

It was a heavy bowl, one of real quality, with a frieze of vine leaves and clear assay marks. The crest, like that on all the silver he had shown us, had been cut into it at a much later date. Soon the table was crowded with silver pieces he'd taken from the cabinet for our inspection. Ted pulled at my sleeve. 'We'll have to get off—it's falling dark.'

'Something here you must see,' our host said, bringing out a large pilgrim bottle; 'Father bought this in the continent before the First World War. It is, I think, the star of the collection.'

It would have been the star in many a collection. Over two feet tall, beautifully embossed and chased, it was a most impressive piece.

Ted blew loudly and, making his mumpy mouth—a sure sign he wasn't very happy—wandered over to the window. Needles stopped clacking and the white head appeared. 'He does go on, doesn't he?' Ted nodded his agreement as a fresh batch of silver was lovingly brought from a cabinet.

'These are my favourite ones. I bought them all from a neighbour, after my Father died, and before I went off to war. They were my very first purchases. There were full tea and coffee sets with trays and a beautiful, very early caddy. Many a time during a dark hour at the front the thought of my contribution to the Fishbolt silver, resting in the centre cabinet, cheered me—and what did I find on my return?' He glowered at the chair back. 'They had given two pieces away.'

The needles stopped once more; there was a pregnant pause.

'I had to, there was nothing else to give. We had no money, and the girl had worked like a slave. If it hadn't been for her there would have been nothing to come back to. You were in a reserved occupation, you didn't have to go.'

'I did—a Fishbolt knows his duty.'

Ted pricked up his ears, and with a quizzical look on his face walked to the table and picked up the coffee pot.

'They had this jumping fish stuck wi' an arrow on 'em?' he asked slyly.

'The Fishbolt crest—yes; why do you ask?'

'Oh, nowt—just interesting.'

The chirpiness dropped from Fishbolt; he looked small and sad as he handled the silver and returned it to the cabinet. 'If only I could get those two pieces back.'

'Valuable, are they?' Ted asked gently.

'To me they are—I'd give £200 each for them.'

Ted looked at me. His head inclined to one side he drew in a deep breath and blew it out in a prolonged 'mmm'.

It was dark when we climbed into the cab and waved goodbye to the stout little man in the Norfolk jacket. I thought Ted would be in a bad mood having to drive in the dark but he was quite ebullient.

The yellow headlights raked the bare hedges, our load of straw hissed as it scraped overhanging branches, and the tyres hummed merrily. Yellow lights shone in farmhouse windows, the first stars pricked tiny holes in the dark blue fabric of an almost cloudless sky, and a shy sickle of a moon laid a ghostly sheen on the grazing cattle.

'We'll unload in the mornin',' he said, as we surged over the bridge by the gamekeeper's. The fox had gone, his mask and brush would be at the taxidermist's, his pelt nailed behind the tool shed door.

'OK by me.'

'Bit of a character—yon fella.'

'You can say that again.'

'That teapot and caddy—£200 apiece. They can't be worth that?'

'Pablo Picasso said, "I value all objects according to the degree of love I have for them".'

'I know, but—'

'Ted, forget it—they won't part with them at any price.'

Vicky massaged my aching shoulders, kneading savagely at that rib of muscle that springs from the base of the neck. I had taken off my shirt and vest and shaken them in the yard, picking the last tenacious pieces of straw from them.

'Ted must have a hide like an elephant,' I gasped, as her searching thumbs found a particularly tender spot.

'He also has business in Richmond,' Vicky laughed. 'When you were milking the goat he went off up Moor Lane in the wagon.'

'What, with the straw still on?'

'Yes.'

Now, a wagon with a load of straw uses a fair amount of diesel and for a penny pinching old devil like Ted to use it for mere transport it had to mean something.

'Towards Richmond—well, he'll not get them.'

I went off to bed early and stretched out luxuriously. It had been an interesting day. Vicky was brushing her hair when we heard the wagon return, dropping into low gear as it climbed past the washfold and squealing to a halt outside Ted's.

Vicky pulled back the curtain and peeped out. I heard the cab door slam. Then Vicky let the curtain drop and patted her chin gently with the hair brush. 'He's got a small parcel,' she said in a low sing-songy voice.

I threw my head back in the pillow and smiled at the ceiling. 'The crafty sod.'

CHAPTER EIGHT

I quite like the approach to Christmas, if it doesn't prove too expensive. There is a boost in the shop's takings as presents are bought, the children are in a state of excited anticipation, and we look forward to a few days of rest—or to be precise, change.

A bit of walling, long walks with the dogs, and lazy evenings spent by a good fire, the children safely tucked up in bed, the soft tick of the grandfather clock.

'Sausages' are packed behind the doors, the log bin filled, the heavy curtains drawn. All the tasks of the day behind us, we talk of the children, how they are growing, how they are doing at school. Then, hesitatingly, we talk of the business, of money being put by for a new van, and the Scotch chest I've bought that we will never be able to sell.

I tap out my pipe and taking the mug of cocoa shuffle slippered feet in the hearth. 'We'll wait till the New Year and shove that chest back in a sale.' It's only a little decision, something we knew we would do anyway, but it cheers us.

We've never been intent on self sufficiency—it is the hardest of task masters—but the smallholding is definitely a plus. A meal that is entirely our own produce pleases us enormously, the leek and potato soup brings favourable comments, the old hen past her prime as a layer fills the old casserole dish and simmers slowly in the oven. 'Free range and corn fed,' we tell ourselves as we set the table, 'the best you can get.'

There is a bit of barter. We swap Rabbit a couple of dozen eggs for a pheasant. Long John brings a hare and, grinning, asks if we want that old wheelbarrow we acquired when we cleared the barn at Melbeck Park. Baz strides into the yard, a green goose under his arm, and wonders if we still have that mud scuppit hung in the apple house. Sometimes we feel we have had the best part of the deal, sometimes the worst, but things even themselves out. The wheelbarrow was worth far more than the hare—we should have had two at least—but when Baz swapped us a home-cured ham for a trio of Muscovies we were well on the right side.

Stephanie, the Reverend Sidney's wife, is a formidable woman—well made with a strong but pleasant face, she takes on the tasks of the parish with an almost fiendish energy. This energy is matched by an admirable organising ability, and when needed, a startling ferocity.

The two youths who thought they would have a little sport disrupting her Brownie meeting can verify the latter, for it was a week before their ears stopped ringing.

Normally when Stephanie calls on us she has a collecting box in one hand and a stick-on flag in the other.

I avoid her. If I see her coming across the green I scuttle into the kitchen and say in a matter of fact voice, 'There's Stephanie.'

Vicky will curse under her breath and clap the flour from her hands. I'm not good with charities, I give too much to one, too little to the other. Vicky has a sliding scale she carries in her head; charity begins at home, with the children's charities closely behind.

'It's you she wants.'

'What for?'

'Go see—maybe she's something to sell.'

I put my untasted tea on to the fender and sincerely hoped she hadn't. I had been into most rooms of the vicarage, and apart from Sidney's collection of botanical books there was nothing of value; they hadn't a stick of furniture worth tuppence.

She gave me what I think was a smile. It was a brief uplifting of weather-beaten cheeks, and a lightning flash of enviable teeth.

'I never see you on the bicycle,' she said, in a rather cool way.

'Don't seem to get the time.'

'Well, I'm here to do you a favour. I have four tickets to the Lalbeck Pantomime—*Puss in Boots* – and I'm willing to exchange them for the bicycle.'

It was a bit sudden. True, I had hardly ridden the

bike since I had bought it at the 50/50 auction at the village fête, but I had grown quite fond of it. It was a sterling machine; a Rudge, no less, in moss green, with chromium dynamo and capacious saddle bag. I had squeezed its brakes and thumbed its plump tyres with pleasure.

'What do you think?'

'Stephanie, I paid quite a bit for that bike.'

She spread the tickets on the counter and thumped on the top of them a bottle of port.

'I'll get the bike.'

'No, I'll send the verger up for it—it's to be a little Christmas surprise for his Reverence.'

Now, Sidney hated that bicycle as much as a man of the cloth can hate an inanimate object. When he had sneaked it into the auction, Stephanie, believing the best about the man, had been sure it had been a terrible mistake.

'Poor Sidney. Someone must have pressured him into parting with his bicycle,' she had told Vicky. 'Hope your man looks after it.'

I had looked after it. True, the tyres were a little soft and it was not lathered in oil, as it had constantly been under the verger's care. The scratch on the cross bar was hardly noticeable, and I was sure a clever man could soon rewire the dynamo.

'When will the verger come for it?'

'Thursday, ten-thirty sharp.'

It seemed to me an inordinate amount of money for just cleaning a bicycle and blowing up its tyres, but Peter assured me that five bob was a fair price. I looked at the bottle of port—it was a good brand, a good year.

'Go on then.'

The verger is a lugubrious man; it is said by some that every time he smiles a donkey dies. Perhaps it's his devotion to Stephanie, his quite considerable work-load, or the domineering unmarried sister he lives with; there are many theories, but there is something in his life that renders him a most unhappy man.

The sight of the bike, clean and shiny and hard tyred, failed to lift his gloom. He raised the rear wheel clear, cranked a pedal and listened to the merry hum of freshly oiled bearings before squeezing the brake. He spun the front wheel, wagged it side to side, then braked that one. There was a lot of sniffing, which culminated in a strangulated nasal moan as he found the scratch on the cross bar.

'That weren't there.'

I agreed with him. It had been caused by the heel plate on one of Baz's boots when he had been larking about on the machine.

'Not a bad one,' I said solicitously. It brought no immediate response; he merely stared at it, his sad mouth drooping lower, little sharply exhaled grunts accompanied his finger as they stroked across the scratch.

'I don't know—that'll take some gerrin' out. When am I going to do it, eh?'

I shook my head in sympathy. 'Busy this time of the year?'

'Busy—when are we not? That's what I'd like to know. Supposing I gets a fundrel next week. Folk never consider that. They don't die to order you know.'

He mounted the bicycle, gave a tinkle on the bell, and rode slowly out of the yard.

'Poor old Sidney,' Vicky sighed, 'it will really make his Christmas when he sees that under the tree.'

'Don't worry. It'll be like new—if we don't get a fundrel next week, that is.'

We don't go out of our way to buy books. A *Wright's Encyclopedia of Poultry* will excite our interest, especially if it hasn't had the plates cut out, and any book on antiques is naturally a bit of a magnet. We pore for hours over *A Guide to Furniture Prices* of 1932. It isn't just that prices are now unbelievable—twelve pounds ten shillings for a brass faced, eight-day clock—it is the wealth of period furniture that was available. A dresser, a plain and simple country piece we would give our eye teeth for, is not recommended at ten pounds. It is better to invest in a more sophisticated piece we are told. 'Where is that piece now?' we ask, stabbing a finger at a William and Mary walnut bureau 'of great quality'.

Ted brings us back to earth. 'You were damned lucky if you had a tenner in 1932. Ar' Billy wor shepherding for fifty pun' a year an' his keep.'

But I have found a charming quotation. A French philosopher whilst visiting these shores apparently wrote to a friend: 'The English are inordinately fond of their mahogany.' He was no doubt referring to the practice of drawing the cloth after dinner, exposing to view that rich, beautiful expanse of cherished wood. A nineteenth-century invitation would be made warmer and more sincere sounding by the offer to 'Come and put your legs under our mahogany.'

It is our favourite wood and that variation of it—rosewood—tends to make me lose all sense of proportion. The richness of its red-brown, the flamboyant tongues of intense black that lick down the grain; it is the prince of woods. There are more exotic ones—amboyna, flashy zebra wood, the rare coromandel—but rosewood used intelligently and embellished with a little ormolu or polished brass is the wood for me. I have been known to pay too much for a rosewood piece.

So when the very attractive blonde woman in the belted trench coat said she had a nice rosewood music cabinet in her car and would we like to look at it, Vicky ballooned her headscarf in the air, tied it firmly under her chin, and said she would go.

She looked at it, but she did not buy it. The attractive woman followed Vicky back into the shop and asked with the sweetest of smiles if she could look around.

Probably in her mid to late thirties, that handful of years when a naturally beautiful woman is in her prime, she has a confidence, a graceful way of moving; the figure is perhaps a little fuller. There are laughter lines beside wise and soft eyes, her hair is no longer tortured by fashionable dictates but follows a natural and easily kept line, and a woman at last understands how important coloration is. The eyeshadow is not as intense, the line of the mouth softer, and the ready smile is sincere. The slight hollowness of the cheeks, the poise, the fascinating way one perfect tooth is slightly twisted over the other.

Her voice was soft and honeyed, beautifully modulated, and one knew that a harsh or jarring word could never fall from such a finely-formed mouth. She was Mrs Minerva; she was the sweet-faced heroine who encouraged her man at the barricades; the perfect soulmate that inspired the weary pioneer to return to the plough and wring another acre of fertile soil from the prairie; the spur of the poet; the anguish of the artist—she was a truly fine looking woman. There was about her much for a discerning man to admire.

She was wearing black, high-heeled boots and a fawn, turtle-necked sweater that was obviously cashmere. A brooch, a shell-cut cameo of high quality, was her only jewellery; her perfume was restrained and subtle.

'I'll leave you my card,' a hand of extraordinarily smooth texture, with exquisitely shaped nails, was withdrawn from a trench coat pocket, 'and I'll call on you again, if I may?' Another sweet smile, and she glided through the door with hardly a jangle of the bell. A hyphenated name, and a good London address.

'That's the type we need; carriage trade—a bit of class, an interior designer.'

'She didn't buy anything,' Vicky replied, in a rather sharp voice.

'How much did she want for the music cabinet?'

'Far too much.'

With that she shook a strand of tinsel from the decorations box and went back to dressing the window for Christmas.

We are always last push up. Charlie's had his winking coloured lights casting a twitching sheen on to the car park gravel for a fortnight now, and a big tree—the annual gift from the estate—is on the green waiting for Ted to round up Baz and Rabbit with his parish councillor's zeal, 'Come on lads, let's be at it.'

Wednesday lunchtime there was a tap on the

104

window. 'Gi' us a hand.'

Baz pulled up his collar as he waved me towards the top of the tree. We carried it carefully, a bouncy bristly load, to the washfold, where Ted was prising up a flat stone. The butt of the tree was inched towards the stone-lined socket; wood wedges thrown from Baz's wheelbarrow, and we were pointed to our places.

Ted, red faced and puffing, stood back. 'On three, lads.'

We groaned and lifted, our heads down, faces turned from the spiky branches, Baz dashing in bravely, his big hands nearly spanning the trunk, guiding it. The tree shuddered as it dropped home, filling the air with dust and a strong scent of resin.

Baz was on his knees, wielding a mallet, driving in wedges; Ted organising, 'A bit more towards the pub, git one in there Baz; that's it, welly it in, lad.'

Rabbit complains. 'It's not as big as last year's.'

He's grumbling because he gets to cut the tree up for logs when it's taken down, but Baz is happy with it.

'Good shape,' he says, throwing the mallet into his barrow.

'That's the important thing, a good shape,' the Colonel agreed. He squinted, his head to one side, lining the trunk up with the corner of Jubilee House.

Ted watched with sly eyes, ready to do battle. 'The tree is plumb enough—just let him start,' he mumbled.

But the Colonel was happy. He called his dog, who had lifted its leg against the wheelbarrow, and with a 'well done chaps' he was off.

The school children dressed the tree as high as

they could reach, then steps were brought and the bigger boys—under the worried and constantly warning directions of Miss Wells—stretched their arms and laced it with coloured light bulbs.

A cable was run under the culvert and then up the wall and into Ted's cow house. There is an electric meter just for the tree, and the Colonel read it, carefully noting the figures in his diary, for the parish council pays the bill.

Thievin' Jack was late—the tree was already lit when his van appeared. It was turkey day, and there were plastic sacks on the van floor, and turkeys with little flags stuck into their plump breasts crowded together on the sacks.

We were having a goose. Baz had reared half a dozen from the breeding trio he was given as a wedding present. They were good and fat he told us, 'An' I'm not dressing 'em for that price—you can pluck 'em yourselves.' He kept one for himself, Ted had one and the remaining three went into the Christmas poultry sale at Lalbeck.

Thievin' Jack had tried to buy them from him, but they couldn't agree on the price.

With the village tree lit, our windows heavy with cotton wool snow, and the first of the Christmas cards strung from the beams, that Christmas feeling began to take hold of us. The children sat at the kitchen table making decorations and longing for snow; Vicky baked and worried, went through her card list for the tenth time, bit her lip in that endearing way, and said she would be glad when it was all over.

I harnessed Topic and took a load of wood round to Nellie May, not good logs but old fence posts and rails I had sawn up. 'It'll be sparky stuff,' I warned her.

'S'long as it warms me old bones,' she grinned.

'When are you coming round?'

She fed a dry crust to the pony. 'We'll see what it's like. I gets up to me fire these days an' I don't want to go nowheres.'

'Come round Christmas Eve, at least.'

'Aye, I'd like that; see the bairns' stockin's filled.'

'I'll get a drop of gin in.'

A thin brown finger trembled a warning, 'I'm not gettin' tiddley, not at my age.' She grunted up the step to the cottage, turned with a hand pressed to her thigh, 'Mind you, a drop of gin is good for old bones.'

'Is she coming?' Vicky wanted to know as soon as I opened the kitchen door.

'Christmas Eve.'

'Good. Have a look at this, Susan's just brought it.'

It was a newspaper cutting announcing a special excursion to York. 'What do you think, take the kids for a treat?'

'Sounds fine.'

'I thought me and Susan would take them—if you don't mind.' There was that fixed, exaggerated smile that told me it had all been arranged. 'You can drive us down to Lalbeck and pick us up. Do you realise the kids have never been on a diesel train?'

It meant another day in the shop on my own. A day of boredom, beans on toast for lunch, innumerable cups of tea, a day of clock watching. There was an auction—the last one before the holidays—but I would just have to miss it. It was a shame, because sometimes a dealer who could see himself being short of money at the festive season would put a batch of goods in, and closing his eyes and wincing just let them go.

I made myself a pot of tea, toed the fan heater on to my legs and trickled my fingers along the shelf of books. I would make the best of the day, closing for lunch, taking the dogs for a walk, and maybe, just maybe, I'd call in the pub for a drink.

Being on the road as a salesman for so many years has put me off pubs at lunchtime; they look wrong. We can see in the unforgiving daylight the worn carpet, the chipped paint; the lighting is wrong, that creamy glow of the ceiling is nothing but nicotine staining. But there would be Rabbit to grumble to, and a good fire.

I did not get to the pub. I did choose a book, a reprint of eighteenth-century designs for the cabinetmaker, and was drooling over the fine drawings when the very attractive woman who had tried to sell us the rosewood music cabinet patted her fingers on the window, gave me a gorgeous smile, and beckoned me to her car.

'This may interest you,' she said, pulling a blanket off a mahogany night table. It was a lovely piece; like the drawings I'd been drooling over, it was late eighteenth century, and the quality of the wood was superb. These once mundane pieces of furniture made to hide the chamber pot, keep the medicine safe, and harbour all those little aids and night time comforts we may need, have quite rightly become very sought after.

This one was a very good example, with fretted handles to its tray top, a horizontal tambour front above false, cock-beaded drawers with original swan-necked handles. The wood was rich, heavily figured and well patinated.

'How much are you asking for it?'

Her blonde hair brushed my cheek as she reached into the car and slid the tambour open, her clear grey eyes laughed into mine. There are worse things than standing on a village green in pale wintery sunshine looking at a choice piece of furniture with a beautiful woman. Her lips parted slightly, a pink tongue curled under that enchantingly imperfect tooth.

'I was thinking of a little trade,' she breathed, 'the night table for the fauteuil?'

There was no doubt in my mind—it was a fair swop. True the fauteuil looked really flash. The little seamstress had done a fabulous job, and the gilding had buffed up nicely, but it was still a 'half age piece'—a copy.

'I have undertaken a commission for a very important person, a Cabinet Minister no less, and the fauteuil would fit in perfectly with my scheme for the master bedroom—what do you say?'

I said yes; what else could I do? When I went to put the fauteuil in her car she placed a well manicured hand on my arm. 'Would you mind awfully just taking it across the road for me—across to my parents?' She pointed at the Colonel's house.

'The Colonel's your—'

'Father. I really have neglected them. I've been so busy these last few years.'

I polished the night table, rubbed a little candle grease into the tambour slides, and placed our best Christmas cactus on it. To my mind it looked far classier than the fauteuil, and it was a genuine period piece.

'To hell with poor folk and potted meat,' I

laughed as I threw the tin of beans back in the cupboard. 'I'll away to the shop, treat myself. Roast ham and the best cheese they've got.'

The dogs seemed to agree; they happily followed me to the shop and back, and then sat quietly under the table as I skipped mustard into my sandwiches.

A warm fire to one's back, a comfortable chair, a full belly, a satisfactory deal, the prospect of an afternoon of justifiable idleness—I was a happy man; and I was happy for at least an hour.

Rabbit dumped the sack in the middle of the shop and waved a big hand at me. 'Just sit where you are. I'll sort this stuff out, an' I'll tell you what I want for 'em.'

Soon all the available floor was covered with gin traps, mole traps, fen traps and a wooden mouse trap that bled dust from every worm hole. There was a pair of scotch hands, a fleam or two, a brass scraper for getting sweat off a horse and a lead miner's candle box.

'Dales bygones—gi' us twenty quid.'

'Twenty quid?'

'Hey! Where do you find stuff like this these days?'

'The tip?'

'Don't be like that, I need some brass. I've had a letter.'

'Tax man again?'

'No. Me daughter. She's coming to see me.'

'Another prodigal daughter returns.'

'Eh?'

'The Colonel's daughter has—'

'I know. I've seen her—she's a snotty bitch. Look, give us fifteen.'

Vicky did not seem too happy with my deals. The

110

night table got grudging approval, Rabbit's bygones none at all.

'She's the Colonel's daughter,' I told her.

'Really.'

'Could be a good contact.'

'You said that before.'

'And guess what, Rabbit's daughter is coming to see him.'

'Really.'

I put her lack of enthusiasm down to tiredness. A long day shopping in York with two children, the waiting on the cold platform. I had only been three-quarters of an hour late picking them up— how could I be expected to hear the phone ringing when I was out hanging traps from the beams of the apple house?

With impish smiles the children banned me from the dining room, where they knelt surrounded by ribbons and holly splattered paper. Vicky sat up to the fire shivering and took the coffee I made her without a word.

After I had milked and brought an armful of wood in she did brighten a little and begin to talk. What Susan had bought, how well the shops looked, the thrill of a rare train journey, but she never mentioned the night table or the return of the long absent daughters.

Christmas Eve day, and things were better. Vicky sang as she rolled out pastry. It was unseasonably warm, there was a frosting of snow capping Penhill, but the gentle breeze was from the west, and a pale sunlight tinted the walls of the dairy. I sat on an upturned bucket and plucked the goose. Christmas, as usual, had been tiptoeing near for weeks, then suddenly rushed at us; there seemed to be so much

111

to do in such a short time. I shopped in Lalbeck, did two small deliveries, and spent a long time going over our modest stock of wine.

At six o'clock I fetched Nellie May. She prodded the goose, sniffed at the stuffing, and took a warm mince pie.

'That's a good fat goose,' she said, tugging a cushion from under the cat and thrusting it into the small of her back.

'I'll give you a little tip. When they're fat like that the only way you'll get the skin crisp is to pour boiling water over it before it goes in the oven—I can't abide skin that isn't crisp.'

She said she'd have a gin. I filled a tumbler full and put in just a dash of tonic and watched her face light up at the first sip.

'Now I'll give you a tip,' I said, leaning over her. 'There's a lot of gin ruined by putting too much stuff in.'

She let out a shriek of laughter that caused the cat to leap from its chair.

'You're right. You go across to the pub an' there's that much damned tacklement floating about in it you can't taste owt.'

She put the half-eaten mince pie into her apron pocket, and wrapping her claw-like hand around the tumbler, she sucked at it.

'I hear Rabbit's lass is coming to see him,' I said to her, hoping it would prompt some reminiscences.

'See'd her this mornin'. By, this is a grand fire,' was all I got.

The children showed her their advent calendar, then squatted at her feet. 'Did you ever spend Christmas in a caravan?' Sally asked her.

'Aye, course I did, bairn, dozens of 'em.' She

112

stared into the fire; her shawl had fallen loose, her thinning white hair curled over the collar of her pale blue cardigan, the fire light flickered over her leathery, deeply creased face. 'Aye, I've had some cold un's, been moved on Christmas Eve—you'd think they'd have left us alone then, wouldn't you?'

She looked up at me, her rheumy pale eyes alight, the thin mouth wet with gin breaking into a smile, 'Them police—blue cockatoos we used to call 'em.' We laughed. The old gypsy pointed a long brown finger at the children. 'You bairns don't know you're born.' Then she too began to laugh, her thin bent body shaking until she spilled her drink.

Peter scrambled to his feet and pushing an intent face near mine tapped my shoulder. 'Dad, dad,' he said, flicking his eyes towards the dresser. I had forgotten Fiery's log. It burned well; that lone and cherished log of bone-dry ash. We pushed our chairs back, rucking up the hooky rugs, and told one another what a grand fire it was. The flames flattened and lengthened, curled around the log, then broke into a hundred dancing stag horns to pierce into the black void of the chimney.

'Come on, bed time.' Vicky's smiling command was met with frowns and wrinkled noses and mild protests.

'The sooner you're asleep, the sooner he comes,' Nellie May told them.

Vicky listened at the hallway door. 'They're off— there's not a peep.'

I brought the presents out of the dairy where we had hidden them in the flour bin. We had to open them all and show them to Nellie May. 'You spoil 'em,' she said a dozen times.

'What are bairns for?' Vicky said, smiling wistfully and primping the satin dress on Sally's doll.

I cut into the blue cheese and poured sherry, and Vicky warmed mince pies on the griddle and refilled Nellie May's tumbler.

The clock in the lounge tinged out midnight. We wished each other Merry Christmas, and I kissed a soft cheek and a leathery one that was salty with tears.

'You never met my Jonty, did you?' the old woman said quietly, 'I was just thinkin' abart him. He was a good man—nowt to look at. Bow-legged as hell, couldn't stop a pig in a ginnel—but he was a good man. Good to me.'

She wiped the tears from her face with her shawl and sighed. 'Ee, we'd some good times. If he'd sold a hoss or 'appens a set o' gears an' had a good do, he'd bring me a drop o' gin.' She leaned back in her chair, her eyes vacant, her puckered mouth twitching as she began to hum.

'I could dance an' all in them days.' The crabbed hands clutched her skirt, and her Oxford brogues— the ones I had given her nephew, Apple Tom— began to tap against the fender.

'Aye, I could dance. Jonty would sit on the van steps, his owd pipe crackin', an' he'd watch me. "Good straight legs you have woman," he'd say, "but pull yer skirts darn—you'll freeten the hosses."'

Her thin chest shook with stabs of silent laughter. Then one hand went to her brow and she slumped sideways, her toothless mouth sagged open, and as the hand sank back to her lap, she began to snore gently.

114

CHAPTER NINE

The bustle of Christmas morning, the warm sloth of Boxing Day behind us, we looked to the New Year with confidence and an eagerness. With no auctions, no trade calling, we decided to paint the shop.

I mixed paint until I achieved a warm primrose that belied the ice etching the inside of the windows, which Peter idly scratched at with his thumb nail.

'There's a man watching us,' he said, in a matter of fact voice. Brush in hand I planted my chin on his head.

'Where?'

'In that horse box. He's got a pair of binoculars.'

At the top of the green was one of those splendid horse boxes; not a large one, built on a Mercedes chassis with wood-panelled sides that were grained and varnished to perfection.

Peter's finger traced along the window.

'See that second slot from the cab? Well, if you watch you will see the light catch the binos.'

True enough, there was some movement, then the binos did catch the light.

'Probably kids, waiting for their dad,' I said, as I re-climbed the steps. I was carefully wiping splodged primrose from the matt black of the beams when Peter turned from the door.

'He's coming.'

He was a very small man, sportingly dressed in check cap and hacking jacket, with a paisley scarf at his neck, and pale fawn moleskin trousers. He walked quickly, slightly bent forward, his thumbs hooked into his trouser pockets.

'Put it on the right way up,' he laughed, as he closed the door behind him and wiped his feet. 'Boss has sent me. He has some stuff to sell. Wants you to call in.'

'When?'

'This aft' OK?'

I looked at Vicky and got in return her indulgent look: raised eyes and a tired, almost sighed, 'Go on'.

A bit of honest trade between Christmas and New Year is as welcome as a catspaw of wind in the doldrums.

'Two o'clock OK?' I asked him.

'That'll do. Cornflower House, Middlethwaite. Do you know it?'

I didn't; so instructions followed. One arm was unhooked from the trousers and it made sinuous curves that signified the road up from the bridge. Stiffened fingers bent at right angles and the head was brought into play with side movements to emphasise the sharpness of the left turn. Then the hand bent back elegantly, and bright eyes flicked up into mine. 'Tucked right in, big iron gates. I'll leave 'em open for you.'

Cornflower House belied its name. It was a square, drab place, hidden up a narrow overgrown drive that was edged in moss and was more suited to a carriage and pair than modern vehicles.

The whole place—the house, the outbuildings— looked cold, damp and unloved. A cube of a house, its dark render was streaked black from overflowing gutters and a mustard-coloured lichen spotted the walls around the lower windows.

116

The horse box was standing at the back door, its ramp lowered, revealing a carpeted interior that was fitted with a low desk and a filing cabinet. The walls and roof were painted cream, and between the ventilation slots hung calendars and unframed prints of race horses. On top of the desk was a thick note pad, a stop watch, and a pair of binoculars.

I pulled at the ceramic knob set in a brass circular mount that was so encrusted with verdigris the word 'pull' was barely legible. The knob came away in my hand, followed by a couple of feet of rust eaten rod.

'Don't work—like everything else 'round here.' The small man had swopped the well cut hacking jacket for a brown warehouse coat that nearly reached to the ground. He held the door open and smiled. 'Come in. I'm Cliff by the way. I've just made a pot—we'll have a drop before we go to see his nibs.'

The hall was freezing cold; flaked paint hung from the ceiling, and above the moulded dado the stained wallpaper curled and ballooned from the walls. A bare, spotted light bulb hung from an ornate ceiling rose, the dusty floor was paved in diaper shaped black-and-white tiles, and matches, empty cigarette packets, and cigarette ends had been cast against the high skirting boards by the passage of feet.

The kitchen was no better. The deep sink was ringed with fat, the grey draining boards piled with unwashed plates. Under the table a black cat laid on an overcoat and suckled three kittens. Everything was painted a sickly green— the cupboards, table, the three old country chairs, the window shutters, the doors and walls up to the dado; above, patterns of damp and mildew gave the walls a peculiar, marbled effect.

Cliff lit the gas ring, throwing the spent match to the floor.

'Suppose I'd better take his nibs one or there'll be hell on.' He poured tea from an aluminium pot and, without asking, spooned condensed milk into the two tin mugs. 'He has coffee,' he explained, turning to watch the kettle as he stirred.

A tray was brought from a cupboard and a cloth laid on it. Cliff arranged the sugar bowl, milk jug and cup and saucer to cover as many brown rings as he could, then poured the boiling water into a jug that had a collar of brown frosting.

'Won't be two ticks. I'll tell him you're here.'

I sat and watched the cat and her kittens. She turned yellow unblinking eyes on me and ignored my friendly tongue clickings and whisperings. The kittens were only a few days old; they looked like miniature hippos, with their sausage bodies, tiny ears and heavy muzzles.

'You can have one if you like,' Cliff said happily as he offered me a cigarette. 'No? Well two's spoken for. T'other one will have to find a home 'cos I'm not drowning it—I've told him.'

'What kind of stuff has he to sell, Cliff?'

'All sorts. There's all sorts—some junk, but some interesting bits—an' if he offers to sell Cornflower, for God's sake don't buy it—it's falling to bits.'

'Cornflower?'

'You'll see.'

There was a row of servants' bells above the door; one started to jangle madly.

'He's ready—now I want a bit of discretion. OK?'

He pointed at me with two fingers that clamped

a cigarette.

'Yes, all in the service.'

'I'll explain when we get upstairs—he's in a wheelchair, you know that?'

'No—who is he?'

Cliff spat a mote of tobacco from his lower lip and stared at the black coconut matting that covered the floor.

'The Honourable Edward Pemberton-Gray, once known around the race tracks and fleshpots of Europe as Teddy P-G, until a hunting accident put him in that chair. And don't get the idea he's got no money—he's rolling in it, just won't spend it.'

He was sitting in a wheelchair in front of a gas fire, a low table at his side littered with racing papers. He looked around at me briefly then back at the fire. He had a gaunt, intelligent face, a salt and pepper military moustache, and from under each side of the ancient tasselled smoking cap he wore bushed iron-grey hair. The broad lapels of his quilted dressing gown were stained with snuff, and on his feet were spurred riding boots that had been polished to a brilliant gloss.

It was not a modern wheelchair, but one of those old fashioned wicker ones, high backed, with broad arms and bicycle type wheels. It was a sad room, gloomy and damp, with faded curtains and a fat, low suite with blackened arms and misshapen cushions. A dark oak sideboard was covered with tarnished trophies, and oak-framed black and white prints hung from the picture rail on ugly chains.

'He's here,' Cliff said.

'I can see,' the Hon. Edward replied somewhat irritably. There was a long silence, during which he massaged his fingers, then without looking around

119

he said, 'Take him upstairs Cliff, and see what he thinks.'

The stairs and landing were bare of carpet, and the walls of any decoration; the ceiling pouched here and there, and under the pouches stood galvanised buckets.

'Hell of a state we are in,' Cliff mumbled, as he held a door open for me. 'Now this is where I want a bit of discretion shown.' Under a linen sheet was a full-size snooker table, in good condition. A rack of cues stood under a pleasantly inlaid marker board, and on a marble topped bistro table stood several empty beer cans.

'I get a few of the stable lads in a coupla nights a week. Old Teddy thinks we have rats in—that's why he wants the other rooms clearing. I keep 'em as quiet as possible, but sometimes they get a bit exuberant and he hears the floor creaking. So not a word eh? I've talked him into keeping the table— come on I'll show you the other stuff.'

There was nothing special, just art nouveau bedroom suites in oak; tall wardrobes with tulip-carved panels, and fly-speckled mirrors, stodgy dressing tables and washstands topped with black marble, cast iron fenders, 1920s jug and bowl sets, the occasional print.

The lumber room proved more lucrative, for in it were three pine chests and a brass and black bed of architectural proportions.

'I'll have to do a bit of working out, Cliff.'

'Give you a tip—he's not expecting much, just wants shut.'

I knew how Fiery's eyes would light up at the bedroom suites and pine, but the fenders and the rest of the stuff were very run of the mill; not easy

120

sellers, and I could be stuck with them for months.

Cliff lit another cigarette and sat on a chest of drawers swinging his legs. 'He's all right is Teddy. He's all his chairs at home—just can't leave the gee-gees alone. Hell of a fella in his day, allus in the society papers, most eligible bachelor in England at one time. Comes from a wealthy family; if you've ever bought a jar of pickles, ten to one you've put money in their pockets. But the accident did for him, he's a semi-recluse now, I take him round in the horse box. We're up on the gallops at the crack of dawn.' The legs stopped swinging, and the ash was cast from his cigarette with thoughtful purpose. 'He's a hell of a judge of horse flesh. It's his hatred of the bookies that lets him down. "Put a hundred on the nose Cliff," he'll say, then he'll smile and say, "no make it two—let's cane the bastards." Aye, he's a character.' Cliff's voice trailed off, 'They certainly broke the mould.'

'What about the bedding? It wants tipping.'

'I'll tell him.'

The Honourable Teddy's face showed no expression at all when Cliff told him my price. 'Let's have it out,' he said, with a wave of his hand.

Cliff was a good lifter; there was a surprising strength in his wiry body. Never once did he groan or ask for a breather as we carried the furniture down the stairs and up the ramp of the horse box.

'Cup of tea time, then we'll shove the stuff for the tip in your van.' Cliff looked disdainfully at the crushed packet of cigarettes.

The Hon. Teddy fisted his wheelchair down the hallway and, meeting us in the doorway, spun it around. 'Come on, we'll have a drink.'

Cliff raised his eyebrows and gave me a quizzical

121

look as he pushed his boss back down the hall and through the double doors into a spacious room that had french windows giving on to a walled garden. Eleven Hepplewhite chairs were set around a long mahogany dining table on which were several silver trophies. A breakfront bookcase was filled with stud books and form books and against one wall on a low plinth, stood a stuffed racehorse, saddled and bridled.

The Hon. Teddy stationed himself at the top of the table and threw a bunch of keys at Cliff, who unlocked a sarcophagus shaped wine cooler and took out a whisky bottle and three glasses. If Teddy was taking money out of the bookmakers' pockets he certainly wasn't putting it into the distillers, for into each glass he poured no more than a thimbleful.

'To Cornflower,' he said, raising his glass.

Cliff and I followed suit, and toasted the stuffed racehorse. Teddy smiled, and folding his arms he dropped his chin on to the stained lapels. 'Bet you'd like to get your hands on some of this stuff?'

I looked round the room, the empty glass still in my hand.

'Very nice,' I said, nodding at a painting by Munnings of a woman mounted side-saddle on a grey.

'Bought that at Christie's, after a particularly good meeting at Haydock Park.' Hung at the side of the chimney piece was a divine little sketch of jockeys by Sir John Lavery.

'Doncaster, '66,' chanted Teddy and Cliff.

It became a little game; me selecting a painting or a trophy, they happily and in unison chanting the year and the meeting that had enabled Teddy to buy it. There was a disagreement over the silver inkwell in the shape of a horse's hoof. Cliff was sure it was Newmarket '72, Teddy equally sure it was Beverly '69. There was a silence broken only by a grunt from one and a bout of sniffing from the other.

'You're right, Cliff; Beverly was the claret jug.' Teddy laughed and threw his keys for Cliff to catch, 'Come on, we'll have another.'

I was driving but I had an hour's work in front of me before I took the wheel—and two thimblefuls of whisky . . .

Again we raised our glasses to Cornflower, then we were back to our game. Every race-course in England had contributed something to the wonderful collection, with the exception of York. I pointed this out to Teddy, who thumped his glass on to the table and wagged a finger at the racehorse.

'You've noticed. There's a reason for that. Cornflower won at York—The Yeomanry Stakes '38. I was a student then. Bit of a rash fella. I'd got meself into a hole, and I put everything I had in the world on her nose—and you came through for me, didn't you old girl?' He winked at the horse. 'Helluva mare; carrying top weight, heavy going and a blizzard blowing and she came through—won by half a length. We've never been back to York since. I managed to buy her at Tatts the following year, and she did me proud. The little mare with the heart of a lion.' He wheeled himself alongside the horse and slapped its belly, coughing at the dust. 'No, it was a traumatic day. I've never been able to bring myself to go to a meeting at York ever since. When the war started I joined the RAF and she went out to grass. Sixteen when she died. I put her to some good stallions, but nothing ever came of it. She just had that spark.'

Teddy jangled his spurs on the chair footrests and flung out an arm. 'To the belvedere, Cliff.'

'Oh no, not today,' Cliff moaned.

'Forward!' Teddy yelled, seizing a whip and slashing at his boots.

We pushed him across the cobbled yard and along a concrete pathway at the top of the garden and into a circular belvedere that was glazed all around and topped by a lead clad cupola. Teddy wheeled around and pulled towards himself a steel contraption on castors which bridged his knees and held, on universal joints, a pair of German naval binoculars and a telescope.

'Fiendishly clever, eh? Look, I can see over the gallops from the old rubbing houses to the Town pasture. If it's an inclement day or Cliff's too busy to drive me up in the 'box, I can sit in here and see everything. Mind you, I prefer going up on the moor—you can pick a bit of gossip up that's useful.'

He spun the chair around, leaving curved tyre marks on the floor. 'Had this belvedere brought from the old place, along with these.'

The whip flicked out towards a long rustic pergola that was overgrown with climbing roses. Here and there pale yellow flowers remained, nipped and shrivelled by the frosts.

'I call 'em my Chinamen. They are Fortune's double yellow. My great-grandfather was a member of the Royal Horticultural Society and he was the first to grow them in the north. They're a bit tender, but they do well here. Fortune himself came to see them growing at the Hall, and my grandfather remembered seeing him. He told Father that Fortune was still wearing the pigtail that he grew when he was in China and he had sat him on his knee and told him how he had smuggled cuttings out of the country. So that's why they are my Chinamen. See this whip? It used to be Fred Archer's.'

'We're not sure,' Cliff said slowly.

'Course it did. I always hold it when I'm picking the winners.' He spun the chair and laughed up at me. 'When I advertise my tipping service I always put "I can see the horses training from my bedroom window!" Well, I can't really put my belvedere, can I? They would think I was a bit eccentric.' His pale eyes twinkled with merriment.

I threw the mattresses and bedding through the landing window into the yard. Mattresses are not easy to handle on one's own. It isn't their weight, but their shape and resilience. I folded them in two and, kneeling on them, tied them with string before sending them bouncing into the yard. Pillows were more fun. I aimed them carefully at a bending and unsuspecting Cliff, following each hit with a convincing, 'sorry'.

I got no response until I threw out the bedding from the boxroom, then there was a shriek of dismay followed by an 'Oi! What the hell do you think you are doing?' It was Cliff's bedding.

*   *   *

They were talking about Rabbit's daughter in the shop and in the pub. She'd been to see Nellie May and Baz and Susan, and every day somebody spotted her walking over the tops with Rabbit's

125

terriers, but I never managed to clap eyes on her.

Reports varied; Baz describing her as a real cracker, Ted thought she was a good looking lass, but too skinny. Vicky met her in Lalbeck and said she seemed a nice woman, very polite, and very well spoken, then added thoughtfully, 'I bet she's a bit flighty.'

I pressed her to elaborate. What made her appear flighty? Had she wicked eyes? A coquettish way?

'No, just gives me that impression.'

Mrs Hall said she was a grand quiet lass, Mr Martin was impressed by her brain, Billy Potts wanted to devour her. Like the blind men describing the elephant, they gave such conflicting reports on the woman I just had to see her for myself.

'How about a brace of pheasants for the New Year?' I asked Vicky. She seemed agreeable, so I put on the better of my two waxed jackets and went to see Rabbit.

He was plucking woodcock under the lean-to, bare armed and hatless, oblivious to the numbing cold.

'Aye, I've a brace—been hung a week. All right?'

'Yes, they'll be fine—not old 'uns are they?'

'No, young birds. I'll get 'em for yer, when I've done this. I'm getting these ready for our lass's supper. She's off to Richmond for the day.'

I clicked my tongue, paid for the pheasants, and hung about at the top of Mill Lane until my legs ached with the cold.

'You've been a long time, did he keep you gabbing?'

'A bit,' I said quietly.

126

She wasn't on the four o'clock bus and she wasn't on the six o'clock one either. 'Get into the pub tonight,' Ted advised, 'she's going back tomorrow. Owd Rabbit'll be sure to take her in tonight.'

Even if it was for just one drink I had to get into the pub. I racked my brain for a suitable ploy as I idly stared out across the green. I suppose I could have just said I needed to see Ted or Baz and disappeared for an hour, but it was New Year's Eve, and to sneak off for a drink without Vicky did not seem right.

Baz solved my problem in a bright and definite way. He and Susan came down just after we had got the children to bed.

'Come on, you can buy me a pint.' He broke the corner off the blue cheese and teased it against the roof of his mouth. 'That's nice.'

'Yes, I think we'll be making more,' I told him. 'Ted says I can have a couple of gallons when I'm ready.'

'Just as long as you don't use the rennet.'

'We did.'

He pulled a face, and quickly withdrew his finger and thumb from the cheese board.

'What's wrong with his rennet?'

'Nowt—really.' He clapped his hands and rubbed them in an exaggerated way. 'Come on, I'm only off the leash for an hour and that ale's waiting.'

It was like opening the door of a bake house. A blue haze hung under the paper-chained beams, and a solid mass of bodies crowded around the bar and between the tables. Baz twisted his body and, raising one arm like the prow of a ship, cut through the noisy crowd towards the taproom.

'Come on, we'll never get served up here.' I

followed in his wake, greeting and apologising in equal measure.

It was cooler and less crowded in the taproom, and beside a proud and freshly shaved Rabbit sat his daughter. She was turned towards him, one hand on the back of the settle, a slim girl in tight, faded jeans and a bright red shirt. Her short hair, an intense black, shone with health and care, bands of highlights flickering over it as she bobbed and shook her head in animated conversation. A small hand, ringless, delicate, twisted a half-empty glass on the table top. The hand came down from the settle, her elbow pressing into hard boards as she pulled her hair up from the nape of her neck, which was thin and startlingly white.

Rabbit pointed to us. She flicked her head around, white fingers still thrusting through her hair, and gave us a steady, appraising look before she smiled.

Her lips were full and pillowy, light pink; her teeth, white, the upper front pair dominant, but not too large. The face oval, with a pert chin and high arching brows over the most remarkable eyes. They were large candid eyes the colour of licked chocolate. They were the kind of eyes a man looked into and smiled and forgot things.

Charlie pushed our drinks through the serving hatch.

'Them's on Rabbit.'

Baz drank deeply then nodded at Rabbit, who beckoned us over. 'Here have you met my lass?'

We were introduced, taking in turn the soft hand, smiling a little too much, hesitant. 'I'm putting faces to names,' she laughed up at us as we bent over the table.

'Don't believe owt he's said about me,' Baz whispered, leaning near her.

Rabbit had both his hands on the table, his face red and smiling, his eyes constantly on his daughter. 'I've just told her that yer an idle bugger who's never had a right job in his life.'

Josephine tossed her head back and laughed; gripping her father's arm she pushed her forehead into his shoulder. 'Is he always like this?'

'It's the best we've ever seen him,' Baz confessed, 'you'll have to come more often, love—we never knew he could be so human.'

It was quite a remarkable night, for not only did Rabbit buy me a drink, so did Ted. He was standing in front of the closed dart board in his best tweed suit, his cap pulled to one side, jingling the change in his pocket, a bemused look on his face.

'Happy New Year, Ted.'

'Aye, same to you.' His beer glass touched my coat. 'What do you make of it, eh?'

'What's that?'

'Well, look in there.' We peered through the serving hatch into the better room; at the bar was the Colonel, with his daughter. She was wearing a black cocktail dress with a single row of pearls, and she was sitting on a stool, her elegant legs crossed, listening intently to her father.

'Look at her and look at her,' Ted's fat finger pointed at the Colonel's daughter then at Rabbit's. He leaned forward, tapped his glass against his chest, and looked fiercely into my eyes. 'And they say crows don't breed pigeons.'

129

CHAPTER TEN

The first sale of the year is always well attended. Dealers shake off their torpor, do mental calculations that are approximate and optimistic and, donning their warmest clothes, make for the auction rooms. There is time for reflection as the everyday unlotted chattels and soft goods are sold.

'I'll never buy another mule chest,' Fatty mumbles, 'unless it's muck cheap. I've got two standing there, and I have had them for yonks.'

The dealers with warehouses who only supply the trade and the runners, who make a precarious living at the best of times, are cautious; but those of us who have shops and a good loyal clientele are better placed. The festive season had been good for us; we had never sold so much jewellery and Mrs Smythe-Robinson had treated herself to the mahogany night table. We were not exactly awash with money, but we had built up our working capital, and if the van could be cajoled into lasting another year we would be able to whittle a bit off the mortgage.

Ours is a great trade for the optimist; this will be the year, we tell ourselves as we root through the mediocre in search of that overlooked gem. Every time I do this I think of Elly finding that Turner sketch, and Martin de Trafford smiling as he pulled the St Louis paperweight from the old sewing bag he'd bought for a pound.

I remember too Old Sarah, who had the biggest junk business in the West Riding. She presided over a saddening collection of trash that was stacked into low buildings round an old stable yard. One loose box was full of old Army great coats devoid of all buttons and nested in by a phalanx of rats. Another—better favoured—held boots, partially worn but finding a ready market amongst the gentlemen who cover many miles on foot and are not too worried about a perfect match at ten bob a pair.

The tack room Sarah used as an office, reclining most of the time upon a Victorian day bed she steadfastly refused to sell.

When a dealer drew into the yard she would spring to the door, a rotten-toothed grin of welcome on her fat face. She wore frayed mittens summer and winter, men's trousers—as often as not with red piping at the seams—and a sweater that could have covered a small elephant. On her feet the pick of the boots.

'The antiques is in amongst,' she would call cheerfully, before giving a cackle and returning to the day bed. Vicky and I, when we were first starting up, did find the odd thing 'in amongst', but the time spent searching and the obligatory bath afterwards made the game hardly worth the candle. Yet we always remembered Sarah whenever we stuck our nose into a really forlorn looking sale. 'The antiques must be in amongst,' we would whisper together.

Sam was sober and uncommunicative. 'Where's it all from?' I asked him, and so did every other dealer in the place.

'Up the Dale,' was the short and clipped answer we all got.

The village hall had never seen such quality furniture. It was a dealer's stuff, of that there was no doubt. The stage was packed with no less than seven marble-topped washstands, four sets of chairs, four tables, a big dresser, two long case clocks and, in the centre—in pride of place—a beautiful Carlton House desk in satinwood.

Fatty Batty tapped me lightly on the shoulder, 'Makes a nice change—more mice than cats for once.'

'Dealer's stuff.'

'Yes—but at the right price?'

'Will it be?'

'We could make it so.'

I looked straight into his questioning eyes; was I being invited to 'stand in'?

'I'd be happy with the Carlton House,' I said quietly.

'Wouldn't we all? I'll have a word with Elly and George.'

I had mentioned the desk in all innocence, never for one minute believing I would be able to buy such a prized piece of furniture, and Fatty's reply took me by surprise.

I was being asked to join the Ring, something we had vowed we would never do. Vicky would never countenance such a thing and though sorely tempted, I was on the point of declining Fatty's offer when he said, 'Leave the tables and chairs alone and we'll not bother you.'

He stalked off before I could say anything, leaving me in a bit of a dilemma, for I had no intention of bidding for them—they were too big for us. Those massive Georgian tables with three or four inserts would have looked out of place in our tiny shop; anyhow, they would be expensive, and deservedly so, for they were all of a high quality.

I collared Long John as soon as he arrived. He took his white smock from its hook and thrust his arms into it, dropping his bearded chin as his fingers searched for buttons and holes. He was a long time answering my question, and before he did he repeated it.

'Whose stuff is it? This goes no further, right?' He leaned forward and whispered the name of a very prominent and respected dealer.

'Never.'

'I'm tellin' yer, it is.'

'Why? Why put it in here? This stuff ought to be at . . .'

'Needs the readies, don't he,' Long John rubbed his fingers together expressively. 'He's doing a bunk. There's only Sam that'll pay him cash—so here it is.'

'Doing a bunk,' I said slowly.

We were talking about one of the biggest names in the trade, a second generation dealer whose showroom was the envy of all, whose reputation was untarnished, whose judgement and knowledge commanded the respect of every dealer in the county.

'Doing a bunk.'

'Spain,' Long John said smugly, 'he's been on the fiddle and things are catching up with him.'

'Fiddle?'

'In a big way, apparently. Now, I haven't told you owt—remember.'

Antique dealing should be a simple trade. Be wary of the fake and flashed-up piece, follow market trends, build up a reputation for knowledge and fairness, take a reasonable profit, and be a good steward to the lovely things that pass through

133

our hands. Moral dilemmas should not be on our daily menu.

Was I in the Ring? Did the stuff in the sale belong to our illustrious dealer, or to his creditors? When Sam handed over that wad of soiled banknotes, who was being cheated?

There is one salient thing about buying at auction: at the moment the hammer falls, ownership of the lot is transferred to the person who is willing to give more for it than anyone else in the room. The auctioneer has a fat percentage— let him worry about the ethics and provenance. My sole worry now, I thought, ought to be how much I could afford to pay for the desk.

I rang Vicky. A prestige piece I told her, a beautiful piece. What should I do?

'Buy it, if you think we can make a profit,' were her final words.

There is something about a Carlton House desk. It speaks so much of the Regency period, although they can be found much earlier, in Gillows cost books of 1762, and Sheraton stated emphatically that they should be in satinwood with a brass gallery.

Mr Sheraton would have liked the one that stood on the dusty stage in Lalbeck church hall that bright, crisp January morning. It was a good one, slightly faded, in need of some minor repair, but it had an air about it that spoke of being left alone for years; at the most only slightly used, it was that thing most prized by our trade—a true sleeper.

Normally I would have admired it, trailed my fingers lovingly over its inlaid surfaces, sighed and made a mental picture of it, then calculated how far I could push the Ring. But here they were, willing to stand off for me provided I left the other stuff alone.

Alarm bells rang in my head—was it a nineteenth-century copy, a half age piece, still beautiful and desirable but not the real McCoy? I took out every drawer and inspected the dovetails, they were thin and precise, and the grain of the drawer bottoms ran front to back. The veneers were thick, hand cut, and the inlaying restrained. All the handles and key plates were original, and the leather skiver, although scuffed and ink stained—was a delightful, faded raspberry colour.

It was worth the thick end of two thousand pounds. I felt a slight sickness in the pit of my stomach, and my palms were clammy. My back was against the wall. The Ring had, by offering to stand off on the desk, put me in a position where I had to show strength or lose face.

I stabbed a finger on to the top of a dust laden piano as I did mental calculations. Sam was usually good for a bit of credit, and quite often we put a van load of mediocrity in one of his sales to pay for a good painting or piece of furniture we had bought from him. It was an accepted and welcome ploy, for Sam is a volume man. He stands beaming, his trilby pushed to the back of his head, his beer belly thrust out, and tells us with great pride that he has 'nigh on a thousand lots to get through'. It is always an exaggeration. A good sale in the church hall will have four hundred lotted items and half as many unlotted ones.

Long John wades through the latter, grumbling, tossing aside the plugless electric fire and unsaleable tie press.

'Come on boss,' he urges Sam, 'let's get on wi'

it—there's half an acre o'bloody junk here.'

Sam cautions him, 'Thee steady on. It's that bloody junk that pays thi wages.'

There is method in John's madness, for he gets to pick over the unsold lots before they are consigned to the tip. A cast iron pan or griddle, a wood fender, the tarnished brass plaque, all end up in the back of his van.

'I can find a home for 'em,' he grins. And so he can, for many a dealer shipping to America will jolt over the track to his lonely farmhouse looking for 'fillers', those cheap and cheerful bits of yesteryear, to pack into the Victorian wardrobe or the Georgian kist.

Long John has a nose for scrap. He scratches the orchard sprayer with his pocket knife and gives me a candid look. 'I thought it wor brass—just had that look about it.' It is flung nonchalantly into the corner with a 'worth a couple of bob is that'. When Sam asks for a pound for it Long John is quick to comment. 'There's a bit missing,' then quietly, 'go on I'll give you a half crown for it.'

The wise do not bid against him—they let him have his perks.

'Been much interest in the desk?' I asked him.

'Like flies round a jam pot yesterday.' His passive face took on a dry look, then he added, 'but nobody of consequence.'

'No de Trafford?'

'Nope.'

'No Jack the Pat?'

'Nope. There's no reserve on the stuff, and so far there's only one proxy bid on it—an' that's nowt to worry about. Derisory, Sam called it, but it'll do for a starter.'

My bolt hole tactic of bidding it to a respectable price against a hefty proxy bid was gone. I would have to put on a show, let the Ring know for once and for all that we had purchasing power. As Sam auctioned off the junk I went and rung Vicky again, telling her what Long John had told me.

'What shall we do?' I asked her.

'Look, do you want me to come and hold your hand? You've been in the trade long enough; just take it to the point where there's a bit of profit left. If it's as good as you say it should sell quickly—anyhow, we need a prestige piece. I've just sold the Askrigg longcase.'

She had that tone in her voice she has when she is bolstering the confidence of the children, an 'of course you can do it' tone—and she'd sold the Caygill of Askrigg clock.

'Right, my dear,' I said, leaning back against the cold glass of the telephone kiosk, 'I'll go back in there guns blazing and pennants flying—but seriously, what do you think I should go to?'

There was a low groan, a click of the tongue, then a low, patronising voice. 'Look if you're so worried about it, leave it alone.'

I couldn't leave it alone—we would lose face. It would become a little incident for the Ring to chuckle over, to point the finger. I could see it becoming part of the repertoire of the saleroom anecdotage amongst them. 'Remember the time we stood off on . . .'

With the sale of the clock we had more capital available, and we were proving that we could sell top of the range stuff—the fauteuil, the night table, and now the clock. It was a local one, a good maker, a fine, slim, well figured oak case—and it had not been cheap.

I went out to the van and rooted the vacuum flask out from under a pile of blankets. £2000 was a figure that kept coming into my head; it must be worth £2000. We had never spent so much at one time, let alone on one piece. Suppose I bought it and it proved to be one of those dreaded pieces that suck up capital and for some inexplicable reason fail to sell. They stand centre stage in the shop or warehouse, a sharp, everyday reminder of folly or pride—or bad judgement.

The trade euphemistically calls them old friends, and we all get them from time to time. We get carried away, we show off, fashions change, the last one we had walked out of the shop; there are innumerable ways of getting stuck with an old friend.

Sam will not stick to the lot numbers; he sells more in groups. The soft goods and everyday chattels, then on to the tables for the better class of smalls, the quality furniture on the stage, rough stuff down the sides of the hall, then finally the carpets, which have been thrown—a yard deep—into the cloakroom.

I drank my tea, did a fair bit of blowing and sighing, and decided I would go to £1800 on the desk. With the van door open and my body half turned in the driver's seat I could see Long John's shaggy head through the dirty windows. They were selling the smalls. There were things I should have been watching—the gold mounted cane, the pewter measures—but I could not bring myself to bid, to disperse capital on bread and butter stuff; it was an all or nothing day.

When Long John jumped up on the stage I cast

138

the remaining tea into the yard, slammed the van door, and with a wildly beating heart marched purposefully into the saleroom.

Long John had his hand on the desk. 'Let's get this out of the way, Sam,' he called cheerily as he gave me a knowing look; he had sensed something was afoot.

I was pleased they were selling the desk first. It would show if the Ring was going to play it as they had said they would. One of my fears had been that they would get a free run at the things they wanted then employ a front man, unknown to me, to bid for the desk on their behalf.

Sam did not waste time, opening the bidding at £600. I let it idle on to a £1000, then with a heart beating so loudly that I was sure it could be heard in the back two rows, I waved my hand. Sam already had a bidder so he pointed at me to show my interest had been noted as he took £100 bids from two women in the front row. One was the new doctor's pretty wife, the other Mrs Smythe-Robinson. Money: that's what those two women with their straight backs and well-cut clothes spoke of.

When the doctor's wife finally shook her head at £1600 and gave her opponent the weakest of smiles, I looked at Sam and raised my eyebrows. Mrs Smythe-Robinson, in response to the bid, half turned in her seat and stared hard at the Ring.

They were stood in a loose group in various attitudes of unconcern; Fatty, hands in pockets, whistled, whilst George studied his own shuffling feet; Elly was engrossed with the nails of his left hand. A flicker of doubt crossed the woman's face before she bit her lip and flicked a glove at Sam. I

139

left it as long as I dared, prompting a melancholy 'you're out at the back' from Sam. Then I raised my brows again, whilst carefully studying a grime haloed light switch.

'Eighteen hundred pounds—nineteen for you, madam?' Sam asked Mrs Smythe-Robinson in a very gentle voice. She shook her head, pressed her lips together lightly, and pulled on her glove. It seemed an age before Sam dropped the gavel; my whole body ached with tension and my throat was lumpy, and behind my eyes a fist of pain began a slow even thumping. It was more than twice what we had ever paid for a piece of furniture—and it needed some repair.

'Here, you look as if you need it.' Canary Mary held out a flask top of tepid coffee.

'Mary,' I said, 'what have I done?'

'Don't you worry, pet. It's a lovely piece. It'll sell, just you see.'

'I've to pay for it first.'

I tried to work out the buyer's commission and VAT on £1800, but even such simple arithmetic was beyond me at that moment. Mary patted my arm and, inclining her head, looked up into my eyes in that warm and reassuring way people adopt before they come out with banalities like 'worse things happen at sea'.

'If it doesn't sell, it would be nice for Vicky, a real woman's thing, a Carlton House desk—and such a bonny colour.'

'And a bonny price.'

Vicky was out of the shop and across the yard before I could get the van doors open.

'Did you get it?'

I pulled the blankets from the desk, '*Voilà.*'

140

She stood silent for a while, then climbed into the van and sat on a wheel arch. Her eyes were bright, one hand supporting her chin, finger and thumb pushing her cheeks up.

'Well?'

'How much?'

'Eighteen hundred pounds, plus.'

Her eyes flicked over the desk. She extended her free hand and carefully opened a drawer, then pushed it shut equally as careful.

'Well—say something.'

'It's nice, very nice.'

'Do you think we've done right?' I purposely put much emphasis on the 'we've'.

She did not answer, but put her arm around my shoulder and drew my head to her cheek. The tension of the saleroom behind me, the worry that had churned my stomach and invaded my head with an almost numbing pain, ebbed away.

We both ran our fingers lightly over the lovely wood, turned, and smiled at each other.

*   *   *

The desk attracted a lot of attention. We put it in the best position in the shop, and trained our two spotlights on to it. The damage, we decided, was not too detrimental, and apart from giving it a polish and gently rubbing the skiver with an oily rag we did nothing to it.

We placed a French carriage clock of high quality on its galleried top, and Vicky arranged several paperweights and an elegant silver inkwell on the writing surface.

Peter spent an hour sorting through the key box

141

and found one that fitted; it wasn't a period one, but it was satisfyingly ornate and Vicky tied an elaborate silk fob to it. We were very proud of our desk.

Mrs Smythe-Robinson viewed it through the window, sniffed, slammed her car door rather viciously, and drove off at speed.

Fiery Frank spread his hands on it, opening every drawer, told us the castors weren't original, then walked around it whistling tunelessly.

'Into the quality stuff eh,' his fingers trailed on the brass gallery, 'it's all right if you can sell it.'

I looked up at the ceiling and groaned. 'Don't say that, Frank.'

'Oh, it'll go—in time—everything sells in time. How much is it?'

'Two thousand five hundred pounds, sir.'

He blew out his cheeks, rolled his head and staggered sideways.

I took the flamboyant little philosopher out into the yard and punished him by upping the price of the inlaid bedroom suite by a fiver. He winced and complained, but he still bought it.

We did not put a price tag on the Carlton House desk, deciding we would keep things a bit fluid. With so much money tied up we knew that if it did not sell in a few months it would have to go off to one of those city auction houses to give us the capital we needed for the start of the tourist season.

It was nice to have these things, but a glance through our day book confirmed what we already knew; it was the cheaper end, the ten to fifty pound items, that kept us viable.

Ted came to see the desk. He stood in front of it, a bemused look on his face.

'Ar' Billy has one just like this.' The big fingers hovered over it. 'But ar' Billy's has drawers down to t'floor. He began to walk slowly around it. 'An' ar' Billy's has knobs, not these tootlin' little handles.' He stopped and, raising his cap at the front, scratched his red forehead.

'What's it made on?'

'Satinwood.'

'Ar' Billy's is oak,' he announced loudly and grinned, with just a flick of his head to drive the point home. 'How much is this then?'

I slipped easily into my big dealer mode; folding my arms I stared out into the grey afternoon. 'Two and a half.'

'Well, if this flimsy little thing is worth that, ar' Billy's must be worth three hundred.'

CHAPTER ELEVEN

The children collect what they call, 'Ted's nice words'. Dumbledore and pettichaps; the humble bumble bee and the garden warbler were the first to intrigue and amuse them, and Peter will smile wryly as he repeats Ted's verdict on a badly faring sheep—'nobbut dowly', he says, in an exaggerated, deep voice.

If the cobbles in front of the shop are iced over, Ted will shout a warning 'mind out, it's slape'; and when a chill north wind sweeps down off the grey tops, flapping his jacket and making him blow on his red hands he complains that it's 'fair snizey'.

A tramp hobbles his way through the village and he pulls the children's legs all day about 'the milepost inspector'. A companion of his youth, a fell runner, is remembered fondly and his fleetness of foot is conveyed to us with a shake of the head and a solemn tone 'by God, but he was snell'.

When a skylark trills from high on a clear day he tells us 'it's a good sign when the laverlock's up'. When the machine-gun rattle of a green woodpecker is heard in Fox Covert he stops and puts a hand to his ear: 'Yon popinjay's at it agen.'

He calls the shy little wren a 'stumpie', and he has a word for Casper McFarlane; but it is unrepeatable.

The trouble between him and the retired ship's engineer arose over a load of logs. Ted sold him the logs, delivered them free, even stacked them neatly outside Casper's boiler house, but the tall thin Scotsman refused to pay full price for them, declaring angrily that, 'they had nae calorific value'.

Ted looked up calorific values in his encyclopedias, put on his gentleman's suit, and confronted Casper. 'Anything that'll burn has a calorific value, and them logs—although there might have been a bit of green elm in 'em—were a good lot, an' I want payin'.'

Casper paid; half the agreed price, and steadfastly refused to give any more. Apparently Ted, quite out of character, had offered violence. A course of action he immediately regretted, for although Casper is as thin as a lat he has enormous hands on long arms, and having spent a lifetime in and out of some of the roughest ports on this globe of ours, he knows how to take care of himself.

Ted had ended up flat out amongst Casper's prize leeks. I got this story from Baz, and had it confirmed by Rabbit who was able to add—

144

happily—that Dolly had given him the steak that Ted had used on his swollen eye, and that it was the finest piece of beef he had ever tasted. It is, as they say, an ill wind.

And it was a wind of sorts that took me up to Casper's place. The gales that lashed across the Dale in the first week in February had wrecked Casper's conservatory, and he was in need of money.

He stood with hands on his hips amidst the broken glass and splintered glazing bars and cursed. 'That bloody Nor' Wester. I heard her go—I hav'nae heard sich a crash since the old Empress of Cathay took the jetty away in Montevideo.'

'It's a mess, Casper.'

'Aye, but I'll rebuild her,' he swung round and fixed me with a fierce eye, 'but this time it'll be teak on oak beams—a real seaworthy job, an' that'll stand these tootlin' breezes we git up here—you'll see. The elements have ne'er beaten Casper McFarlane. Why, mon, I once put new fire bars in the old *Rose of Tralee* as she wallowed in a force eight off the Cape.' He held out his enormous hands. 'There's skill in these hands, and there's a mickle o' brain in this old heead.'

'What do you want to sell, Casper?'

His eyes blazed, and the dewdrop on the end of his hooked nose trembled but continued to defy gravity.

'Treasures, mon—treasures.' He stepped delicately through the rubble and signalled to me to follow him.

The house was oppressively hot. Down the hallway stretched two runs of six inches diameter steam pipe, so hot that one could not bear one's

145

hand an inch from them, let alone touch them. Casper tapped the upper then the lower one with a spanner, smiled, then bent to peer at a large, highly polished pressure gauge. This gave him more satisfaction than the tapping of the pipes, for the smile became a wide grin.

'She's up ta pressure—an' that's wi' oot the booster.'

He did a little jig, an inelegant figure in baggy khaki shorts and fisherman's smock, a blue woolly cap pulled down over his ears.

'I'll show yer the boiler afore ye go,' he promised with the wag of a finger. 'Now laddie, the treasures await. A veritable cornucopia of good taste.'

I have never considered stuffed parrots to be in the best taste; Casper had three. I got their life histories, their little habits and peccadilloes, even how much they had cost to be mounted. They were Amazonian parrots—the best, I was told. The one in the glass case was called Captain Holt.

'He was my first master, aboard the old *Star of Madagascar*. What a queer, biling fella he was. Used to inspect the ship every Sat'day morning, walking around wi' white gloves on, an' Gawd help ye if them gloves got mucky. Nae shore leave, extra duties, boat drill till wa' could do it wi' our een closed. Aye, he was a queer fella alright—so I called ma first parrot after him and taught him to screech "I'll make a sailor oot o'you, Mister".'

Casper laughed out loud, throwing his head back then hurriedly bringing a handkerchief from the pocket of his shorts to catch the dewdrop. He blew loud and long, then held the handkerchief in front of him and inspected it.

'Aye, we've had many a laugh, me an' Captain

146

Holt here.'

The next parrot was mounted in a very natural manner on one of those Tee perches, its head turned slightly, its beak open.

'This here's Chief Engineer Coles—or Coley, as we used to call him. He wasna' a man, he was the De'il incarnate, a blusterin', cursin', drinkin' man who couldna' keep his hands to hisself. A brutal man who made my life a misery when I was fourth engineer on the old *Drumness Castle*.' He poked the parrot, making it rock.

'I taught this one to say "oil Number Four, oil", for he was a man who should ha hed an oil can carved on his tombstone—except he went doon to a wattery grave wi' the old *Prince of Denmark*.'

Casper folded his arms and gave the last parrot a mean and icy stare. 'An' this here's Mrs McFarlane, named for the woman who blighted thirty years of my life. She used to say "Ar' ye no caming hame Casper", and I used to tek great pleasure—great pleasure—in thrustin' ma nose to her beak and saying, "No I bloody aint".'

I opened my jacket and loosened my tie, for the huge pipes which snaked around the room made it uncomfortably hot.

Peggy James, that fine and upstanding woman who cleans for Casper, goes into the broom cupboard and takes all her clothes off on arrival; dusting and polishing clad only in a thin nylon overall. She is in no danger, for her employer—in spite of his occasional lapses into violence—is a very moral man.

'Well then, how much for they parrots?'

'Sorry, Casper.'

'Sorry, sorry. What the hell dae yer mean, mon—

fine specimens like that, part o' my life, parrots wi'
a history, an' yer no interested.'

He dabbed his nose with the handkerchief and
gave a long low moan. 'I thought you'd jump at 'em.
Well, no matter; on to other things.'

He had a good writing box made from porcupine
quills, a stuffed armadillo, and some Arabic knives,
wickedly curved blades and handles so heavily
ornamented they were difficult to hold.

'This is the stuff, Casper,' I told him.

'Bazaar stuff.'

'It sells.'

'We'll hev a look in here.'

He led me into what was his den, his retreat
from the world. 'I no allow the woman to come in
here, understand? It's a room for men. I want nae
prissying in here, nae smell o' perfume.'

It was a small room much the size I imagined his
cabin as Chief Engineer would have been. There
was a roll-top desk against one wall, a leather
armchair scuffed and stained and bagged down in
the seat until it looked the most comfortable chair
in the world, and a small table covered with nautical
books. On the walls were photographs of ships and
a watercolour of the Pool of London on a grey day,
packed with shipping.

Casper stacked the books on the table until there
was enough room for him to sit then indicated that
I should take the chair. He coughed, folded his
arms, and stared at the ceiling.

'What do ye think of that little picture?'

'It's super.' I got up and had a closer look at
it. Choppy oily water in the foreground, a tug,
workaday and rust streaked, dug in its stern as the
screw bit and the tow line came taut. Two shadowy

148

figures stood on the bow of a lighter, behind them massed ships, smoke stacks and masts and over the grey broken line of warehouse roofs, a sun setting behind ragged clouds. It was beautiful. Everything was right; the perspective, the tonality, the composition—it was from the hand of a master.

'No, it's more than super, Casper—it's gorgeous. Is it for sale?' He shook his head, and took off his woolly hat and turned it over in his big hands.

'No, I couldnae sell that. There's tae mony memories in that picture.' He raised his head and looked at it, then with a guffaw pulled his ear. 'Ye'll think 'am an aud fool, an' ye can laugh at me if ye want, but I put everything I had into that picture.'

'You painted it?'

'Aye, it's no bad, if I say it ma'sel'.'

'It's brilliant.' I had just lowered myself into the chair, but I sprang up again and went to the picture. It was dated 1932 and signed C.M. Casper rose and joined me, his finger tracing over the glass.

'That there was the *Star of Madagascar*, ma first ship, and this here picture is how I first saw her, in the Pool on a grey February day. I was fresh down frae Scotland, a raw young lad, and when I stood an' looked at they ships—that power, that majesty—I knew there was no other life for me. I had nae salt watter in ma veins—we were a croftin' family—but I went along to the shipping office, told a wee lie or two, an' I got my first berth. They were hard days to be a seaman. Ye had to tek yer turn at trimmin' the bunkers, an' I chipped rust an' painted till ma arms were dropping off—an' the grub was atrocious, but it was still the life for me. Rose ta be a Chiefy, torpedoed three times, been round the world more times than I can remember. Seen sights

149

every man should see, an' seen sights nae man should see.'

The finger dropped from the glass; he chewed his lip and breathed down his nose. 'Forty-two years wi' the same line. They had twenty-seven grand ships when I joined 'em; now they've one dredger an' a wee little thing that brings timber o'er from Scandinavia.'

'Casper, how does an old seadog come to—'

'I know, I know, why do I live here? I'm asked that mony a time. Well, look.' He went to the tiny north-facing window. 'See, we're 600 feet above sea level, an' that way it's forty-eight miles as the crow flies to the North Sea, and this way forty-eight and a half miles to the Irish Sea. What better place to swallow the anchor?'

'Do you think we could open a window?'

'Aye, why not.' My clothes were stuck to me, and I felt a little sickly.

'Casper. Have you any more watercolours?'

'Drawers full.'

And so he had. I got the background to every one as he cast them on to the table like a man dealing outsize playing cards.

'A wartime one that; destroyer escort in the Atlantic. That's the old *Melbourne* on her way to the breaker's yard.' He paused, a set look on his face. 'Was there ever a more beautiful ship? The *Mauritania*.' He let the picture drop slowly. It showed the liner three quarters on, showing the port light and ploughing through an indigo sea on a tropical night. Lights punctured the side of the ship, and from her funnels trails of smoke rose lazily into a wide and cloudless sky.

He showed me a beautiful watercolour of a

ferry under Brooklyn Bridge, the jagged skyline of Manhattan in the background. There were sketches of hulks on the River Plate, and of feluccas plying the glassy waters of the Nile, a busy corniche delicately suggested behind them.

There was the rattle and throb of a lorry reversing up Casper's drive. He went to the window pulling the curtain back and pressing his nose to the glass.

'Coalmen—I want a word wi' them. They are no palming me off wi' inferior stuff this week.'

I took the pictures from his arms and began to look through them, distracted now and then by shouts and curses from the yard. The argument grew quite heated, and I found myself at the window looking out on to a scene that could have been lifted straight from one of those complex modern plays that we lesser mortals have to have explained to us.

Casper and the two smudge-faced coalmen were squatted, miner style, on their hams, on the back of the wagon. In front of them were two pieces of coal. A large Alsatian dog sat on a pile of empty sacks, its ears cocked, watching them intently.

Casper picked up one of the pieces of coal. 'You're no tellin' me this is deep-mined coal—it's bleddy open cast. This is deep mined.' He picked up the other piece and waved them both under the nose of the older coalman, who clasped and unclasped his blackened hands before shaking his head and taking the coal from Casper.

'Casper, it's all deep mined—it's all from Eckleton Main, we don't buy coal from anywhere else.'

Casper snatched a piece back and turned it

151

before his eyes. 'Whisht, mon, if that's Eckleton Main I'll eat ma tam—it's as grey as a louse's liver; I've thrain better stuff o'erboard afore I'd insult ma boilers wi' it. This stuff just makes clinker.'

The younger coalman lit a cigarette and holding it alongside his ear, fondled the dog with his free hand.

'I don't know why we bother,' he said in an angry voice. 'We trail up here into the bloody wilds with a ton and a half of our best stuff and every time we have this bloody inquest—do you want it or don't you?'

Casper cast his eyes over the full sacks. 'There should be a bit o' leeway on price, ye ken. I mean, I'm worried aboot the calorific value.'

'No!' exclaimed both men in unison.

'Alreet then; this time.'

The younger man jumped down and, flattening his back against the wagon, reached over his head for the ears of a sack. 'Why don't yer convert to oil, that's what I'd like to know.'

Casper was on his feet throwing a piece of coal with demonic force into the mud of the yard.

'Oil! Oil! Are my ears deceiving me, did this cretin say oil? Have ye ever been in an oil-fired boiler room laddie? Experienced the unnatural stench? Had your ears numbed wi' the roar o' they forced burners? Choked yer lungs oot wi' all manner o' devilish gases an' fumes? Do ye not know laddie why there's all these fires at sea? Well, I'll tell yer laddie—it's split fuel tanks and weepin' fuel lines. I wouldna raise steam wi' oil if . . .'

The elder coalman, still squatting on the wagon, said something I couldn't hear and smiled slyly.

Casper dropped his lean body into the leather

152

chair. 'It's like talking to stoops. But what can I do? They're the only ones left who'll deliver. Not that I'm awkward, mind. It's just that I will no feed my boiler wi' inferior stuff; it is a false economy lad. I do not know if ye heard, but the fool suggested I convert to oil.'

I pretended I had not heard; I wanted to get Casper back to the watercolours.

'Are you willing to sell any of these?'

'Aye,' he answered in a tired voice. 'I'll sort through them, there's only one or two I want to keep.'

'Most of them are commercial, but these sketches of engine rooms—clever stuff, but no appeal to anybody who's not, well, keen on engines and boilers.'

'I understand, laddie. I did them mainly for my ain records. There was something so complete aboot them old cathedral type engines, all that polished brass and copper, the shining crossheads, cylinder rods gleamin' like chrome—and the power, that so smooth yet tremendous power. Have ye ever heard MacAndrew's Hymn? I used tae mek all my apprentices read it.'

His chin dropped on to his smock, there was sadness in his voice. 'I had the last of the best years; when ships had a heart in them, a beating, pulsing, warm heart. When the first plumes feathered out of the smoke stack you felt her coming alive, and when ye were up tae pressure an' ye watched the gauges flicker as ye opened the valves it was like being in control of a magnificent, primitive beast.'

We were silent for a while, Casper smiling down at his smock, me going slowly through the pile of unframed pictures marvelling at the skill of the man.

'Self-taught. I did buy a book or two, an' allus went roond the art galleries when I was ashore,' he said brightly, slapping the arms of his chair. 'Come on laddie, I'll mek ye a cup o' engineer's tea.'

'Do you still paint Casper?' I asked, as I followed him into the boiler room.

'What is there to paint?'

'Landscapes—ever tried landscapes?'

He took two tin mugs from a shelf, spooned tea into them, and held each in turn under a brass pipe, turning a cock and sending a spluttering, coughing rod of superheated water into them. Casper blew steam from the mugs and peered into them.

'I've tried landscapes, but I can no get into them. They always lack something—I've been having a try at birds, an' I quite like that. Aye, I may be able to do something wi' birds.'

The tea was as black as ink and bitter to the taste.

'Thick enough for a mouse to skate on,' Casper observed, flicking a tea leaf from its surface, 'just as it should be.'

He leaned against the whitewashed wall of the boiler house, tin mug held in front of his face, one hand in the pocket of his shorts.

'Well. What d'ye think?—grand is'na it?'

It was grand; a great, matt-black, horizontal boiler, its domed top with a thick crust of insulation, its sides hemmed with a tracery of pipes. Valves and gauges, all highly polished, were set at eye level, and from around the fire box door a pinkish glow emerged to tint the walls and scrubbed, concrete floor.

'She's just on tick over now,' I was told proudly.

154

'I hev a small vertical engine through there, drives an o'er head shaft wi' fast an' loose pulleys to a lathe, a drill an' a milling machine. I can mak ony part ye care tae name.'

I had no doubt he could; Casper's skills with machinery were well known in the Dale. It was his skill with the paintbrush he had kept concealed, and impressed as I was with his boiler house and workshop, it was his watercolours I wanted to talk about.

'How many pictures have you, Casper?'

'Hundreds—I've been painting forty year, and the only one I've ever framed is that one o' the Pool.'

'With a bit of careful handling they could pay for the building work.'

'It's an awfu' lot o' money that's wanted,' he replied doubtfully.

'Let me take two or three, frame them up and put them in the shop.'

'Tek what yer want, Laddie.'

We walked out into the cool air. Casper stooped and picked up the piece of coal he had thrown into the mud with such vehemence. 'Ooh! They're no bad fellas but ye have to discipline 'em fra time to time.' He rubbed the coal on the grass and put it in his pocket.

'Them parrots nae guid then?'

'Fraid not.'

'Na'er mind. I shouldna' sell 'em anyway. They represent the three most cussed and awkward specimens o'humanity I've come across in a lifetime o' travellin'. Speakin' o' awkward and cussed folk, does that muckle great empty headed clown o' a farmer still live next door to yea?'

'Ted? Yes, he's still there.'

'He's a great wallop o' a festering idiot.' Casper clenched his fist and shook it. 'He threatened me, mon. Threatened me wi' violence, an' him stone-cold sober. A devious money grubbing fella that. I laid him oot yonder. Tried tae palm me off wi' inferior goods, then threatens me—why there's nae words to sufficiently describe that, that . . .' The big Scotsman let out a bellow that was more expressive than any words, and gazed down at the spot where the unfortunate Ted had lain.

'Accusin' me o' being tight—I've never been one to keep ma pennies in ma pooch. A generous man; I've always been a most generous man.'

*   *   *

I framed three of Casper's watercolours and set them in the main window on little easels. Vicky printed neat cards, and we agonised over what prices to ask.

'Let's shock them,' Vicky said, with more than a grain of devilment in her voice.

'Right, seventy-five quid apiece.'

'A hundred.'

'All right, a hundred-and-ten.'

He was the type of man you would not have expected to have a fiver in his pocket let alone £330. He bought all three of Casper's paintings. He never asked about the artist; in fact he said nothing other than 'I'll have them', and 'thank you'.

I rang Casper with the good news; he was delighted.

'Brilliant—I'll be doon for the money, an' how many more do ye want?'

'Frames are a problem, Casper; but bring half a dozen, we'll see what we can do.'

I found frames for two more and we put them in the window. As Vicky wrote out fresh cards I told her, 'We can't go on like this, finding old frames and chancing to luck to sell Casper's paintings. He needs promoting, and I know just the woman.'

The lady artist who had painted Fiery Frank and done the lovely sketch of our house had put little stickers on the back of her work, giving her address and telephone number.

I rang her and told her of the superb artist I had discovered.

'You still got them damned dogs?' she asked, with a chuckle in her voice. 'I'll be up there tomorrow, if he's as good as you say he is.'

She had not changed at all; still sporting the huge, floppy hat, tall and thin, hollow cheeked, she stood and stared silently at the watercolours. Picking up the one of feluccas on the Nile she took it to the window and angled it against the light. 'Beautiful—when do I meet him?'

They were so similarly built they could have been brother and sister. Fiona held Casper's hands in hers, and looked solemnly into his eyes. 'You're a wonderful, wonderful man.'

Casper grinned sheepishly. 'Yer embarrassing me, woman.'

We went into the house. Fiona squatted on the floor and Casper surrounded her with paintings. 'I'm self-taught, ye know,' he said apologetically.

'You're a genius,' she mumbled.

We had engineer's tea made for us, and Fiona was taken to marvel at the boiler house.

'I shall take you in hand,' she told a high-spirited

157

Casper, tapping him on the chest.

'Yer think I can mek enough for the building work?' he asked.

'My man, when I've finished with you, you'll be rich enough to build the pyramids.'

The following day Fiona called in to the shop and took Casper's paintings away with her. 'I have contacts—I studied at the Slade, you know. I'm taking him to London, I have a friend who specialises in maritime subjects, and I know he'll be thrilled with Casper's work.'

I drove them to Darlington station and left them on the platform, the loud confident voice of Fiona, her arms stretched around a big portfolio of pictures, chivvying Casper good humouredly.

He, self-conscious in a new hounds-tooth jacket and vivid green corduroys, scrubbed pink as a schoolboy, inching a battered trunk along the platform, grinning sheepishly and telling Fiona gently she was 'bletherin', like an old ewe'.

They were away for three days, and returned like conquering heroes, a taxi from the station, new luggage, Fiona laughing through an armful of flowers, pulled to the shop door by a radiant Casper sporting a white yachting cap and holding at arm's length a parrot in a cage.

'Is he no a beauty?' It was a splendid parrot; the intensity of the green and the orange was marvelled at. We laughed when it squawked, watched it smilingly as it paraded sideways along its perch, and stared into its eye—an intense and liquid black, ringed with orange and yellow, radial flecks in the two annuli making it look like a colourful ammonite.

The children cautiously poked fingers through

158

the bars and offered peanuts. 'What's his name?' asked an excited Sally.

Casper drew in a long breath, laid a big hand on the cage finial and looked at the bird.

'I have been pondering over that all the way up in the train.' He looked at me; his eyes twinkled, the mobile mouth held the ghost of a smile. 'Your faither knows I have a bit of a system aboot naming me parrots—aye, and I think we'll hev to call this yun Ted.'

CHAPTER TWELVE

Snow on high ground was forecast. The steely sky darkened in the north-west, no wind disturbed the tangled mass of Russian vine or shook the uppermost branches of the apple trees. A line of bleating sheep, a grey snake with a back-bone of black blobs, filled the trod down from the very top of the fell.

'We're in for it—they know,' said Baz, nodding towards the sheep. He had put old red rubber tubing from a milking machine on the handles of his wheelbarrow, and his boots were thick with dubbin. There was a time when he and Rabbit paid off their rates by snow shifting, a time when the village cared less about being under a foot or two of snow.

'If you got your sheep down an' had plenty of fodder for 'em, a bin full o' tatties and a flitch of bacon hung in the dairy, you didn't bother as long as you could get your milk out at the station. Mind you, there's been times when we couldn't get it out for two or three days—but the dairy still took it, they were very good that way.'

There are snowdrops around the base of the Russian vine and if we bend down we can see in its fine matrix the cosy, podgy blotches of sparrows outlined against a threatening sky. The blackbird stands motionless on the apple house roof, a sharp and elegant profile for him. The goat is restless; she wanders backwards and forwards behind the fence, treading a muddy path, rearing up on the gate with a clatter of hooves and cocking her head so she can see into the kitchen.

The Colonel pulls his British Warm about him, and with a fast, stick-swinging walk does his round of the village. His trilby is cocked forward, crushed on to his head, and all we get is a curt nod—no time for Colonel-ish, clipped observations this morning. The black lab trots at his heels, panting a little, head down, sleek as a seal.

Dolly comes out of the shop. She's thrown a coat and headscarf on, but she's still in her powder-blue slippers. Her bag, made from multi-coloured lozenges of leather, is full. She's satisfying some atavistic need to 'stock up', buying flour, suet and a big box of oxo cubes. Mrs Lewis listens with heavily intent eyes, her flowered overall crisp, well ironed.

'If you've a few eggs and some flour you can always knock summat up.'

I open the door for Dolly; she smiles in acknowledgment, and extends two fingers from her purse hand to pull it closed.

'They say we're in for it.' She sounds half pleased, as if an annual snow-up is a tribal ritual to be gone through, to emerge from stronger and more confident, more resilient, and then to belittle

160

it proudly. 'Nowt like we used to get when I wor a bairn, I've known Altonshotts cut off for three weeks at a time.'

Around midday a light wind got up from the west, then veered northwards and intensified, until gusts of it plucked the empty milk bottles from the window-sill, rattled the dustbin lids and toyed open the garden gate into a steady clack, clack.

The first flakes came, tiny ones in flurries, and soon the yard was salted grey. I took the goat in, giving her a good measure of mixed flakes and spreading more bedding. The hens were already on their perches, feathers ruffled, heads pulled in, but the ducks waddled about the yard, their clumsy bills stabbing here and there. Blown sideways by the gusts, they squawked their complaints and ran with stretched necks to the lee of the barn. They are noisy and dirty, and they continually get in the way, but they are now a part of the place. In summer we erect a low fence, our 'duck barrier', to stop them getting into the house, and in winter we dissolve the class barriers and herd them together, the haughty Silver Appleyards and aristocratic Muscovies mixing with the lowly Khaki Campbells and Aylesburys. They fratch a little, sort out a pecking order, and become one noisy, homogeneous mass whose overriding concern is food.

I fed them early, broadcasting wheat over the barn floor, and watched them probing the straw with busy necks. It kept them occupied and out of the snow, which was now thickening into larger flakes that sat on my coat for a second, a silent splattering of the unique, magically snuffed to patches of prosaic wetness.

The ones who said we were in for it smiled to

161

themselves, wise owls peering through the flurries at a white village green and a road that had turned light grey and showed tyre tracks. 'It's settling, I said we were in for it.'

The school bus came early, squares of yellow light filling its windows, engine droning as it climbed Moor Road in low gear.

'Where's the sledge?' Peter yelled through the window pane. There were snow flakes on his eyebrows and his face was pink and excited. 'We gor' out early.'

'Got,' his mother corrected, then smiled. 'Your Dad will get your sledge out, you nip into the shop for me.'

Vicky was sewing; she bit the thread off and looked around for her purse. Sally came through the door, shoulders hunched, on the point of tears; Darren Metcalf had put some snow down her neck. Vicky fished it out and blew down the child's back, then kissed the neck, turning tears to giggles.

'I'll gerrim tomorrow for you,' Peter boasted.

'It's get, and you won't. Now,' counting coins on to the table, 'do you want some chocolate?'

I fed Topic and stood in the stable door, looking out at a quiet and neat, white world. Peter rushed back from the shop.

'It was full,' he complained, then making tyre screeching noises and with stubbing feet ran in a big arc, ending up thumping his small body against the back door.

'It was full,' I could hear him say, as the wedge of light from the door was scythed away. I stood, as I often do, leaning on the jamb, listening to Topic's steady munching. I like the warmth of the stable; I like the horsey smell. The cat spends a lot of her time in there on wintery days. Topic blows down her nostrils, making the cat's ears flick and her fur turn, but she will not be moved from her nest in the hay. The cat lords it over this warm domain; barely tolerating the dogs, watching haughtily any intruding duck or hen, she shows off her superiority by leaping on to the manger and curling her paws under her, blinking, and feigning sleep.

'You said you'd get the sledge,' I was gently chastised into action by childish and accusing voices.

Every year I say I'll grease the runners before we put it away and every year I forget, so it was into the workshop for emery paper and the light brown rust falling like snuff on to my boots.

The runners, shiny now, were caressed with knowledgeable fingers. 'Real,' Peter breathed, 'she'll go like the wind.'

'Let your sister have a go,' I called after them as they ran up the garth, scarves flying, happy mouths smudged with chocolate.

All evening it snowed steadily, the track on the road covered over, the pyracantha bent under its white load, and an eerie silence fell over the village. Occasionally a far-off engine would roar, then fall to a persistent drone as wheels clawed for grip.

Baz threw a sack full of logs into his wheelbarrow and took them to Nellie May, completing his good deeds by fetching her bread from the shop and a bottle of stout from the pub.

He stood in the kitchen doorway and rubbed his hands vigorously. 'Just been to see the owd lass is all right. We're in for it; the grit wagon has had to turn back, can't make it up Wren's Bank—that's a bad sign at this time of the night. There's two cars

163

stuck up by Tinker's Pond, and Thievin' Jack's left his van in the pub car park, so we're all right for a bit of sausage.'

Behind him the snow fell, big flakes catching the light in their purposeful descent, a business-like snowing, silent and malevolent.

Baz looked over his shoulder, tapping a mittened hand on the door handle. 'Are you going across there tonight?'

I looked at Vicky, who shrugged, then back at Baz. 'Yes, it'll be quiet—might nip across for one.'

'There'll be nothing for me tomorrow but a bit o' snow shovelling, can't go walling in this stuff. I'm up to here in work.' The mittened hand went to his forehead. 'If it keeps up I'll have to take a man on.'

'Isn't Rabbit helping you?'

'Rabbit is about as predictable as a baby's bottom. He swears he'll be there, put a full day in; sometimes he turns up, sometimes he doesn't. He throws his shovel down as soon as the pub opens, and he's forever wanting a sub. I had to tell him last week, "Rabbit, subs is adding up to more than the job's worth." He just grins—you can't do owt with him.'

I rather liked the idea of Rabbit being so individualistic, uncluttered by ambition or greed, never constrained by the work ethic, paring his labours down until income near enough meets expenditure. A sixpenny overspend on your annual budget did not bring misery when you lived in Ramsthwaite and you were rich in favours done; calling them in when your throat was like the Sahara, or one of your terriers needed the vet.

It was good to know that Baz was keeping busy. His cottage was now one of the best in the village, having sprouted a trellis porch, had the sag taken out of its roof, and been re-pointed. We were not sure about the whitewashed stones that now lay along the foot of the banking, and the lace curtain at the window of the garden shed. People shook their heads, whispered about outside influences, petticoat rule. Some smiled and bewailed the ruination of a good man, but all had to agree that Baz had never been happier.

Nowadays we had to be told of an impending visit to the pub; unlike his bachelor days when he was to be found in the taproom every night, busy with dart or domino, or idle gossip, a pint glass rarely out of his hand.

'I'll be across about eight,' I told him, 'I've a chicken to pluck.'

I didn't get the chicken plucked, and I didn't get to the pub until nearly ten o'clock. At a quarter to eight I yanked the kitchen curtain back and clicked my tongue at the billows of snow as a now mettlesome wind drove against the window pane.

'That's all we need, a wind to get up and drift the stuff.'

Vicky pulled out her work basket and stretched the frayed collar of a shirt across her thigh. 'I shouldn't worry, we've enough food in to feed the Russian army.'

'It'll ruin trade, who's going to . . .' I was broken off by a loud hammering on the door: it was Mucky Marion. She had thrown a blue gabardine over her head and shoulders, and stood shivering, her plimsoled feet hidden in deep snow.

'That goat o' yours—it's in me privy. You'll have to do summat, I can't get the door open for it—and I want to go.'

165

Elspeth was gone; dimples in the snow led from the goat house across the yard and out on to the green. I grabbed a torch and a length of billy band and followed a complaining and barely audible Marion back to her cottage.

Kneeling in the fresh snow I shone the torch under the privy door and saw four white feet. It was Elspeth. I called her name, and got a low whinny in response. 'Come on girl,' I coaxed, gently rattling the sneck and pushing the door. It would open a hand's span and no more, for Elspeth was wedged between it and the toilet pan. I couldn't imagine what had caused her to go walkabout on such a night. The odd occasions she has escaped from her house or the orchard she had merely wandered about the yard or trotted down to the stream to crop the watercress.

Marion's dogs started a ferocious barking, and took no heed of her shouts until she kicked the door and gave vent to an ear piercing 'Shurrup!'

I managed to get an arm around the door and seize one of Elspeth's legs, but she is a big strong animal, and I couldn't move her.

Butting her buttocks with the door and shouting encouragingly things like 'gurrup yer bloody thing' was equally ineffective. I stood with my torch casting a yellow disc on the snow and thought hard. How had she managed to close the door behind her?

She's a contortionist, an acrobat, and a clown— an intelligent animal, inquisitive with a blasé, unflappable attitude to life. If I had sat down with pencil and paper I could not have designed a more efficient goat trap. She had obviously curled herself around the door after first poking in an insatiably

166

nosey head. Could she be induced to re-curl herself around the door?

'An apple, Marion, have you an apple?' She had; one of those dark little russets that have a skin like brown parchment and flesh so crisp and aromatic that no goat can resist it.

'Now watch this,' I said confidently.

'Just hurry up—I'm wantin' to go. And another thing, it's eaten me smalls off the line. I'll want compensation for them.'

'All right Marion, just shush a minute and I'll have her out.' Elspeth craned her neck around, and before I could withdraw the apple in a tempting way she had it firmly clamped in her jaws and out of my hand.

'Another apple, Marion.'

The next time I got her to reveal her head and gazed into one of her frank and unblinking eyes. 'Come on, old girl,' I pleaded, 'just a bit more, just let me get your collar.'

But the goat would not shift. Two more apples taken from my extended arm, a feverish scrabbling of fingers for her collar and then I sank on to my wet knees in defeat.

'Come on,' Marion pleaded, wringing her hands.

'Can't you use a neighbour's?'

'They don't like me goin'. I don't know why. I think it's 'cos I'm the only one left with an outside bog.'

'I'll have to leave her in till the morning. I'll come and take the door off—if I can.'

'You'll do no such thing. I want it out, an' I want compensation.'

She stabbed a finger between my shoulder blades; her dogs, responding to her raised voice, began to bark again.

'Hey, I've just thought,' she laughed, 'supposing we put me monkey in—it could lead it out, or pummel the damned thing out; it don't like goats.'

'I don't think that's a good idea, Marion.'

'Well, have you a better one?'

I hadn't, and lights were beginning to appear in bedroom windows, showing black silhouettes of peering neighbours. I shone my torch under the door again at the four white feet and cursed. There were little pools of dark water on the concrete floor and trodden squares of torn newspaper.

A bedroom window opened. 'Are you frozen up?' a woman's voice called. Marion stepped sideways on to the garden, looking down at her feet sunk into the snow then up with a smile at the enquirer.

'No, it's his damned goat—it's gor in and wedged the door.' She stood with her body bent slightly backwards, her face still smiling, mittened hands pulling the gabardine to her throat. 'Hey! do you mind if I use yours?'

The silhouette turned sideways, obviously consulting someone; there was a pause, then the hand on the stay pushed the window wide open, 'Aye—come on.'

I walked around the toilet shining my light on it, although there was no real need to, for the filtered moonlight was sufficient to pick out the bricks, the old iron hooks for washing lines, and the ventilation holes high under the roof, the hallmark of a Victorian privy builder who knew his business.

Bedroom lights went out as warm kitchens and television sets regained their authority. Marion returned. 'By they've got it nice in there; they've an

168

enormous rubber plant at the top of the steps, and their karzi is all carpeted—and soaps. Hell's bells, I've never seen as many soaps—jars and dishes stacked with 'em. Ay they did smell nice, an' their stairs are—'

'Marion, another apple,' I interrupted, grabbing her arm. 'I've an idea.'

I took the apple and tied the billy band around it, making a cage; then, knotting on a further length, I led Marion to the back of the privy and upturned a bucket.

'The plan, Marion, is this. You stand on this bucket and dangle the apple through this hole. She can't resist a good russet. What she'll do is climb up on the seat to get at it. When she does I'll have room to shove the door open. OK?'

'I hope it doesn't mark that seat; I scrub that seat regularly,' Marion muttered as I handed her up on to the bucket.

'Now, just let it down a bit. Don't let her grab it or I won't have time—you're all right, you won't fall?'

'Just get the damned thing out,' she answered, quite irritably.

I lay down in the snow and shone the light under the door.

'Got the apple in, Marion?'

'Aye.'

'Well, she's not seen it. Can you jiggle it a bit?'

'I'm jiggling.'

Elspeth never moved; her hooves were set on the concrete as if they were glued to it. I broke a branch off the lilac bush and poked her heels with it. She gave a little kick of annoyance and moved sideways slightly, prompting me to try the door

169

again. I stood up and pushed strongly, making the goat bleat, but she would move no further. Despair welled over me, I leaned my head against the door and groaned, 'You stupid, stupid animal.'

I heard Marion's bucket clatter and then some very unlady-like comments about goats, snow and buckets, then a shouted demand: 'Oi, come an' get me up.'

As I helped her to her feet the light in the helpful bedroom went on again.

'I'm bloody fed up,' she yelled, 'I'm makin' a spectacle of myself. I'm off to make a cup of tea, and you can get that bloody goat out of that bloody privy by your—bloody—self.'

I stood on the bucket and carefully pulled the string out of the ventilation hole. The apple had gone.

I climbed into a neighbouring garden and borrowed a clothes prop, and poking it under the door tried to prise the goat to one side; but as I could raise it no more than six inches or so Elspeth just stepped elegantly over it. My trousers were soaked, I was frozen, and I had run out of ideas. Elspeth would have to stay there until morning and we could take the door off.

'Come on in,' Marion called from the kitchen door, 'I've made some tea.' The dogs jumped up, sniffed excitedly at my legs, and licked off the patches of snow that stuck to them. From high in the airing cupboard the monkey watched me, a puzzled look on its wizened face.

Marion tore the lid from a cardboard box and, leaning her forearms on the table, pushed out her upper teeth with her tongue and stared thoughtfully at her two brown, stained ovens.

'Let me see: a good bra, two pairs of knickers, me black slip—oh, an' five apples.'

The pencil stub tapped on the cardboard, the teeth were sucked back in. 'Go on, we'll call it a tenner and be straights.' She pushed the list into my hand and gave me a cold smile. 'I'll throw the tea in for nowt.'

'Very kind.'

'Hey, yer gettin' off lightly. Think how I have been incommoded. I was just set to do a bit o' baking and I thought I'd pay a call. Can you imagine the fright I got finding a damned goat in there.' She raised a mitten, and a grubby forefinger flicked out of it and stabbed at my chest. 'Another thing, if there's any damage in there I want compensating, understand?'

'Yes, Marion.'

'I don't know what I'll do if I'm taken short.'

'I'll be around first thing tomorrow, take the door off.'

'Make sure you are, I don't like using other folk's.' The finger tapped, faster this time.

'An' bring the money. It's not proper, not havin' a change of underthings. Just think yourself lucky there's still the sales on in Lalbeck, otherwise it would cost you a lot more.'

'Yes, Marion.'

'Gawd, I wish I'd a drop of gin in. It's fair set me in a dither, all this worry. Is the pub open yet?'

I pulled a soggy fiver out of my back pocket and laid it on the table, mumbling something about having a drink on me and how sorry I was. The monkey leapt from the airing cupboard and did a chattering dance on the table, then bounded into Marion's old pram and, squatting on the folded

171

down hood, looked from me to Marion and back with quick little darts of its head.

'She don't like her routine upset,' Marion said. Her tongue went behind the upper set again, and she rested her knuckles on the table and looked at the monkey before she peeled the note from the table.

'First thing tomorrow,' I promised, with my hand on the door knob. I half opened the door, and there on the path stood Elspeth, a square of newspaper hanging from her mouth, her head bent sideways in that enquiring and endearing manner.

I called her a sod and threading my belt through her collar I led her home and managed to overcome the enormous desire to boot her angular rump as I pushed her into the goat house.

I took off my trousers and rubbed my legs with a towel.

'Get me a whisky, will you?' I asked Vicky in a weak voice.

She was standing with her arms folded, swaying slightly back on her heels and grinning. 'Might be funny to you, but I've lost the will to live,' I said, slightly annoyed.

'You'll regain it when I show you this.'

She held out a cheque, one of those large, impressive ones, splendid copper plate on pale buff paper. I read it balancing on one leg, trying to bring life back to the numb toes with some brisk towelling.

'£2,250—only. Jack the Pat—the Carlton House?'

'He's staying at the pub; his car is stuck in a drift. He wandered across just after you'd gone, and was taken with the desk. Couldn't leave it alone, patted

172

it and patted it, opened every drawer, ended up on his knees in front of it. How much? How much? he kept asking, so I said two and a quarter and stuck to it—did I do right?'

'Do right! I'll say you did.'

I threw the towel into the hearth and danced her around the kitchen, disturbing the cat and drawing the dogs from under the table. The staircase door was opened, and I saw two blonde heads appear over the banister. They watched us in silence for a while, then with impish smiles they crept down the stairs and stood at the kitchen door: Sally clutching her teddy, and Peter with his head against the jamb, his toes wriggling madly.

We showed them Jack the Pat's cheque and let them squat in front of the fire. Whilst Vicky heated milk for cocoa I told them of Elspeth's escapade, falling on my knees, pretending to shine a torch and cursing the goat again, but in a bowdlerised form.

'You're winding them up—they'll never get off to sleep,' Vicky warned. But there was a sense of occasion—the biggest sale we'd ever made. Elspeth's naughtiness, now being laughed into the family's history with that gay, carefree giggling of happy children.

We shooed them off to bed, smiling as they chuckled their way up the steps and across the landing. I pinned Jack's cheque to the dairy door and pulled on dry trousers. 'I never got that whisky.'

'Baz is waiting for you across the road, remember?'

*   *   *

The pub was very quiet. Mucky Marion was in the

lounge hugging the fire, a gin and tonic in one hand, the other rifling in a bag of crisps she held in her lap.

'I've just been tellin' 'em about that bloody animal of yours,' she said without looking up, as I slipped a folded tenner into her hand.

Charlie was reading the newspaper, spectacles on the end of his nose, his body slumped over the bar, the heels of his boots hung over the cross bar of the stool. Baz and Rabbit were the only ones in the taproom; sitting on the settle, their legs stretched, staring vacantly through the open door into the lounge.

'Where's Jack the Pat?'

Charlie folded his spectacles, then the newspaper.

'He's off to bed—he's fagged out. Ethel's goin' to take him a bit of supper up later.' Baz and Rabbit looked at each other in a knowing way, raising their eyebrows and pulling their mouths.

'Gettin' looked after,' Rabbit whispered. 'He's allus had women pandering round him; I don't know what he's got that I haven't. Allus seemed a bit of a puff to me.'

I felt I had to defend my good customer's name. 'He's all right Rabbit, bit of a ladies' man, but a very astute fellow. Hard working and a good business head on him.'

Charlie brought the pints I'd ordered, and when he had thrown his tray on to the bar and gone to sit with Marion, I leaned towards my companions and told them in a low voice: 'Mind you, I think Charlie's a bit naive, letting Ethel, you know ...'

'Naive! You should talk,' Rabbit laughed.

I suddenly remembered that the antique dealing

174

romeo—that suave, slim-hipped, brilliantined and silver-tongued swine had been alone with my Vicky for the best part of an hour. Now he was in bed—fagged out. I felt my face flush, felt an ache in my chest. I swallowed hard and turned my glass slowly.

'Why—what do you mean?' I asked warily, avoiding Rabbit's eyes.

'Well, I mean, paying Mucky Marion for two pairs of knickers—she's never had two pairs of knickers in her life.'

CHAPTER THIRTEEN

Is it ostentatious to wear three ropes of pearls, a flesh pink trouser suit and a fetching little pill box hat made from flamingo feathers when one is cleaning out the dovecote?

Some may consider it so, as some people consider Rabbit's massive and torn overcoat an unnecessary encumbrance on a hot day, but we know the necessity; the indispensability of that coat. The pearls, the trouser suit and the hat? What else could Amelia possibly feel comfortable in, even when performing this most mundane of tasks?

She gave an ear-piercing 'yoohoo', a flashing smile and pushed her way through the raspberry canes. 'Won't be long darling,' she trilled, advancing with the brass shovel held out in front of her. She deposited the little pile of dried droppings on to the compost heap, and with raised eyebrows and a pert mouth disappeared once more into the dovecote. Several journeys later, as I was still pondering on the fact that I was witnessing what must be the most elegant and civilised cleaning out of a dovecote ever, Ted's tractor skidded to a halt in the lane.

He swept open the cab door and, half rising from his seat, glowered over the hedge.

''Ave you told her yet?'

The flamingo feather hat, the palest pink an artist's palette could furnish, rose over the raspberries. 'Told me what darling?' Ted slammed the cab door and, stabbing a heavy hand on to the throttle, roared off down the lane.

Amelia picked her way round the bushes as daintily as her twenty stones would allow her. 'Now, darling, what have you to tell me?' I silently cursed Ted. I had been blackmailed into this task; not an easy one by any means, and now I was really on the spot. My carefully rehearsed speech, my planned demeanour, out of the window.

Amelia looked down at her dew-sodden Turkish slippers, turned slightly and raised her head to give me the benefit of her noble profile, then looked down into my eyes.

'Well, darling?'

The ability to think on one's feet is a gift.

'Just popped in to—er—tell you—that, the props, I've managed to get the props.'

A pink arm encircled me and crushed me to a scented sea of pink. 'Splendid!'

There is no doubt that in her youth she had been an imposing looking woman; her hair was still corn gold, her complexion clear, and her violet eyes as magnificent as ever. But the tall willowy girl who had first stepped on to a stage half a century ago to thrill an audience with her voice had, over the years, thickened out somewhat.

And that was the real reason for my visit. She was undoubtedly an asset to the Lalbeck Amateur Dramatic Society and her insistence in always taking the female lead had led to productions playing to packed houses—but for entirely the wrong reasons.

West Side Story was a good example. The power and range of her voice still captivated, but when she had sashayed on to the stage as Maria, clad in a leather mini skirt, fishnet stockings and a black blouse that revealed more than it covered, the soaring and accomplished notes of the beautiful song 'Tonight' had been completely drowned by laughs, cheers and cat calls. Subsequent performances saw not an empty seat in the entire hall. Luckless ones who could not steal a ticket or trick their way in bribed the stewards to leave the curtains undrawn and placed boxes against the wall, thrilling as the very window panes vibrated against their noses. The line between life and art had never been so distinct.

A cub reporter delegated by the *Stockborough and Lalbeck Times* to cover the event was beside himself. He wrote a review which owed as much to P. G. Wodehouse as it did to *Roget's Thesaurus*; only to have it cast aside by a world-weary editor with the words 'Think son, when she storms into this office, it'll be thee she's after.' Our fresh-faced scribe had blanched and wisely re-penned the review.

Amelia released me and, taking my hand, led me through the french windows into the conservatory. 'Sit there, darling, whilst I make some tea.'

The cane settee creaked ominously as she lowered her bulk into it. 'Sugar? Milk?'

I shook my head; perhaps a little digitalis, I said to myself, for my task was getting harder by the minute.

The Colonel called it delegation; I called it blackmail, because he had retracted from an agreement to sell me the double barrelled Greener shotgun until I had taken on the task of telling Amelia that she should not play the female lead in the forthcoming production of *Showboat*.

Her voice, her acting, her very stage presence, were all of a superior nature—it was just her size.

Mr Martin was about to fulfil a lifelong ambition to play Gaylord, and had dug his heels in; he would not stand down for a taller man, and he would not take part in a farce. At every rehearsal, when he had to plant a kiss on Amelia's cheek he had teetered on his toes until his calf muscles ached, stretched his neck and arched his back until his spine creaked. But to no avail—he could not negotiate that enormous bosom; so Amelia stood centre stage regal and imposing, but unkissed.

After the last rehearsal, when Amelia had bestowed the favoured with 'kissy, kissy' sprinkled 'darlings' and 'sweeties' like confetti, donned her cloak and flounced off into the night, silence had fallen over the village hall.

A silence of despair, broken after several moments by Ted's loud and lugubrious voice. 'Shoo's too big, shoo spoiled *West Side Story* wi' them thighs—like forty gallon oil drums.'

We all knew it, and no one more than Mr Martin. The Colonel suggested he wore small stilts, but this we immediately dismissed as frivolous; his trousers would have to be lengthened by at least ten inches.

178

It was not for the first time the Colonel had felt the loneliness of command as we all shuffled off to the pub leaving him to lock up, and, as the producer, face the inevitable—she had to be told.

What is a man of parts? That's what he called me as he advanced through the crowd thronging the bar and almost pinioned me against the wall. 'You're a man of parts, little job for you. Go and tell Amelia that she's to relinquish the role.' His extended little finger tapped against my glass, 'Then we'll talk about the Greener.'

He refused to listen to my pleas, turning his back to me and glaring at some visiting churl who had unwittingly occupied his favourite stool.

*   *   *

I sat opposite the pink clad bosom, it seemed as if there was nowhere else for my eyes to rest. It flowed from under her wattled chin into a wide flat expanse like the glacis in front of a Maginot fort, difficult terrain for any man, impossible for the slightly built Mr Martin. The sheer area, the daunting angle, the breathtaking enormity of the woman's chest, rendered her—irrespective of other shortcomings—a most unsuitable Magnolia. She was Wagnerian, a magnificent Brunhilde; clap on the horned helmet, buckle on the breast armour— she was engineered for the part—but Magnolia?

Amelia placed a hand on my knee, threw back her head and closed her eyes.

'It's a part that needs to be played with hot blood, like I played Maria. Did you see my Maria, darling?'

I confessed that, sadly, I had missed it.

179

She half opened her eyes and viewed me from under long lashes. 'I was magnificent—packed house every night, curtain calls, the atmosphere was electric. Women sobbed, strong men clapped hands to their eyes to hide their tears.'

Closing her eyes she raised her free hand, the crimson lips parted to reveal perfect teeth, the huge pink glacis rose and swelled, the wattles vibrated as the first piercing notes of 'Tonight' knifed into my ears. I thrust my head back into the cushions, my whole body tingling as if from an electric shock. The teacups rattled, the curtains billowed out of the open window, a huge cheese plant hugged its waxy leaves and trembled, the raspberry canes bowed towards the hedge, and in the field opposite terrified sheep leapt the stone wall and scattered over the moor.

I had heard her sing at rehearsals, but never like this.

'You're surprised with Amelia—I can see.'

'A unique voice,' I answered lamely, now viewing in a fresh light the once seemingly absurd stories I had heard about men's bow ties being blown off at Glyndebourne, and the cracked ceiling in Salzburg. Now I quite believed that she had rid Lalbeck church of deathwatch beetle after a rendition of 'Onward Christian Soldiers'.

My head was still ringing as I eased myself out of the cane chair and walked steadily towards the french windows.

'You came to tell me about the props, darling?'

'Er, yes I've got some trunks, boxes for the levee scenes,' I lied, as I quickened my pace up the garden path.

The Colonel thrust his head through the shop

door.

'Mission accomplished?'

'Not exactly, done a preliminary reconnaissance though.'

'Good man, good man, but time is ticking on—get her told before the next rehearsal.'

'Colonel.'

'Yes.'

'What about her replacement, we're well—'

'Don't you worry about that, my man, all taken care of, leave the strategy to me. You just get that woman told.'

'Wilco,' I answered brightly, and inwardly wondered if the Greener was worth it. Vicky was no help at all. If anything she was on Amelia's side. Wasn't the woman a professional? Didn't she fill the hall? How many charities benefited? All negative thinking, but just after lunch she did say something which put the seed of an idea in my brain.

Clattering the dishes into the sink she said, 'When they had this problem in the films they stood the hero on a box or dug a hole for the heroine.'

It was feasible, the stage was made up of boarding on simple trestles. A nine-inch deep gully from the wings to centre stage—Richard could make one in no time. True, Magnolia would have the appearance of being on tracks, but it was a brilliant idea.

'Put it to her,' the Colonel said.

'Might work,' conceded Ted. I went off with high heart, even though the Colonel had dampened my powder a bit. The stern statement that I was to make it clear that even if she agreed it was to be her last performance worried me a little.

'Only solves the problem of height. There is her age to consider,' he snarled.

Amelia narrowed her eyes, threw out her chest and shrieked, 'What! Amelia Hawthornthwaite walk in a trench—are you mad? Have you taken leave of your senses? I will do no such thing. I am a professional, and I will be treated as such or I will withdraw from the production.'

Having weathered the blast quite successfully and seeing a glimmer of hope, I pressed on. 'Mr Martin is a little embarrassed in the romantic scenes.'

'So!'

'Well, we've considered all kinds of solutions, but none seem feasible; except the trench.'

'Stretch his legs, stretch his neck, stretch any part of his anatomy you like, Amelia Hawthornthwaite walks in a trench for no man.'

'It will only be—'

'No!'

'We will light the stage from—'

'No! No! No! No!'

She sank into the cane sofa, one hand splayed across her bosom, the other shielding her eyes. We remained in silence for some moments, then she said very quietly, 'It's that little military man who's put you up to this, isn't it?'

It was a moment of terrible temptation, I could have dropped the Colonel right in it; but I thought of the Greener, and instead refuted her.

'No, it was a general decision, they pushed me into the role of spokesman—much against my will.' Her eyes sparkled with malevolence.

'He's had it in for me ever since that unfortunate incident in *Annie Get Your Gun*. Stupid little

182

man, prancing about the stage in jodhpurs and a waistcoat.'

'Unfortunate incident?'

She ignored me and, with many grunts and creakings, rose from the sofa and drew herself up to her full height. 'Tell them Amelia Hawthornthwaite is deeply offended at such a suggestion, and that she withdraws from the production until a full apology is forthcoming.'

I dutifully reported the conversation to Ted and the Colonel at the next rehearsal.

'She'll wait till doomsday for an apology from me,' snorted the Colonel.

'Me too,' Ted added happily.

'What has she done to you, Ted?' I enquired.

He didn't answer, just sniffed and hammered a guardrail on to 'Cotton Blossom'.

I stood behind him confident and happy; my mission was accomplished—shortly the Greener would hang in my gun cupboard. When that warm feeling of confidence flows over us we are emboldened, we push back frontiers.

'Ted, I thought you liked big women?' His hammer clattered on to the stage, he turned and briefly made a mumpy mouth.

'Are you making that bloody paddle wheel or aren't you?'

I squatted on the stage and assembled Richard's clever plywood cutouts. The axle of the stern wheel was to extend through the backdrop and be turned by a small boy, Peter in fact.

The boy was thrilled with this limited role, because it meant that for four nights it would be eleven o'clock before he crept into his bed.

Canary Mary was to be the new Magnolia;

183

true, she was of ample proportions, but nowhere near the size of the statuesque Amelia. She had understudied the part and had connived with the Colonel to have Amelia disposed, for before the retired opera singer came on the scene Mary had had her share of the leading roles. She has a sweet voice, a complete lack of any inhibitions and, like a lot of robust women, she moves with an enviable grace. Her demands were slight and readily acceded to. When she sang the duet with Ravenal in Act One her dress was to be bright yellow taffeta, and the livery of the Cotton Blossom was to be changed from black and white to primrose and white.

'A much happier combination,' she smiled.

Vicky, as assistant wardrobe, got busy with needle and thread, I with paintbrush.

The company took on new heart; cheery chatter, much laughter and a sense of relief now marked rehearsals. Only Mr Martin was unhappy; he and his wife had been hatching a little plot which had gone awry. True, Canary Mary gracefully bent to receive his embrace in a manner Amelia had never been able to bring herself to do; and she was not averse to supporting the slightly built man when he craned forward on the tips of his toes to deliver his kiss—but Mr Martin was not happy. Everyone else thought Canary Mary made an admirable Magnolia.

We had had a good month. The Carlton House desk had really bumped up our takings, so I had a merry heart that Saturday evening as I filled out the paying-in book.

Mr Martin rapped on the shop door and pointed to the closed sign, a warm smile playing under his clipped moustache. I slid back the bolts and showed

184

him in. Not a man to beat about the bush, our bank manager. You overdraw by the least bit and he displays all the warmth of a rock in an ice-bound pool.

He folded his arms and waited until I had seated myself behind the counter.

'I'll come straight to the point—I'm not happy with Canary Mary.'

'Oh dear,' I replied gently.

'She's not right for the part. I would like you to use your good offices and have a word with her, get her to step down.'

'At this late hour who will take her place? It's dress rehearsal next week.'

He looked a little sheepish. 'Fact is, Mrs Martin and I have been working on the thing together, and we feel she could really make a go of it.'

'Too late. Anyway, why me? I was the one who had to tell Amelia. Let somebody else do the dirty work this time.'

He folded his arms and stared at the ceiling, then he said very slowly, 'Let's see, isn't it time we reviewed your overdraft facility?'

I looked down at Jack the Pat's lovely cheque, the one we danced around the kitchen and kissed a thousand times.

'Ten o'clock Monday morning OK?' I asked him happily.

CHAPTER FOURTEEN

All the visible signs of the coming of spring; the greening of the Dale, the fields alive with new lambs, and the absence of that blistering chill in the north wind are welcome and assuring. But it is the hanging out of Bed and Breakfast signs and Baz's geese starting to lay that are the real harbingers of the longed-for season.

Ted stood in his barn, khaki shirtsleeves rolled up, and pulled his ear as he looked over the bales of hay. 'Might get an early bite in the bottom meadows—but yer can be caught out,' he warned. 'I've known us have a foot of snow on Lady Day.'

We did not need to heed his warning, we had hay enough. Our own good sweet hay, loose and made in the old fashioned way. I brought a cart load up from the barn in the field we rent from Nellie May, leaving trails of wisps on the overgrown hedges. Ted shoved his big hand into the load, grabbed a handful, sniffed it, then thrust it back. 'Aye, it's all right.'

Topic thought it was all right and so did Elspeth and the children's rabbits. I enjoyed forking it off the cart and under the dutch barn; it's precious stuff, hard won with the sweat of our brows, so I sheeted it up and weighted the edges with wall toppings. The cat crawled under the sheet, a little mobile lump too noisy and hampered to be of danger to the mice who were soon attracted by the warmth and seeds.

The hay had been there a week when I found that one of Ted's Rouen ducks had made a nest.

There were three eggs in it, so I started to look out for a broody duck. Baz has Silkies that will sit at the drop of a hat, but it is better if we put them under a duck. Duck eggs incubate for twenty-eight days as opposed to twenty-one for hen's, and sometimes the sitter—if it be a hen—gets bored with the extra time and leaves the nest. Then there is a frantic dash to the airing cupboard with a cap full of eggs, and a search round the village for a broody of any kind.

'Just to bring 'em off,' we plead.

'All right, but I want it back. Damned good hen, that.'

We were lucky; a Muscovy started to sit, and the Rouen eggs—now eight in number—were gently put under her. She hissed, pecked at our hands, then shuffled herself comfortable. We smiled and began a watchful wait. Every day when I threw corn out for her I thought of those deep keeled, quick growing French table ducks; and Ted's face when he saw them.

Vicky was not sure. 'You should have given him the eggs back.'

'Serves him right for keeping our Barnevelders.'

'You don't know for sure they were ours.'

'Course they were. All he's got is piffling little White Leghorns and there he is with a sugar bowl full of superb brown eggs.'

'Well, it's not the same.'

I could not see why, but we were not going to argue, not that day, for my old boss and his wife were coming to see us. But as usual I had a sale to go to.

'Try and get back early,' Vicky pleaded. I promised I would do my best, for it was a very ordinary sale, nothing had excited us at the viewing, but there were a few good pieces of pine I liked. We kept wondering when the pine boom would end, but the demand for well stripped and finished pieces showed no sign of abating, so we kept on buying.

* * *

Fiery Frank is a rapacious pine buyer. His cheery greeting upon jumping from his van used to be followed by, 'Owt in my line?' Now it's invariably, 'Any pine?'

The Ring will go after any prestige bits of pine; an old double corner cupboard, especially if the upper half is barrel backed, or a really fine housekeeper's desk. The run of the mill they disdain. Long John will buy when finances allow, and there is always a 'new face' in this section of the trade. Clutching tape measure and clipboard they flash in, buy at top prices for a few weeks, then disappear. We do not strip pine—it's too time consuming. We sell it all 'in the paint' with the exception of any unusual or rare pieces that take our fancy, and these we send out to be done.

There was one such piece in the sale, a Victorian estate desk. It had never felt paint or varnish, and had worn into a deep rich colour. It had numerous drawers, shallow cupboards set in the sides and, fitted to the front of it, a game rack. Were the good and prompt paying tenants rewarded with a brace of pheasants? It was not large, no more than a yard square, and was fitted with carrying handles. I really liked it, and had been warned by a worried Vicky not to go mad. When I reminded her of the Carlton

House desk she had sighed and wrinkled her nose.

I was at the saleroom early enough. Bundles of soft goods were still being held aloft before an unenthusiastic crowd, the dealers pressed around the one functioning radiator, and the auctioneer had that flat tone in his voice. With the exception of the estate desk it was a drab array of goods and chattels that filled the old chapel.

Canary Mary sat on the end of the front row, a welcome splash of colour; her hands were thrust up the sleeves of her bright yellow mac as she shivered and shuffled her feet. I squatted beside her. 'Done any good?'

'No. A bit of hand-worked linen, an ornament or two. There's nothing here, I don't know why I've come. I fancy that pair of vases, though.' She pointed to a pair of glass vases badly overpainted with hideous birds of paradise.

'All right I suppose.'

It was going to be a long sale, so I went to the back and sat on a chest of drawers, pulling my coat about me and making myself as comfortable as possible.

Canary Mary bought the vases. I didn't know how much for, because a state of torpor had descended upon me. I huddled in my great coat, clacking my shoes together gently, and staring at the floor. I could not decide what to go to on the desk. Vicky and I had come up with a figure at the viewing, but I'd already upped that twice, firstly in the van then upon seeing it once more.

Canary Mary stood in front of me, her sale bag bulging. I smiled at her and thanked her for the chunk of 'yellow peril' she offered.

'You've got the loot, now you're off home to

gloat.'

'Some loot. It's been a waste of time—be lucky if I make a couple of pounds out of this lot.' She shook her bag and stumped off with a lugubrious 'See you'.

I chewed on the cake without enthusiasm. Yellow peril needs to be lubricated down the gullet. I spilt crumbs, big yellow crumbs, that rolled down my coat and scattered on to the dusty floor. A night time treat for the saleroom mice.

I flung the last piece of cake into a waste bin and returned to my reverie.

Eric had always been a good boss. An engineer of the old school, he'd risen from the shop floor to a seat on the board of one of our old established machine tool companies. The young Glasgow apprentice had excelled at night school, applying himself diligently to both work and study, attending the kirk regularly and marrying his childhood sweetheart. A very self disciplined man, fair and hardworking, and not without a sense of humour, he always backed the engineers against the 'clerks' as he disparagingly called all accountants and planners.

We had had our arguments, our fall-outs; always over a design problem, a marketing ploy or something similar. If things had got a bit heated at a meeting and we had parted with glares and without a handshake, the following day he'd be on the telephone, his soft Scottish voice with a chuckle in it. 'Now you wild Yorkshire man—simmered down, have we?'

Since the early days of our marriage Vicky and I had longed for an antique shop of our own. When I was travelling the length and breadth of the country

190

I spent every lunchtime haunting junk shops in search of a bargain, anything I could repair, or a chair for Vicky to re-upholster.

Most things I picked up could fit into the car boot, but the purchase of a quickly fitted roof rack extended my range; now the odd chest of drawers and longcase clock could be bought. I was careful to keep my activities quiet, for although I never let them impinge on the company's time, they frowned on such things.

I smiled to myself as I remembered the time I had bought an Edwardian seven-piece suite; lashing the settee and ladies' and gentlemen's chairs to the roof rack I had managed to stow the four dining chairs inside the car. It had been re-upholstered in a garish blue, and as it made an eyecatching load I had secreted the car down a side street out of view of the head office. The journey home had been slow, for the settee pitched alarmingly every time I braked, but it proved one of our better buys. I repolished the walnut frames and Vicky changed the nightmare blue for a sedate beige.

They were starting on the white goods; rust frilled radiators and cookers sticky with fat. I hid myself behind a wardrobe and waited impatiently for the estate desk to come up. Fatty made an innocent looking tour of the saleroom to spot out the competition then seated himself right under the auctioneer.

The senior steward slapped his hand on the desk, 'Lot 186.'

The auctioneer peered over his glasses. 'Looks interesting. Let's have it out lads.'

Two stewards carried it in front of the rostrum and stood each side of it, unsmiling guardians of the star of the show.

I never got in the bidding and neither did the Ring. The auctioneer asked for £100, and could not conceal his surprise when a tiny woman in the second row fluttered her hand. 'That a bid, madam?'

It was, she confirmed. A portly farmer in his Sunday best wagged a thick finger lest the auctioneer fail to see his interest and brought the gavel down prematurely. The bidding see-sawed between the two until the farmer twisted his lips and shook his head. 'No! Let her have it.'

Fatty rejoined the Ring; they stood in silence for a moment, then I heard, 'Bloody crackers—it's unusual but not that much.'

Finally Elly's flat voice, 'It's over the top, is that.'

The tiny woman was explaining to a steward; it was for her daughter—'She's an artist, you know.'

I bought the worst pine chest in the sale, as badly a proportioned set of drawers as I'd ever seen, and with a split top. Fiery would groan—but he'd buy it. I rammed it into the van, and was shutting the doors when Elly appeared at my elbow.

'You know them vases Mary bought?'

'Yes, the painted ones.'

'You're a pal of hers. Go down and buy them off her for me, would you?'

He pushed three five-pound notes into my hand. 'Try her at a tenner, but go to fifteen if you have to.'

Mary stood the vases on her pine sideboard. 'You say they'll give me fifteen for them?'

'That's it, goodness knows why they want them. They're nothing much.'

'If the enamelling was taken off—what then?'

192

'Still a pair of mediocre vases.'

'They must have seen me buy them. I only gave four pounds for them. Why this generosity? It's not like them.'

We went over the vases again. Very pale green, a few crissles, clumsy pontil marks, and the amateurish painting, they were nothing special.

'What should I do?' Mary asked.

'Up to you, I'd sell them; you said you'd had a poor day—at least you'll be a tenner up.'

*　　　*　　　*

A slate grey Jaguar was pulled up in front of the shop; our visitors had arrived. I drove the van into the yard and left the atrocious chest and mediocre vases in it—there's a bit of the snob in all of us.

Eric looked thinner and smaller, but his chatty wife Morag was still as round and jaunty as a robin.

Vicky had taken them into the lounge, settled them into the best chairs and thrown an apple log on the fire—it was a day for showing off. The children had been paraded, told how they had grown, how Sally had her mother's hair and Peter my eyes.

Eric shook my hand vigorously, and Morag jumped up to plant a kiss on my cheek. Then we settled in front of the roaring fire with tea and crumpets.

I was horrified to hear how the industry had shrunk. World famous names were no more; the company itself hardly manufactured anything, being mainly agents for imported machines. But the sadness was countered by tales of old colleagues: Phillip now had a caravan park in

Wales, the happy-go-lucky David a restaurant in the Cotswolds, and the studious Harold a second-hand bookshop in Sheffield.

Eric and his wife were booked in for the night at The Ship. They had arranged for an evening meal and cordially invited us to join them. 'The wains as well,' Morag laughed.

Sally and Peter were thrilled; this was really grown up stuff being taken to the pub for an evening meal. Peter had recently enjoyed a week of late nights turning the paddle wheel of Cotton Blossom. *Showboat* had been a great success, and when the cast had taken their final bow on the last night, Canary Mary had called the blushing boy on to the stage and to thunderous applause given him a sloppy kiss.

I took Eric around the smallholding as the evening drew in, showing him Topic and Elspeth, the hens and the ducks, and telling him of our plans to replant the orchard and become as self-sufficient as we could.

The garden looked sad, but the dairy was still cluttered with the last of the root crops; potatoes in boxes covered with sacks, nets of onions, carrots and parsnips stacked root down and covered in sand. Garlic hung in clusters from the roof, the cast-iron egg rack was full, and in an alcove rested two cheeses, maturing nicely.

The russets had kept best, each one wrapped in newspaper. I pulled one out and bit into it, the wrinkled, tough skin was like sandpaper but the flesh was sweet and juicy. They are a nuisance to pick are russets, and ours seemed prone to scab, but I like the scent of them. When we gather the windfalls in an old zinc bath Elspeth nudges aside the pippins and searches out a russet.

I tapped the cheeses as Mrs Lewis does; we were sure that both were blue.

'They live like kings,' Eric told Morag when we got back to the lounge.

The meal went well, simple fare beautifully cooked and in abundance. I had taken a bottle of Rioja across, and Charlie the landlord had waved his hand depreciatingly when I had offered to pay corkage. Soon Vicky was looking anxiously at her watch. It was way past the children's bedtime, so she and Morag hurried them across the green as Eric and I slunk off to the taproom.

We were a bit overdressed, which brought a 'hey-up, two bleedin' aristos' from Rabbit. As we settled at the chimney table away from the clacking dominoes, the Colonel peered through the serving hatch at Eric—he was sure he knew him from somewhere.

Baz rose from the table, stretched and yawned. 'I'll have to be off, early start tomorrow.' It brought protests from the other domino players, 'Come on, just one more Baz—me luck's turned.' But Baz scooped the coins into his pocket said his goodnights, and the door clattered shut behind him.

Ted joined us, then Rabbit. His terriers, edging under the bench, watched him until he was seated, then they dropped heads back on to paws. It was country talk. Ted held forth on curing bacon and the best way to get the calf bed back into a cow; Rabbit on catching 'mouldies' and the finest trail hound he ever owned.

'Won a lot of money wi' that dog, there was never the like of him from here to the Scottish border.'

Eric bought a round of drinks, then another, staying protests with a 'No, you're my guests'. Ted and Rabbit grinned, and launched into more country talk. This time it was fresh water crayfish, muzzle loading guns and tickling trout.

When Charlie called time Eric got a crushing handshake from Ted, slaps on the back and an invitation to hunt the horned hare.

'Horned hare?' Eric queried when we were standing on the pub doorstep.

'Forget it,' I advised him as Morag tripped across the green towards us.

'They're well away—both off them out like a light. You've two grand wains there.'

Her voice was a little wistful; they have no children. She left Eric and me looking across at Bullpen Farm, the cold night air deliciously fresh on our faces.

Eric pulled out a cigar. The lighter, flaring, showed the creases in his face, the slightly gaunt cheeks. From the moors came the faint bleat of sheep, nearer the soft 'phoo phoo' of an owl. Lazy smoke rose from chimneys and coiled against a layer of light sky before losing itself in a rolling cloud.

We talked quietly of old times, old friends, triumphs and disasters. I told him of our early days; how we had started in antiques, picking up things here and there—old Stanley selling them for us on commission in his tiny shop.

'My company car often had its boot stuffed full of antiques,' I confessed.

'And not only the boot,' Eric laughed. 'I once saw your car parked down Sussex Street with a super parlour suite on its roof—I was really

196

tempted to make you an offer for it.'

CHAPTER FIFTEEN

Eric and Morag came across to say goodbye.
They had sat up in bed until the early hours of the
morning talking over the idea of his resigning and
them coming to live up the Dale. Capital was not
a problem. 'We could buy a caravan park—a small
hotel,' he told us excitedly.

I told them that it's not all roses round the door,
woodsmoke and pigeon pies; there are long hard
winters to get through. We are not exactly 'ten
miles from the nearest lemon', but there are some
real drawbacks: a visit to the theatre or cinema
takes on the magnitude of a small expedition; to the
swimming baths and back, and half the day is gone.

They would find it easier than we did, being
relatively wealthy and having no children, but
there is still a lot of adjusting to do. It takes time
to fall in with and accept the slower pace. Not to
become frustrated queuing at the Post Office whilst
the latest village wedding is discussed in detail, or
waiting for local tradesmen who have an almost
Spanish concept of time.

'I'll get straight to it,' says Baz. We smile, for we
know that it will be three weeks at least before he
pushes his wheelbarrow into the yard.

Eric was adamant, 'We've had enough, it's
getting me down.' Morag agreed; she had seen him
age alarmingly these last few years.

It would be a good move for him, so I made light
of the problems, telling him: 'The difficulty is, Eric,

197

measuring yourself; you've no yardstick to go by anymore. There are no thrills to be got wresting an order from competition, no cut-and-thrust meetings. You have to settle for the really simple pleasures; taking a warm egg from the hen's nest, bringing a basket of shining apples from the orchard, a cracking log fire after a long walk with the dogs.'

'It'll do me,' Eric said quietly.

Morag was effusive; she fancied a small private guest house: 'We could have a Burns night, and Eric, we could get a licence and you could specialise in whiskies. Get all the different malts and the like.'

As we stood and waved them off the telephone rang. Vicky called from the shop. 'It's Fatty—wants a word with you.'

I paused at the door and watched the glistening roof of the car disappear behind the estate wall. They'll be back, I said to myself.

Fatty has a grand voice, deep and gratey, every word clearly enunciated, and I heard very clearly his simple request to put the pair of vases I'd bought from Canary Mary into the auction at Lalbeck church rooms, but I still said, 'What?'

He repeated his request adding, 'There's nothing sinister in it—just a bit of a jape. Put them in under your name,' he added, then rang off.

'They're not hot are they?' Vicky asked, a note of concern in her voice.

'No, don't think so, but I'll check with the stewards at the saleroom.'

The vases had apparently come, along with a mass of goods, from a deceased estate, so I dropped them off at Drunken Sam's.

The house was a tip. Every room was piled high

with cardboard boxes of various sizes, pictures and prints were stacked down the hallway, even his kitchen floor was littered with stuff for the forthcoming sale.

Sam did not look good. He was slumped on a stool in front of the cooker, peering at a pan full of sizzling bacon. He was unshaven, and his grey hair had not felt the comb for a day or so. A tartan dressing gown was draped around his shoulders, and his feet were thrust into matching slippers. The sink was full of plates and pans, and on the table his huge black cat daintily selected pieces from last night's fish and chips, its gently swaying tail brushing an empty whisky bottle.

'This is the only drawback,' he muttered.

'What is?'

'Cookin'! Living on yer own is grand except for the cookin'.'

Sam's wife had struggled for years trying to wean him off the drink, finally she'd thrown the towel in and gone to live with her sister.

Sam had settled into an easy-going way of life, doing a sale a month, looking after his cat and seeing a bottle a day off—whisky if he was in funds, Long John's lethal brew if he wasn't. He was getting to look old, but was still as sharp as a pin when he was on the rostrum.

'What yer brought me?'

'Just a couple of vases.'

He forked the bacon on to a plate and criss-crossed it with brown sauce. 'Secret is regular eating—every morning at nine o'clock I have half a pound of bacon—sets me up for the day.' He trailed the stool up to the table and, wiping a knife on his dressing gown, gave me a friendly smile.

'Any reserve?'

'No, they've to go.'

'What I like to hear.' He pushed the cat gently off the table with the back of his hand. 'Come on Sheba, let's have a bit of decorum. Yes, the only thing is the cookin', everything else is a plus.'

'Think she'll ever come back?'

He paused, fork aloft dangling bacon.

'Bloody hope not! For thirty years I thought there was something wrong wi' me ears. Now it's bliss, isn't it Sheba?' He cut a piece of rind and sucked the brown sauce from it before dropping it to the cat.

'No, when I get home now and hangs me cap up I know I'm welcome.'

'Long John acting as porter again?'

'Aye. He curses, belches, farts and insults all me customers, but—' he shook his head sadly, 'you can't get the staff these days.'

Sheba jumped up on to the cluttered draining board sending a plate crashing to the floor. 'There it goes again,' Sam muttered through a mouthful of bacon, 'that bloody gravity.'

*   *   *

'The remarkable thing is, Vicky, he knows where everything is, who it has come from. Everybody gets paid out quickly, and to the penny.'

'He's like you, love.' She patted my cheek. 'Not as daft as he looks.' I probably should not have dipped her nose into the Yorkshire pudding batter, but Apple Tom is adamant on one point—women and horses have to be kept well in hand.

With the coming of spring the goat began to milk

better. There was not much for her to forage in the orchard, so I tethered her in the rough ground behind the barn, letting her nibble at the brambles and elder that stood waist deep. She made a den in the centre, and lay there shielded from the nippy wind that skipped down from the fells.

Elspeth had milked through into her second year; it was time she had a kid. Long John kept a billy: a disreputable, cantankerous and smelly thing, heavily horned, his gingery tattered coat hanging almost to the ground. But over any she-goat he exerted a magical power. They licked and nuzzled him, butted him playfully, rubbed themselves against him, then submitted happily to his carnal desires.

The last days of March had promise in them. Early morning mists cleared, revealing pale leaden skies that brightened on the horizon to a gleaming almond, then the faintest of blues pushed away the feather clouds and the Dale was washed in a lustrous sunlight that had more than a tinge of warmth in it.

I watched Elspeth closely for signs that she was coming into season. She gets more vocal and restless, then the tiny pink triangle under her tail becomes swollen and brighter.

'She's ready,' I told Vicky as I lifted the goat into the van. We tied a hurdle across to stop her being thrown about, and spread a good depth of straw. A plastic bucket half full of carrots was ignored as she raised herself up between the seats and bleated in our ears. She is so inquisitive she is a good traveller; never becoming agitated, her bright eyes miss nothing. She pushed her soft nostrils against our ears, nibbled our coats, flicked her ears forward at a passing wagon, then discovering the seat belts, chewed away at them.

We found Long John in his workshop. The waterwheel which powered his polishing machine was rumbling away happily, spraying a haze of water droplets that shone like jewels in the sun. The crabby bachelor was hunched over the spinning buffing wheel, slowly turning a brass jam pan in his black hands.

I poked him in the back for when the wheel is in full spate the noise is deafening. There is the rumble of the wheel, the splash of water hitting it as it spews from the leat, the jangle of things lying about the floor of the trembling shed waiting to be polished and the cheerful clinking of glistening pans, kettles and fire-irons that—having been polished—hang from the rafters.

He turned and grinned at us, his black beard splitting wide and revealing his yellow teeth. 'I'll just finish this,' he mouthed, stabbing a black finger at the jam pan.

Vicky and I leaned over the fence and watched the waterwheel. Technical College problems of a thousand years ago came back to me, foot pounds of energy into horsepower, percentage efficiencies. 'Bet he gets at least two horsepower out of that,' I said slowly.

It is an overshot wheel, cobbled together from parts of a quarry conveyor and parts of a bucket elevator, but it has rumbled away for years, providing Long John with free power. It had not rained for days, but this big fell takes some draining, and the beck was sweeping down the leat peaty brown, then bursting into a frothy arc over the wheel.

Long John joined us, wiping his hands on an oily rag. 'I'm getting as much done as I can. The sale is the day after tomorrow.'

'Sam's? In the church rooms?'

'Aye, like to have a bit of stuff in.'

'We've brought the goat up to see the billy. I think she's ready.'

John clicked his tongue and shook his head. 'Not here I'm afraid—he's gone walk about again. Having a lot of trouble with the daft old sod. Last week he was in Sottenghyll, got knocked into with a car or summat, came limping home, one horn shattered, covered in blood. I had to take the horn off and cauterise it. Soon got over it though, he's a tough old goat.'

'Wasted journey,' Vicky sighed.

Long John pretended to dust her nose with the oil rag. 'It's never a wasted journey when you come to see your Uncle John. Follow me.'

We followed him in single file across the farmyard and down the ghyll to where the old pheasant pens were. One of them was filled with brushwood. Long John poked amongst it, his great boots cracking the twigs.

'Here we are.' He bent and carefully filled his cap with tiny eggs. 'Quail,' he announced cheerfully, handing the cap to Vicky. We picked out the eggs gingerly, beautifully pointed eggs of beige splattered with greys and intense browns.

'I haven't a docker, John,' I told him.

'Eat 'em. Don't bother rearing quail. There's plenty here, they breed like rabbits. Never known owt as fertile—unless it's that old billy of mine.' John opened the van door and looked at Elspeth. 'She's in good fettle,' he said.

'Time she had a kid.'

'Sorry he's off. When I get him back I'll give you a ring. Meantime, a little liquid solace.' He pushed a bottle of Swaledale Lightning into my hands.

Vicky nursed the eggs in her bobble hat as we rocked and swayed down the track. 'What do we do with them?—I've never had quail's eggs before.'

'We put them away for the time being, and don't tell the kids.'

*　　　*　　　*

Early morning on the first of April I took a handful of hay from the barn and fashioned it into a passable nest. I put it into the hutch with Sally's rabbit and placed a quail egg in it.

Vicky threw back the curtains in Peter's room. 'Gosh it's snowed.' An excited boy in his pyjamas leapt to the window; the disappointment on his face soon turning to a smile.

'Every year,' I laughed, 'never fails.'

Sally was not to be caught, she had heard her Mother in Peter's room. But when she went to feed her rabbit her shriek was audible in the kitchen. The breathless child held the little egg in a trembling hand. 'Nibbles has laid,' she shouted excitedly. Peter hurried to disillusion her.

'They're having you on. Rabbits are live bearers,' he said loftily. A charmingly bent index finger wavered in front of me as a slow smile spread across Sally's face.

'You!' she yelled. I took flight; letting her chase me through the shop I leapt into the van and drove to Lalbeck.

The church rooms were packed. It is not just

the content of Sam's sales that draws the crowd; the church rooms are centrally heated, and the new plastic stacking chairs are as comfortable as stacking chairs can possibly be—besides, Sam is always good for a laugh or two.

We are given a good opinion of the baking bowl, told that they are not made like that anymore, that it is the best he's seen these last twenty years. 'Give us a pound.' The hands shoot up. Sam does his one, two, three trick, smacks the desk with his gavel as the fluttering hands wither out of sight.

'Three pounds, yours luv. By there's been some good bread made in that bowl.' The new owner is congratulated, nodded and smiled at. 'Now, this ironing board. I want you to have a good look at this ironing board . . .'

The last thing we want in the world is an ironing board, but we crane our necks. 'Let's see her set up, John.' The brown-smocked John obliges, big hands, fingers spread, press on the brown stained cover.

'A good 'un—give us a pound . . .'

And so unwanted goods find new owners, each coming under much scrutiny, fifteen seconds of fame for a bowl and board alike. Long John wrestled another board from under the pile. 'Now, this is a better one,' Sam informs us seriously, and without the blink of an eye.

I remembered Long John telling me when we set up the cottage sale the previous year, 'This bugger can plait sawdust.' Sam plaited away.

Big Rosie wondered why she had bought the meat safe. 'It'll come in,' she told her friend, who nodded her head absent-mindedly; she's wondering where she can put the cane table she couldn't resist.

Canary Mary sat in the front row, watching

intently. Sam rarely plays his one, two, three trick on her. She straightens her back, glares at him, her voice loud and confident, 'Oi! I bid a pound.'

The vases were on the table below the rostrum, and in the company of mixed tumblers and soup bowls they stood out, looking more than they were.

Fatty put his fingers to his lips when I asked him about them. 'You'll see.'

Slowly the tables were cleared, Long John collapsing and stacking them against the wall. He worked around the vases until they were the last item on the last table. I went to the back and propped myself against a plywood wardrobe, ready for the furniture, and looked at my watch. It was a quarter to twelve.

'Let's have a look at 'em, John.' The vases were held up to Sam. 'These are bonny—a bonny pair of vases, and perfect. They are perfect aren't they, John?' They were pronounced perfect, and Sam asked us for a tenner. 'They'll make it,' he confidently predicted.

Fatty opened the bidding at a fiver and a serious faced Canary Mary offered ten. The bidding rose steadily a fiver a time until the price stood at ninety pounds. Sam was sweating, the clean shaven jowl wobbled as he flicked his head from Fatty to Mary. There was a pause at ninety-five, it was Fatty's bid and Sam stared appealing at Mary.

'Come on, fill it up. Make it a century, Mary.' She stared back at Sam, her hand hovering on her cheek. 'Come on! you'll lose 'em luv,' he coaxed.

'One hundred—now sir. Let's see what you're made . . .'

A vase crashed to the floor and burst into a thousand fragments. Sam's jaw dropped open as a gasp burst from the crowd; he pushed his brown fedora back, then clutched at his sweating brow. 'John! John! What 'ev you done?'

'Sorry Sam, I'm sweating a bit and,' he shrugged his shoulders, 'couldn't help it.'

Sam looked at me, his mind no doubt feverishly working out what he would have to pay me. Fatty was laughing helplessly along with the rest of the Ring, and the crowd, now over the shock, tittered and chattered.

A good auctioneer soon regains any lost composure.

'Come on, we'll sell the remaining one.'

Fatty, his body still shaking with mirth called out, 'A fiver.'

And Mary countered with, 'Ten.'

The bidding skipped along, soon bringing a deathly hush over the saleroom as Sam turned his bewildered looking face to Mary and asked her for the second time to, 'Fill it up, make it a century.'

She had no sooner done so than the second vase crashed to the floor. Sam crushed his hat to his face and dropped his head on to the desk.

'John! John! What the hell are you doing?'

Fatty and the Ring started to clap, Sam lifted his hat to see the grinning face of Long John pointing to the calendar as Lalbeck clock began to chime midday.

Sam pushed his hat back, picked up his gavel and grinned broadly; then, one hand to his brow, he began to laugh. 'You buggers! You buggers!—I'll get you for that—I nearly had a bloody heart attack!'

CHAPTER SIXTEEN

April is my favourite month. Spring has got into gear; the garden comes alive with thrusting spear points of pea and bean, and the deep green of the early potatoes stars the brown earth.

The blackthorn hedges are stippled white with blossom, finches gather in chattering groups, and far off down in the estate woods we hear the first cuckoo and, eyes closed, make our secret wish.

April is the month of promise. The garden is surveyed; cabbage here, onions and carrots intermixed to fool the root fly, and with the sun warm on our faces we wax confident—this year we will not buy one vegetable. I plan to decimate the vast rhubarb patch, root out a gnarled old apple tree, and take the sod off a good slice of the orchard. More onion ground, more potato ground is planned, but Vicky forcefully paced off a good sized square of it.

'I want a herb garden here, there's nothing like fresh herbs.' Her argument was irrefutable. We have mint; the bottomless buckets we planted it in have failed to contain it. There is mint between the raspberry canes and the blackcurrants, it pops up in the cold frames and it forms a pale green collar around the foot of the water butt.

'We must have tarragon and basil—and rosemary,' I was told, and I agreed readily; they are worth growing for their names alone. 'Coriander and borage,' and I was into the shed for my spade.

There was the castor to repair on the canterbury, the foot to glue back on to the livery cupboard, but they could wait. I hung my coat in the crook of an apple tree and, watched by an inquisitive goat, set the line band parallel to the wall. A moment's reflection, then it was advanced another yard into the orchard—no point in skimping.

Soon I was panting, and the pauses for brow wiping became more frequent. Ted's head appeared over the wall. 'What are you on with?'

'Herb garden.'

'You want basil and you want rosemary.'

'They are in the plan, Ted.'

'Don't forget to curse the basil, you always curses basil when you plant it—don't know why.'

He disappeared, and I had another barrowload of turf ready to tip before he was back. 'And parsley. You sow the seeds and it goes to see the devil before it comes up.' His laugh trailed off into the cowhouse as I bent my back to the barrow handles.

At lunchtime the children hurtled into the yard and, ignoring me, burst into the kitchen. Two minutes and Sally was at the fence. 'Mum says you've to come—it's ready.'

'I've a little surprise for you later,' Vicky told us as she poured out the tea. I pleaded with her and so did the children, but all we got was a firm, 'No, wait and see.'

We heard nothing of school, and they didn't want to know what I was doing in the orchard. Frequently we had a 'go on, tell us', and occasionally a long drawn out, 'Mum, Mu-um,' coupled with an ingratiating smile, but Vicky can be hard.

'Finish your dinner—no clean plates, no surprise.'

Eventually we were led into the shop. In the window Vicky had set up a gypsy table, covered it with an ornate cloth in the centre of which stood a crystal ball, alongside it a colourful headscarf and a pair of dangly earrings.

She had neatly printed on a small card: Complete fortune telling set for sale. 'Bought it this morning, an old woman brought in the ball and this cloth. I dug the gypsy table out of the store and set it up for a laugh.'

Peter weighed the ball in his hands, turning his back to keep at bay his clamouring sister.

'How much?' I asked.

'I gave a tenner for the ball and the cloth. It's a very ornate cloth, but look at this.' She lifted the headscarf up and pointed to four regularly spaced holes. They were hemmed and stitched, and were obviously purpose made—but for what? The cloth was heavy and handwoven and was made from two symmetrical pieces stretched together. It had rounded ends, and the wide borders contained patterns of flowers and scrolling foliage.

I scratched my head. 'Got me—can't imagine what it's been made for. Probably some part of a magician's prop—have you fixed a price, because that gypsy table cost fifteen quid?'

'No, just did it for a laugh, thought it would be a good window piece to get attention.'

'Quite right,' I laughed as I looked up to see a puzzled Dolly peering through the window at us.

'Can you see anything?' Peter asked his mother. So we sat her on a stool and she bent her head over the ball, headscarfed and earringed, a theatrical wave of hands silencing us.

'The mists are clearing—I see much work ahead,

a time of toiling and hardship . . .'

'Is it ever anything else?' I muttered.

'But then there are going to be many rewards—much rejoicing—great fortune—and two children are going to be late for school.'

Vicky was right, the fortune telling set was an attention getter, and to our surprise we had several genuine enquiries about it. The well preserved seamstress from Lalbeck spent half an hour poring over it before deciding to patronise Jack the Pat instead and buy the coromandel vanity box, and Canary Mary squealed with delight on being shown it.

'You'll not get anything from it in here,' she pronounced, 'the ambience is all wrong.' She was right; we got nothing from it. When I hovered over it all I could see was the distorted pattern of the cloth. Peter and Sally stroked it and, grinning, told of ogres and tall dark strangers.

As usual Canary Mary had no money, but she was sure she would come across something we would be eager to swap it for. I'd been caught with this ruse before, keeping things back for her for weeks only to be eventually told she had changed her mind.

'Can't keep it, Mary. Sorry, but we've a business to run.'

She half closed her eyes, pursed her mouth, and called me a pig.

* * *

I like digging. There is something very satisfying about turning over the brown earth, cutting clean, square blocks of soil, casting them forward, breaking them with a twisting spade. The simplest of tools, honest labour; the reward of seeing a dug patch grow, dark and neat, full of hope.

I let the hens into the new bit of garden, stretching wire netting across to keep them from the sown part. They rushed in, legs scratching in wide arcs, heads stabbing at the worms. The neatness was destroyed in an hour, then they lay on the dark earth, one leg folded under them, the other stretched, and ruffled their feathers. Happiness for them is friable earth, a warming sun, and worms.

They were sated, their crops were bulging, so I gently herded them back to the orchard, happy at the thought of the free protein they had got.

Vicky called from the back door. 'Have you a minute? There is a woman interested in the fortune telling stuff, but she only wants to buy the crystal ball—what shall we do?'

'Ask a high price for it.'

'How high?'

I rather liked Vicky's little set-up. I'd noticed a number of people looking at it, pointing and laughing, and it was the start of the tourist season. It could be a good thing for us. 'Thirty quid!'

'Don't think she'll wear that,' Vicky replied, pulling her mouth wide.

'It's getting a lot of interest—thirty quid!'

'I'll try.'

Vicky tried. Refused twenty-five, and polishing the ball on her apron, set it back on its plinth.

'Well, we know it's worth twenty-five.' I consoled her as I bent my head over the ball and stared into it. 'She'll be back.'

There is no pattern to our trade. We go weeks

without anything brought into the shop then we get a spate of it. Vicky bought the crystal ball and cloth, then I bought a wax bust of Wellington under a glass dome and a silver-plated tea urn, and we got a house clearance—all in the space of three days.

The clearance wasn't up to much, for as usual the relatives had had their pick, clean patches on the wallpaper showing where several pictures and a barometer had been.

Nevertheless there was some decent bread and butter stuff. A set of tall oak dining chairs, a table that would have been better had it not lost its spare leaf, and a brass bed were the best items. I filled a clothes basket with cheap trinkets and packed them around with newspaper—good tray lots for Sam to squeeze the last penny out of.

The soft goods were poor. Curtains that were faded and stained, drawers full of musky bed linen fit only for cleaning cloths, threadbare carpets ready for the tip.

In the hallway were three small rugs, faded and worn. I pondered over them; were they worth keeping? Finally I threw them into the back of the van; they would come in useful for packing material.

Vicky searched through the clothes basket, yanking out several pieces of crested ware. 'We can sell these, we're always short of smalls.'

I am very furniture orientated and I often completely ignore the porcelain and glass at a sale, so Vicky works hard to redress the balance, chiding me over my shortcoming. 'We sell on average one piece of furniture per week; we can't live on that.'

'Don't forget the shipping stuff—Fiery Frank is a good buyer—he'll take the table and chairs, and the brass bed,' I told her.

Vicky is never convinced. She is sure that the shipping trade will come to an end in a year or so, and it is a wildly fluctuating market. The dollar gets strong and we, tucked away in a tiny village up the Dale, feel the flexing of its muscles as the price of shipping goods falls; not greatly, but it is a narrow profit margin trade to start with.

I like it. I like filling the van, having bedroom suites and mirror-back sideboards crammed into the barn. It is a volume trade, a trade of haggling, deals, of setting one thing off against another. I buy a massive sideboard, heavily carved and with ponderous handles; Vicky thinks it is hideous. It is brought home with difficulty, moved into the barn with more difficulty utilising trolleys and sack carts, polished, worried over and finally sold for a tenner profit.

'A prestige piece, keep 'em coming,' I tell Vicky as she wrinkles her nose.

'Risking a double hernia for ten pounds.'

There are times I agree with her, and dream of the days when we can make fantastic profits trading solely in Georgian silver, a few choice items in a cardboard box on the back seat of an MGB.

There was no time for dreaming. The table and chairs wanted a wipe over, there was a load for the tip, the cutlery to sort through, Fiery Frank to ring up.

'And ring Otto up too, let him have a look at these rugs,' Vicky shouted. She was kneeling on the storeroom floor, the rugs turned over in front of her. 'They are all hand knotted—could be something.'

Our prospective buyers were tardy. Fiery said he

would be across next week, and Otto merely asked us to keep the rugs on one side for him—he would get to us when he could.

'You were right,' Vicky laughed, as the decrepit camper van pulled up in front of the shop. 'It's the crystal ball woman. You said she'd be back.'

'Thirty quid, not a penny less,' I warned.

She was a tall, angular woman, wearing a long cerise skirt and a wax jacket. On her head was a scarf patterned with signs of the zodiac, and her thin concave face was framed with jet black hair. She smiled politely and extended a bony hand towards the ball. 'May I?'

She turned it gently in her hands, her long fingers forming a loving cage, her dark eyes caressing it.

'Did we agree on twenty-five?'

Very firmly I said, 'The price is thirty.'

She smiled and, going to the window, tapped upon it. The van door opened and a painfully thin man, shabbily dressed and with a wild mane of ginger hair, got out and shuffled into the shop.

'It's thirty pounds,' the woman told him.

He shrugged his shoulders. 'What do you think?' Another shrug. She continued to turn the ball then, bringing it near to her face, her fingers became still; she closed her eyes and pressed it to her cheek.

'It is warm, Raoul,' she whispered. Raoul shrugged again, his yellow face impassive. 'We have to buy it, Raoul.' He reached into his pocket and brought out a wad of notes that would have choked a donkey. She peeled off three and dropped them on the counter. Again she closed her eyes, and clutching the ball to her chest, she bent her head and kissed it. Low incantations slipped from her trembling lips.

215

'We have to break the bonds, Raoul,' she said at last. From her jacket pocket she took a square of red velvet and wrapped the ball in it. She turned and kissed Raoul. 'We are a family again,' she laughed.

'Bet we could have got more from that ball. Did you see that money?' I told Vicky when they had gone.

She shivered. 'They gave me the creeps.'

'You can break up your little tableau now.'

'Wish we hadn't sold it,' she answered biting her lip.

'Fancy yourself as Madame Vicky, gazing the crystal, casting the bones?'

'No, just have a feeling.'

'Well you didn't predict much—hard work if I remember rightly.'

'And great fortune,' she reminded me with a grin.

Fiery loved the shipping stuff we had gathered together, but Otto, when he finally appeared, was not enthusiastic about the rugs. He hissed through his gold teeth and spread his big pink hands. 'Caucasian village rugs. Mid-nineteenth century. OK but very worn—too worn.'

'Have they no value?' Vicky asked.

'Yes, a little, for their interest. See, they are woven with the Turkish knot, and the wool is harsh course stuff.' He sighed, lifted a be-ringed hand and pushed the fingers deep into his cheek. 'Probably a tenner each—no more.'

A tenner sounded all right to me, but Otto declined to buy them. 'Keep them for interest. Hang them on your wall. They help you learn.'

Vicky apologised for wasting his time. 'Sorry, I

thought they were worth looking at.'

'Don't worry dear lady. Otto always glad to see friends.'

'It was this that started me looking at the weave,' Vicky said, taking the gypsy cloth from the corner where we had stowed the remainder of the fortune telling set.

Otto seized it and strode to the window. 'Where did you get this?' he exclaimed.

'We had it brought in a couple of weeks ago.'

He bunched the cloth in his hands and turned it over, pushing his monocle to his eye.

'Thought so, thought so,' he muttered excitedly. He squatted down and spread the cloth over his knees stroking it with his fleshy hands, a childlike look of wonderment on his face. He looked up at us and laughed; his monocle fell and swung on its gold chain. 'You know what this is?'

'No,' we replied in unison.

'This is a Mongolian saddle rug. See, Otto show you.' He got to his feet and spread the rug on a marble top washstand.

'Woven in two pieces and joined in middle—see. This is Senneh knot—see.' We craned forward, for the light in the storeroom is poor. 'And these four holes, they go under the saddle bosses, to keep it in place. This too is mid-nineteenth century.' The fingers pressed into the cheek once more, then he picked up the rug and carried it to the window again. 'No, Otto wrong—it is earlier.'

I looked at Vicky and raised my eyebrows.

'What's it worth, Otto?'

'How much you want for it?'

'Much as we can get.'

Otto laughed and took out his cheque book.

217

'Here, young man. Write in what you want for it.'

Otto delights in this kind of thing. He is a gregarious and generous man, but he is no fool. He knew the problem I wrestled with as I took my pen. Otto is rich; his yellow and black Rolls Royce stood in the yard, his house is stuffed with treasures, he owns a chain of modest hotels—and he is our most valued customer. When we buy at auction for him the resulting little brown envelopes are most welcome and often keep us financially afloat.

Otto's gold teeth gleamed, his pale blue eyes twinkled as they watched me. If the worn rugs were still worth ten pounds each, the saddle rug, in good condition as far as we could ascertain, must be worth much more. But how much? Were they rare? I had never seen one before; but surely there had been hordes of Mongolian horsemen, and logically hordes of saddle rugs. I finally decided the rug, considering the excitement it had caused Otto, must be worth at least seventy-five pounds.

Not wishing to kill the pig I wrote fifty pounds on the cheque and gave it to Otto. I watched his face closely, but it betrayed no emotion as he pulled out a fountain pen and smothered the cheque in lilac ink.

'Here you are, dear lady.' He presented the cheque to Vicky with a flourish, and hanging the rug over his arm shook me by the hand.

'Goodbye dear boy.'

We waved him out of the yard and went into the kitchen. Vicky had brought the headscarf from the storeroom and, flinging it over her head, she did a little sinuous dance. Ending up in front of me she leaned back, half closed her eyes and stroked a finger under my chin.

'Didn't Madame Vicky predict great fortune?'

'Yes,' I laughed, 'fifty quid isn't bad.'

She pulled the cheque from her blouse, and with a devilish grin spread it to my face.

Otto, with many slashes and strokes of the lilac ink, had cancelled the fifty pounds and written in its place two hundred and fifty.

CHAPTER SEVENTEEN

I like the name Leonora, especially when it's coupled to a phonetically pleasing surname like Petherbridge. It has a certain cachet, a certain ring to it, and bearers of such names have a tendency to grow into them.

Not many mousy, thin, hesitant Leonoras of mature years are to be found; instead we have large, confident types, ones who will drive a hard bargain.

Their husbands, on the other hand, can be mousy but interestingly so; they have that hidden streak of deviancy which is found in many English men. Such was Albert Petherbridge. Small, wiry, with a quick intelligence, an outwardly unflappable nature, and a dry sense of humour, he was in all ways the opposite of the excellent Leonora, without being any the less excellent.

She is the guardian of the household, the main provider—she's a head librarian—and the one with the full and active social life; as the calendar behind the kitchen door testifies, for at first glance it resembles some exotic and colourful lichen. Leonora has a battery of coloured pens, and a

219

system. Red for the WI, blue for the church, green for meals-on-wheels and a delicate saffron—which would delight Canary Mary—for the Women's Luncheon Club.

The system consists of various lozenges, squares and asterisks, and is simple and easily understood.

Albert consults the calendar after his part-time job at the garage is finished, a lozenge of brown, and he smiles; his dear wife has an evening meeting. He waves her off with a light heart, pours a generous whisky, and settles himself in his tiny study with his stamp collection.

The Petherbridges had viewed the calendar together, found not one geometric shape commandeering the afternoon of Wednesday, and had consequently suggested I called that day between two and three of the clock; for they had things to sell.

And good things they were too. A delicately inlaid corner chair, several pieces of Worcester, plated entrée dishes and a games table—in want of a little repair, but very desirable.

Leonora, in her efficient way, had brought home one of those yearly published price guides of antiques. It lay on the piano with several pieces of paper, no doubt marking the sections on porcelain, games tables and corner chairs. These publications are admirable, but they do tend to be a little ambitious.

The price guide was placed so I could not fail to miss it, and Leonora stood straight backed and stern eyed. The intent was obvious; the good woman would brook no timewasting. I would be expected to reel off a good and acceptable price for each item, count out the money in notes of an acceptably low denomination, and tiptoe away with the goods, quietly closing the garden gate behind me.

A smiling Albert brought mugs of coffee and perched on the end of the sofa. A flick of Leonora's eyes dislodged him and brought him to his feet.

'Any good to you?' he enquired, cautiously.

'Yes indeed, nice things Albert. Had you a price in mind?'

Another flick of the fierce eyes withered the words on his lips.

'No we haven't; have we Petherbridge?'

It is better if you can get an approximate idea of what people expect. Sometimes we can set an unacceptably high price for a well thought of piece against the undervaluation of another, and we make everybody happy. But Leonora knew how to handle dealers—do your homework, get them to make a firm offer for each item, and if the offers are not acceptable, consign the stuff to the saleroom.

Any article requiring repair presents the dealer with a problem. Not only is there the cost of the repair, but there is the question of acceptability when it's done and, especially with cabinet work, the fact that the piece lies in an unsaleable condition for many months—money tied up.

I took out my notebook and doodled away, watched intently by the Petherbridges. Mentally I upped my prices several times until there was nothing much left in it for us. Leonora drummed her fingers on the piano, flicked open the price guide and did some noisy breathing.

'We'll think about it, won't we Petherbridge— we've always been ones for straight dealing,' she

221

announced coldly when I gave her my offer. Then she flounced off, leaving Albert and me feeling a little uncomfortable.

'Come on, I'll show you something,' he said cheerily, leading the way into his study.

He had just bought a Bermuda one shilling green, and it lay in the centre of his desk under a slab of glass. Lights were switched on and a magnifying glass offered. 'Beauty, isn't it?'

I've always been fond of stamps, especially British Colonials; they have a subtlety of colour and a quality of engraving which is quite captivating. It was a lovely stamp, and Albert beamed at my approval. 'She doesn't understand—most women don't,' he whispered as he poured two whiskies out and directed me to a chair.

It was the instant I sank into the chair that I saw the clock. It hung opposite Albert's desk, a simple round clock, beetle hands and a white face on which was the magic word 'Lalbeck', and underneath that 'NER'.

'Albert, you've got the station clock.'

'Aye, it was the wife's father's—damned good clock, excellent timekeeper.'

'Is it for sale?'

'For sale! For sale! Not likely—she'd flay me alive if I parted with that clock.'

'If you ever do, Albert, give me first chance.'

'That I will—but don't hold your breath.' He bent over the stamp again, a faint smile playing about his mouth.

I didn't hear from the Petherbridges, so I assumed the stuff they had to sell had been sent to the saleroom. It did appear in Wilson's sale a month later, now highly polished, and a plastic bag containing the loose bits of the games table tied to one of its legs. A note written in Leonora's strong hand informed us that all the missing pieces were in the bag and that the table was Victorian. It was a buoyant sale; it always is when it contains stuff you've priced up privately. The corner chair, the Worcester, the entrée dishes, all made very good prices; but I was able to buy the games table, slightly over what I'd offered originally, but it was very desirable—and all the bits were there.

The Petherbridges were at the back of the saleroom, he quietly glum, Leonora wearing a little smile.

'You did well,' I told them, 'you picked a good sale.'

Leonora inclined her head slightly, the smile turned to a smirk and she lifted her eyes to the dirty, peeling ceiling of the saleroom. 'You bought the games table.'

'Yes, it's a nice piece.'

'At considerably more than you offered me for it.'

'Not considerably more—just a bit.'

'I see,' she said slowly, and brushed past me.

One good thing about Wilson's is that they pay out quickly; right after the sale if you insist. Leonora was standing straight backed in the tiny office insisting, so I walked Albert out into the scruffy yard.

'Look Albert, when I came to your place I offered as much as I could. Just misjudged the games table a bit.'

'Don't worry. Done it myself with stamps. Sometimes you make an offer, then when you get home and have a bit of a think . . .'

223

'Yes. Albert, I've been thinking about your NER clock, and—'

'Forget it!' he burst out quite brusquely; then, as if apologising for this out of character behaviour, he put his hand on my shoulder and added quietly, 'Look, it would have to be something really special to make me part with that clock, really special.'

I'd thought a lot about the clock, been tempted to boast to Ted that I knew of its whereabouts, pictured it above my desk ticking away. I'd told Vicky about it, about how I'd give almost anything to get my hands on it.

'It's a clock,' she'd replied in a down to earth way. 'Just a round wall clock.'

I spent a hour educating her on railway clocks. Their fine fusee movements, the part they had played in one of the finest and most efficient transport services the world has ever seen. Here, I explained, was a clock that was all that and more, for it was a local one. It had hung in the ticket office for more than half a century, thousands of watches had been set by it; the 'farmers' express' timed by it and the curiously named 'Bonneyface'—the afternoon passenger train—had made it tremble as it thundered through Lalbeck. A very desirable clock indeed.

*   *   *

On the first of May old Mr Hall came and plaited Topic's mane and tail. It was a bright but cool day, so we decided to harness her up and have a drive.

'Down the lane to Richard's!' shouted Peter.

'Why not take the games table with us,' Vicky suggested, so we wrapped it in an old blanket and,

224

after checking the plastic bag of bits was still intact, stowed it under the seat.

If we take the green lane from the bottom of the village and then sneak across one of Ted's fields we can regain the main road a bare two hundred yards from Richard's workshop.

The hedgebottoms were thick with celandine and white dead nettle, and in the fields sturdy lambs stood hock deep in lush grass. The sycamores were in full leaf, but the ash trees still held theirs tightly in sticky wraps.

Topic was getting fat. She ambled rather than walked, shaking her head and chomping at the bit she hadn't felt for some weeks. Her winter coat hadn't all combed out, and in spite of the gay streamers she sported on mane and tail she looked a scruffy pony. It's not the most comfortable of vehicles, our coup cart, and there is a tendency on a chill day to lose all the feelings in one's legs. I got out of the cart and led her on at a brisk walk. Soon I was joined by Vicky, but the children stayed put; they are of the firm opinion that third class riding is preferable to first class walking.

We walked in silence, one each side of Topic. The dull stubbing of the pony's hooves, the creak of the harness and a little desultory birdsong were sufficient to blot out the drone of the cars on the distant highway.

Although it was Sunday, a thin plume of smoke arose from the chimney of Richard's workshop. The glue pot was boiling away on the stove, and a pleasant warm fug greeted us as we pushed open the door.

'Working on the Sabbath,' I teased him.

'There's not enough days in the week, not

enough hours in the day,' he replied cheerfully.

He was obviously packed out with work, and we felt a little guilty bringing him more; but we were regular customers and prompt payers—the latter a quality which rarely fails to appeal to a cabinetmaker.

'Let's have a look at it,' he said with mock severity when I told him about the games table.

'Simple glue and pin job—that's all,' I replied, waving the plastic bag of bits at him.

'And I suppose you want it yesterday?'

'No, tomorrow will be fine.' He took the bag and hung it above his bench. When Vicky and Sally left us to seek out Gwen and her daughter we gravitated to the stove, not in search of warmth, but because it was the only uncluttered part of the floor.

Peter leaned against the setting out bench, hands thrust deep into his pockets, a studious look on his face.

'Richard,' he said at length, 'could I have a piece of half-inch dowel.'

Richard paused, stool in hand, and smiled at him, 'Only if you tell me what wood it's made of.'

'Ramin!' shouted Peter.

Richard's big hand ruffled the boy's hair as he laughed, 'Go on, cut as much as you want, bairn.' He sat straddled legged on the stool, and flung wood offcuts into the stove. 'I've seen that games table before. Leonora Petherbridge brought it in some weeks ago. Had a fit when I gave her my estimate. You see, not all the bits are there—one or two missing.' He slapped my knee. 'So it's not just a spin and glue job, and you can't have it tomorrow, or next week or the week after that.'

'Damn the woman and her straight dealings.'

*   *   *

I pulled the harness from Topic and, watched by the cat, gave her a good rub down. She had raised some sweat on the trot back home, but she seemed better for her little work out, going at her oats with a new fervour.

'They're bred to work,' Ted had told us. 'There's nowt looks worse than a Dales pony that's run to fat.'

She wasn't exactly a barrel of lard yet, but I resolved to work her more, get the gleaming coat and hard muscle back. The saddle lay gathering dust, for Sally hardly rode any more. I had no doubt the pony would carry my weight, and I toyed with the idea of riding her. The thought of a brisk morning canter on the moor, a brief stop for a pipe whilst the dogs got their wind back did appeal, but we have to be realistic. The smallholding was taking up more and more of our time; many mornings it was nearly lunchtime before I could climb into the van and make for the salerooms.

I left Topic's mane and tail plaited up. It seemed a shame to destroy such a lot of neat and meticulous work after only a few hours. Mr Hall had put her tail up in a traditional Yorkshire bob, weaving in ribbons of red and blue. Her mane was tightly braided and decked in the same colours.

'Red and blue for a black, red and yellow for a grey,' the old man told us.

What colours for a bay, a sorrel or a chestnut, I'd asked. He'd sniffed, stroked the ribbons out between thin fingers.

227

'Depends.'

'Depends on what?'

'Where you come from.'

He'd turned back to the pony, combing out her mane, an unlit cigarette bobbing between his lips, and skipped over the problem of the ribbon colours. 'She don't need a roll, do you old girl? We used to weave rolls in when they were a bit ewe necked—give 'em a nice curve—but this girl don't need one, she's a neck like a railway arch.'

I stroked the neck like a railway arch and listened to her steady munching. I spend hours in the stable—just watching and listening, and the cat does too. The general noises of the pony, her snuffles, blowings and pawing excite no response in the cat, but the rustle of a mouse brings that instant jerk into wakefulness.

I faked such a rustle, pushing the stem of my pipe through the hay. She was fooled for only a brief moment; then, giving me a baleful look, she re-curled her paws, closed her eyes and returned to her meditation.

I thought back over the day. The surprisingly cold morning, Mr Hall shuffling into the yard, hands full of ribbons and raffia, Richard's warm workshop, Peter stowing his lengths of dowel under the cart seat. Eventually my thoughts turned to the games table and the missing pieces. Devious Leonora: her and her straight dealing.

In the course of our trading we acquire many pieces that are incomplete. We stand the lamp in the cupboard, confident that we can find a burner that will fit, the delicate cruet set patiently awaits a matching mustard pot, and the fine Sunderland lustre teapot grows root contemplating the prospect of a matching lid. Stopperless decanters bow the shelves of our stockroom, and ranks of wine glasses wait to be marshalled into sets.

Our expectancy in this quarter is low, for experience has taught us a lesson we stupidly ignore. These things are best got rid of, they are money tied up, precious space occupied, countless hours of fruitless searching, frantic tryings on and attempts at matching up.

Occasionally we are rewarded; the mortar complements the pestle, the stopper fits the scent bottle; these are then jubilantly borne into the shop, saleable at last.

As it is with goods, so it is with ideas. They tumble around in our head for months, then things will come together and fit as snugly as the stopper did into the scent bottle.

I'd thought about the Lalbeck station clock, and Albert's words kept coming back to me, 'It would have to be something special to make me part with that clock.'

Now, Canary Mary had a rather special stamp she vowed she would never part with. It was a Victorian five-pound orange, used and slightly damaged.

Long John had found it in a roll top desk he'd bought from the estate, and not recognising the significance of the denomination—five pounds in Victorian times—had responded gallantly to Mary's comment about its pretty colour.

'It's yours, my dear,' he'd said, handing it to her in a charming way.

Now Canary Mary, like the majority of us, has financial crises, usually in her case brought on by the frequent repairs to her little egg-yellow Citroën.

We've told her a thousand times to wear her glasses when she drives. There are parts of the Dale where she is regarded as the patron saint of drystone wallers: they raise their caps as she passes by, for no one else puts so much work their way.

I bolted the stable door behind me, and in response to Vicky's window tappings hurried into the kitchen. 'Theory is,' I told her, 'stamp to Albert, clock to me. Problem: how to get the stamp off Mary.'

'You on about that damned clock again?'

*　　　*　　　*

It was a fortnight later, coming back from a futile house call, when I noticed the gap in the wall at Three Mare Close. Not a huge one—a yard or so of stones down, the toppings cast no more than a few feet into the field.

Narrow tyre tracks bolstered my suspicions, and when I pulled up in front of Canary Mary's they were confirmed: the little car had a crumpled nearside wing.

She was wearing a lemon silk housecoat, about her shoulders hung a bright citrine shawl with two appliqué sunflowers and on her feet were slippers of crocus yellow.

She arrayed herself on the pale cream chaise longue and patted an ample thigh as an invitation to her two cats, Amber and Topaz. They leapt on to her knees and sprawled luxuriously under the caresses of her heavily ringed fingers. Cyril was out walking with Piccalilli.

'You seen my car?' she enquired.

'No,' I lied.

'In a truly civilised country walls would be set further back from the road.'

'Bad, is it?'

'Bad enough.' She brightened and fixed me with a wide smile. 'I've some nice things to sell. Come with me.' I raised a hand to stay her.

'Stock coming out of my ears. Only thing that might tempt me to part with money would be a bit of indulgence, something small with perforations—and orange coloured.'

She pulled a face and heaved a deep sigh. 'It was a prezzy; you shouldn't sell prezzies.'

'I know, I was there when he gave you it. And I know this, if he thought that selling it would ease your path in life, he would insist you did so.'

'You think?'

'I'm sure.'

I rang Vicky at eight o'clock to tell her where I was, and it was another hour before Mary and I agreed on a price.

'Don't let Long John know how much, will you?' she whispered as I left. The agreed price was supposed to barely cover the cost of repairing the little car. Before I climbed into the van I took a look at the damaged wing and resolved that next time round I would be a panel beater instead of an antique dealer.

*   *   *

Leonora flung open the shop door, leaving a sad looking Albert to close it behind him. It was a fine sunny morning; the Muscovies had started laying, swifts scythed and shrieked over the village green. I'd sold an expensive little bijouterie table, and on

231

the wall behind me ticked the Lalbeck station clock.

Leonora fixed me with a stern look. 'Petherbridge had no right to let you have that clock.'

'A bit of straight dealing, madam, that's all.'

'It's not all. You know very well Petherbridge has a weakness when it comes to stamps. I've called in to let you know that I'm not at all pleased—not at all pleased.'

She looked up at the clock, snorted several times, then stalked to the door. 'Sometimes I think Petherbridge would swap me for a damned stamp.'

Albert gently closed the door behind them then opened it enough to squeeze his little head back into the shop.

'If you ever get a Cayman Islands penny scarlet—'

'PETH—ER—BRIDGE!'

The window rattled. I just managed to catch the expensive little fairing which trembled its way off the top shelf. It was my favourite one—the one of the scolding wife.

CHAPTER EIGHTEEN

Warm sunny days tempt me out of the shop and into the garden; rain and a howling west wind and I'm in the kitchen feeding sticks into the fire and cursing the slow kettle. I listen for the shop bell and feel a little guilty, for we have a rule—quiet times, no customers, we sit and polish or dust the shelves. A bright, sparkling shop with spotlights reflecting on rosy copper and burnished brass, glassy mahogany

232

and mellow pine. A well brushed carpet, clean windows, and people will be tempted to buy—well that is the theory.

Vicky is a good shopkeeper; I am not. When I'm not at an auction or there is no urgent job about the smallholding, I dutifully take my turn in the shop, my frequent tea-brewing trips causing Vicky to slam the iron on to the table.

'What you need is a samovar.'

It is not a bad idea. The square behind the counter is thickly carpeted, the smokers bow comfortable, the little shelf packed with favourite books and things. Place the fan heater judicially, weak lemon tea on tap, one wildly spendthrift customer and I'm sure my feet could find a cosy place alongside the waste basket and so make shopkeeping bearable.

There are compensations. The doorbell jangles, we look up from our book, and our eyes are delighted: we have a character.

He was short and portly, immaculately turned out in pin-stripe suit and bowler hat, and his bright grey eyes peered at me over round, wire-rimmed spectacles. A plump pink face scrubbed to apple shininess, a prim little mouth and snub nose, and a chin that had one of those unbelievably deep dimples that children try to peer into. I laid my book aside.

'Good morning.'

'Good morning to you, sir. May I look around your excellent establishment?' I indicated gracefully that he should feel free to do so. The pert mouth gave a pert smile. 'What a lovely smell of polish, sir. I do love the smell of polish.'

He leaned his rolled umbrella against the

counter, and with his hands clasped behind his back he hummed his way around the shop with an occasional 'ha' and a frequent little cough, which caused him to raise a pudgy hand with equal frequency. 'I must apologise for the cough, sir; seem to have a tickly throat.'

He coughed his way around the dresser, past the partners' desk and along the shelves.

'Jolly nuisance,' he smiled apologetically.

He seemed in no hurry, scrutinising every single object in the shop with care. When he came to the glass-topped counter and bent to look at our small display of antique jewellery the little cough exploded into a body-shaking spasm. Tears ran down the plump cheeks and into the immaculate white handkerchief he drew hurriedly from his pocket. 'I'm terribly sorry, sir,' he spluttered.

'Stay there!' I ordered him, and hurried into the kitchen.

Nellie May makes a concoction of angelica, coltsfoot and yarrow which is the most effective cough cure I've ever encountered. The children hate it, protesting loudly and holding their noses when it's administered, and I must agree it is not the pleasantest of medicines. We usually dilute it a little with warm lemonade, but as none was to hand I topped up the little tumbler of brown liquid with a measure of Swaledale Lightning.

'Drink this,' I said, offering it to our friend on a small tray. He thanked me profusely and gulped it down. After a long pause during which he stared motionless at the floor, he breathed heavily, pushed his glasses up his nose, gave an almost imperceptible burp, apologised and smiled in a slightly tortured way.

'By jove, sir, that reaches the spot. That is very, very kind of you, sir.' He blew out his cheeks and swayed slightly.

'May I, sir,' he said, indicating the duet stool. He sat down gingerly and, removing his bowler hat, displayed a head of close cropped silver hair.

'My name is Goodchild, sir. I'm a butler.'

He was such a pleasant, unaffected man, and he seemed so vulnerable with his old world courtesy and his outmoded clothes. I held out my hand. 'Pleased to meet you, Mr Goodchild.'

'No! No! Goodchild, sir. That's the form, only the others below stairs call me Mister—and I am pleased to meet you. What a interesting shop.'

'Thank you, Goodchild.'

He leaned forward, his eyes sparkling. 'That medication, sir—most efficacious, most efficacious.'

I thanked him once more, and asked where he was staying.

'That excellent establishment across the road. That hostelry, sir, is run exactly as I would run it. Clean, staff sharp as pins, with just the right touch of rural charm, and the food—plain as a pikestaff but of premier quality, and cooked to perfection.'

Goodchild retrieved his umbrella and folded his hands over it. 'Cough completely gone, sir,' he laughed.

'Staying long, Goodchild?'

'Alas only another day, sir. The Master is back next week, and things must be absolutely pip-pip for his return.' As he leaned forward this time his voice was heavy with respect. 'Very old family, sir— fifth baronet.'

I raised my eyebrows, as I felt it was expected of me.

235

'Good employer?'

'The very best, sir. Can't beat the old families.'

'Been with them long?'

'Started as a pantry boy straight from school. Mind you, the staff has shrunk since then. Do you know, sir, we are down to one gardener.' I sympathised. 'And the temporary staff we get, sir, it's unbelievable. Do you know, only last month we were having a house party so I rang up the agency for a second footman. You will not believe this, sir—they sent a man with an earring.'

Goodchild leaned back, his face stern, his prim mouth pressed in distaste. 'Sent him packing, sir—footman with an earring. What next!'

He stood up and, putting on his bowler hat, adjusted it carefully. 'I will not waste your time, sir. I have seen several things I wish to purchase. Would you please reserve for me the brass milk skimmer, those two buttermarkers, the Art Deco cottage *sucrier* and the ivory-handled corkscrew. I shall return on the morrow with the requisite amount of money, which I ascertain to be exactly one hundred pounds.'

I gathered the articles together and put them alongside the till. 'They'll be here, Mr Goodchild, wrapped and ready.'

'No, sir, Good—'

I stopped him, and with a raised finger. 'In this establishment a customer of your magnitude is accorded the utmost respect.'

He hooked the brolly over his arm and shook with laughter.

'Really, sir, you are most kind.'

His hand was on the doorknob when Vicky burst into the shop. Her hair was awry, her apron stained and her face shone with sweat. In front of her she held a small saucepan. 'This damned sauce!' she gasped. 'I can't get it right.'

Goodchild released the doorknob and raised his hat; his snub nose twitched. 'Bearnaise, if I'm not mistaken, madam?'

Vicky smiled weakly as he sidled across the floor and took the pan and wooden spoon from her. 'Too hot, madam,' he pronounced after sniffing and trailing the sauce from the spoon. 'You've let it get too hot after putting in the egg yolks and butter, I'm afraid.' He pursed his prim mouth and his grey eyes twinkled with gentle devilment.

'May I be permitted?' the devilish eyes flicked towards the kitchen. Vicky and I looked at each other, then at Mr Goodchild.

'Why not?'

Taking off his jacket he donned a frilled apron and set to work on a new sauce, instructing Vicky at every step. We had bought an extravagant amount of Theivin' Jack's best steak. Vicky had been determined to do it justice, and I, equally determined, had decanted a bottle of Mr Johnson's excellent Rioja.

The children were taken with Mr Goodchild. They leaned their elbows on the table and watched his every move. 'Ever thought of going into service young man?' he asked Peter. The boy shook his head. 'Can be a good life, a full and satisfying life.' Peter did not look at all impressed. At that time he was going through a military phase, his heroes the pink-faced recruits who frequently marched through the village, sweating under heavy packs.

Mr Goodchild smiled indulgently and stirred the sauce. 'By jove, sir, if cook could see me now. How she would laugh.' The sauce thickened and shone to perfection, hot plates clattered on to the table.

'Will you join us, Mr Goodchild?' Vicky asked.

'Very kind, madam, but no. I have a meal booked over the road—but it is kind of you.'

Mr Goodchild served the steak and poured the sauce over it. Commandeering the tureens, he cradled each in turn and, skilfully manipulating two spoons in one hand, he filled our plates with carrots and peas and finally potatoes. The wine he served with a flourish, then standing back he beamed with pleasure. 'What a pleasant scene, sir—wait till I tell cook, how she'll laugh.'

The steak was superb, the wine elegant, and the sauce delectable. 'Mr Goodchild, at least you'll join me in a glass of wine.'

'Indeed, I think I will, sir.'

We sat before the fire as Vicky piled dishes into the sink and the children retreated to their play corner. Mr Goodchild approved of the wine.

'Very good, sir, very good indeed. You know, cook and I often draw the cork on a bottle. Winter's evenings when the house is quiet we draw up to the kitchen range, a little table between us, and out comes the bottle and the cards. Cook is a first-class poker player, and I too am not without skill in that direction.' He stretched out his short plump legs and sighed contentedly. 'Spent hundreds of hours playing in the pantry when I was a footman—used to be quite a vice amongst us downstairs.'

'And those upstairs?'

He half closed his eyes and whispered, 'Not half, sir. The Master's quite a sporting chap, and so was his father.'

We finished the bottle and stared into the fire

238

in silence for a while, Mr Goodchild smiling and patting the chair arm with a plump hand.

Pleasant company and a good wine, I'm sure the poets have penned many a line about the feeling of well being and generosity they give rise to. Taking his shoulder gently and leaning forward, I looked him frankly in the eye.

'Mr Goodchild, we give ten per cent discount to trade and friend alike and I would like to think of you as a friend.'

'Most kind, sir, most kind.' He beamed and stood up and held out his hand. 'Must be off now, sir. I'll take a turn round the village whilst the light holds.'

It was nearly midnight when Rabbit returned the foot pump. The peace was shattered by the roar of an engine; a single yellow beam of light scythed around the yard and died along with the engine noise. A healthy thumping on the door set me drawing the bolts hurriedly.

Rabbit held out the foot pump. 'Ta. Got her goin' yer see.' With the flourish of a gauntleted hand he indicated an old and sad-looking motorcycle leaning against the orchard fence. He was wearing a massive leather jerkin on top of his overcoat; on his head was a pudding-basin helmet, and around his neck hung a pair of flying goggles.

'Might need it again, OK?' He grinned and nodded at the foot pump.

'Yes, OK—anytime Rabbit.'

'Just off to see cousin Leopold—he has a sidecar for me.'

'Rabbit—it's midnight!'

'Aye, thought I'd wait till the roads were quiet. I've been reckonin' up, it's fifteen year since I last had her out, bit rusty. That's why I'm putting the chair alongside.'

The machine, an ex-army BSA 500, was not an easy starter. Perhaps a fifteen-year hibernation under sacks and bales of straw saps the will of a machine. Rabbit kicked the starter, tickled the carburettor, and cursed.

'Come on, yer bloody thing,' he yelled.

'Petrol,' I suggested gently.

'Better not be, I'm broke.'

Rabbit shook the bike between his legs, his ear cocked to the swish in the tank.

'No, there's plenty in there.'

More cursing and kick-starting brought a burst of life to the engine that died away under his frantic throttle twisting. He dismounted and pushed the bike into the pool of light that spilled from the kitchen window. 'Have you a screwdriver?'

I have never liked motorcycles. It was purely for economic reasons that I owned a small red Excelsior-something in my student days. Cold rain trickling past scarves down chest and back, legs frozen numb and the high proportion of time I spent pushing the thing home reinforced a natural dislike of things on two wheels.

At half past one the following morning I hated motorcycles. The BSA was in the kitchen, leaning against the dresser, its eviscerated carburettor laid on spread newspapers in the centre of the table.

'Found it!' Rabbit yelled gleefully, holding out for my inspection a tiny hair he'd poked from a jet. 'Wouldn't think a little bugger like that could stop such a powerful machine, would yer?'

I didn't think anything, I just yawned, and prayed that his callused banana fingers could coax all those little bits back into the carburettor; that the carburettor would go back on the bike, that it would 'fire up' as he called it, and that man and machine would disappear from my life.

It was nearly two o'clock when the engine burst into life and Rabbit, straddling it, happily adjusted his goggles.

'Grand night for a ride over the moors.'

'Rabbit, you're never going to Leopold's at this time?'

'Course—why not? He hardly sleeps, he's one o' them insomoniacs.'

*   *   *

It was a bleary-eyed shopkeeper who greeted Mr Goodchild. Vicky had wrapped his purchases up very neatly, and I laid them carefully alongside my black coffee. He tapped each little parcel lovingly. 'The corkscrew is for myself, the buttermarkers and the *sucrier* for the two maids and the skimmer for cook. By jove, sir, how she will laugh.'

Mr Goodchild emptied a linen bagful of money on to the counter. 'Ninety pounds, sir. Think you'll find that correct.'

'Ninety? I thought —'

'The ten per cent for friends, sir, remember?'

I remembered—vaguely—and started to count the money. There was one ten pound note, three very screwed up five pounds, a healthy bundle of pound notes and a pile of coins of all denominations. I was soon overfaced.

It looked right, and I felt Mr Goodchild was not the type to work a fast one on me, so I made to sweep it into the till.

'No! No! Count it, sir. I insist.'

241

So I counted it. Piles of fifty pences, twenty pences and ten pences soon covered the counter. 'Ninety pounds, Mr Goodchild—spot on.' He dropped his purchases into a Gladstone bag and hooked his umbrella under his arm.

'Might I say, sir, it's been a pleasure doing business with you. My regards to your lady wife and your admirable children.'

He raised his bowler, smiled, opened the door with a smoothness that hardly jangled the bell; then closed it behind himself with a dignity that befitted a man who had buttled for forty years.

I did not have a good day. It was well into the afternoon before I came around. I walked the dogs down Mill Lane and, looking over Rabbit's hedge, saw his motorbike under the lean-to, a swish Watsonian sidecar attached to it.

It was reminiscent of a 1930s speedboat, with a razor-sharp prow and a little chromium plated rail around the foredeck. I smiled as I pictured the poacher and the 'insomoniac', their grey heads bent in Leopold's barn in the early hours of the morning wedding this piece of elegance to the decrepit motorcycle.

A grey day, most of it spent cooped up in the shop; a string of irritating things, nothing worthwhile achieved, does not promote—in spite of tiredness, a good night's sleep. A pint or two in congenial company does. So I made my way through a heavy drizzle to The Ship.

The pints were available, but not the congenial company; there was a deep gloom in the taproom, and the cause of it was the admirable Goodchild. He had fleeced them all at cards the previous night.

Ted had lost a tenner, Mr Wall five pounds,

Baz six, the Colonel fifteen. As each despondent drinker called his losses out like the disjointed numbering at a regimental parade I made a mental note. Eighty-five pounds I had got it to, when the Biggles-like figure in the corner staring into an empty glass muttered something obscene, then in a clearer voice. 'A fiver.'

Heads turned towards Rabbit. The little fat man with poncey ways had got a fiver out of Rabbit?

Ninety pounds. I started to chuckle. The heads of the shorn sheep turned towards me with puzzled looks as I raised my glass high in a salute to the admirable Goodchild.

'By jove, sir, how cook will laugh.'

CHAPTER NINETEEN

Everyone knows what the wages of sin are. The first week in June we good villagers of Ramsthwaite discovered just how lucrative were the wages of sloth. Rabbit got fifty pounds for letting a television company film in his garden.

The pretty girl with the clipboard had toured the village peering over walls and through hedges, making notes, tapping a pencil on perfect teeth. When the reason for her search became known—they required an unkempt and overgrown garden—she was assailed from all sides.

'Come look at mine, it's a tip,' Ted insisted.

Mr Hall peered up at her with rheumy eyes, 'Mine's a disgrace—an absolute disgrace.'

I proffered ours. 'It's not exactly overgrown, but we have a corner that is waist high with brambles—

243

and we can provide a goat, and poultry, if you wish.'

It was all to no avail: Rabbit was streets ahead; he had half a century of neglect to boast of. Upon hearing of the girl's quest, Thievin' Jack left his travelling butcher's shop full of bewildered customers and sought her out. 'Come up to my place—it's just what you're looking for. There are parts of it I haven't set foot in for twenty year.' But the girl had found what she wanted.

Rabbit did cut a little amphitheatre of grass in the centre of the garden. A place for his terriers to sun themselves, and where on a fine day he could sit and study form, the racing pages of the *Daily Mail* spread on an upturned peggy tub.

The overgrown blackthorn and elder that almost swallowed his decrepit ferret cages and pantile-roofed lean-to are always thronged with birdlife, and the variety of flora would send any botanist reaching for his notebook. It is a long thin garden that Rabbit proudly tells us is 'nigh on a rood and a half'.

It was a children's programme they were making, and the young actors—a boy and a girl—had to run through the garden pursued by a villainous type of fellow. To our dismay no extras were required, so we watched take after take, unappreciative of the minor variations that caused the director such anguish. A massive truck throbbing with generators was parked on the green, black umbilical cords snaked through the hedge to feed huge arc lights.

Miss Wells brought the children out of school to watch. The pretty clipboard girl squatted on the banking, gave them an outline of the story, and told them when they could see it on television. They were thrilled; the girls excited and envious, the boys excited and in love.

At lunchtime the children chattered happily; out of the window went nursing and soldiering—Sally wanted to be a girl with a clipboard, and Peter a sound man.

'They've been filming at Sottenghyll,' Peter told us.

'And the man who chases them is really awful,' Sally added, rolling china-blue eyes in emphasis.

Ted had cut Nellie May's land for us, refusing payment with a shake of his head. 'Naw you helped me last year when I broke me leg—it's all right.'

'Let me give you something for the diesel.'

'It's all right!' He turned his back and climbed on to the tractor, leaning out to give me shouted advice. 'Leave it today, might have a bit of rain; it runs off wi' no harm when it's laid. Turn her over tomorrow.'

We did not have rain. A crisp wind brought a swift-moving sky that cleared to give us one of those beautiful bright invigorating days. I felt frustrated not turning the hay, for it was a day for outdoors, a day to doff one's coat, breathe in deeply, and get things done. I harnessed Topic, and throwing hammer and nail bag into the cart set off for the bottom land. There is always a bit of fence repairing to do.

Sparrows and chaffinches were busy in the fresh green hedges and as I turned the mare's head into the hay field a heron rose from the windrows and with an unhurried flapping of its wings cleared the barn and disappeared.

'Clean land and clean water.' The voice came from behind the hedge; it was Praying Billy.

He stood up, brushed wisps of grass from his

245

sober suit, and put on his black hat.

'Herons, only where the water and land are clean. I've been watching it for an hour. Stalking along the windrows like a haughty old dowager she was, stabbing her beak here and there.'

'Sorry I disturbed you.'

'It's all right, I've had me hour of contemplation, must be off on God's work—it's never done, you know. It's a sinful world we live in.'

It is also a world of broken fences; so, tying Topic to the barn, I filled my pockets with nails and started working my way around the field nailing a rail here, wedging a post there. The fencing is made up of slab wood from the estate sawmill. Irregular in section and still carrying bark, it looks raw and intrusive when new but it soon takes on a grey colouring and begins to host a wealth of lichens. Then we have a fence that is cheap, effective, and pleasing to the eye.

I was late for lunch. The children had eaten theirs, Sally was in the orchard, and Peter had disappeared into the workshop.

'What's he doing in there?' I asked Vicky.

'Don't know but he's certainly busy with something.'

For several lunchtimes I had seen, through the dusty shaving-frilled workshop window, the boy's bobbing head, his tongue curving to his upper lip as he concentrated on planing and drilling.

'I'll go see.'

'No, don't,' Vicky said hurriedly, 'I think it's to be a surprise, because he's shooed Sally away several times.'

We left the boy to his secret labours and studiously avoided the workshop.

246

When Ted pronounced, after scouring the sky, that the hay was turnable, Vicky dashed indoors to prepare sandwiches and flasks of tea whilst I gathered together hayrakes and forks.

Peter emerged shyly from the workshop, in his hands a beautifully made miniature hayrake. 'I made this for Sally. Last year she was towed to death with that big rake.'

'So that's what you wanted the dowel for,' I said, with a smile.

Sally was delighted with her little rake. Peter had exactly copied a full sized one, shaping the teeth, bending an ash bow and mortising it into the handle and head.

He had sanded the handle to a pleasing silkiness and burned Sally's initials into it.

'Come on, let's go haymaking,' Sally shouted, shouldering her rake and marching proudly around the yard.

We attacked the laid grass, forking and raking it, teasing out the thick bands of it until half the field looked as if it were covered in a green froth; the other still lying under shiny regular swathes.

'Time for tea,' Vicky called. Rakes and forks were thrown down as we raced towards the cart. Topic was grazing the hedgebottoms, but sensing the possibility of a crust she trotted down the field after us.

'There was a heron sat there yesterday,' I told them, pointing with my sandwich, 'and behind that hedge was Praying Billy.'

'We've seen him,' Sally said, pulling apart a sandwich and peering into it.

Peter stretched his legs and chewed away. 'I like him.'

'I do too,' I confessed. 'It takes a lot of courage to do what he does.'

Vicky poured tea and lemonade. She had put on a loose overall and pulled her hair up under her headscarf. I had thrown the tailboard of the cart down and she had adopted it as a table, setting mugs and plates on it.

She knelt, and with Topic looking over her shoulder, brought order to the alfresco meal.

'Two sandwiches each, or no buns,' she warned. Boiled eggs and cress, Thievin' Jack's best roast ham with a smidgin' of mustard, all in home-baked bread; we were soon at the buns.

The children fed crusts to Topic then flopped on to the grass. Vicky, cup of tea in her hands, giggled as she walked towards me on her knees. 'Nearly forgot, Praying Billy came in the shop yesterday. He wants to buy those leather-bound volumes of *Henry's Commentaries*, but will only give fifteen pounds for them.'

'What are they priced at?'

'Twenty.'

'Let him have them—religious books are poor sellers.'

After the previous year's lessons in haymaking from Ted I worked the field filled with confidence, forming footcocks with skill and speed. Why didn't some curious tourist stop and ask relevant questions? I could have leaned on my rake, a stem of sweet grass in my mouth, and awed them with my knowledge. There we were, a whole family at honest toil. Vicky's overall and scarf, my checked shirt and corduroys, bunched under a broad belt, wielding the tools of yesteryear. Surely a picture worthy of comment—the odd photograph. But our only audience, fratching rooks, one cheeky blackbird and occasionally, from the top meadow, Ted. He was, as he later put it, 'keeping us right'.

Hay that is to be stacked loose has to be drier than hay that is baled; otherwise we get the dreaded heating up. But too dry and it loses feeding value, so a delicate balance has to be struck. Hay has to be turned on the boot, sniffed at and worried over before we can reach that point where, with a glance at the sky, we can say with deep satisfaction, 'Right, let's have her in.'

The pub-bound experts favoured pikes. 'There's a good crop,' Rabbit said, rasping his fingernails under his unshaven chin, 'I'd put it in pikes, hay'll stand in pikes—bring it in at yer leisure.' Billy Potts, having listened to the farming forecast, agreed with him.

Baz wasn't sure, but Ted was adamant. 'I've seen more hay ruined in the last day than I've had hot dinners—I'd be down there now piking it up.'

So we built pikes. Forking the jockeys into heaps that would make a cart load, combing them with forks until the outer hay lay in a way which would throw any rain. It was hard work, arm aching, back aching work that left us all dog tired.

The first big drops of rain pattered on to the cart bottom as I backed Topic into the shafts. I urged the pony into a trot, and she willingly threw her head into the collar and made for her stable at a good pace, joggling our tired bodies together as we crouched under a tarpaulin.

The children went to bed unwashed, as I saw to Topic and staggered around the place in driving rain, locking up the stock. Then Vicky and I sat nursing mugs of tea, easing our aching limbs and smiling at each other.

'Well, it's safe,' Vicky sighed.

'Yes, he's right again—our knowledgeable neighbour. You mark my words, first thing tomorrow morning his beaming face will be thrust over that wall—'telled yer'.

Vicky laughed, then winced and arched her aching back.

Monday morning we were late up. The children hurriedly dressed, ate half a breakfast and scuttled across the green as the last deep dong of the school bell faded.

'We're having an easy day,' I told Vicky.

The rain had washed the dust from the world, leaving colours as bright and sharp as a new paintbox. Tiny rivulets trickled across the yard, their bottoms alight with glistening pebbles, the apple trees bled diamonds from every twig, and the rushing beck gurgled and happily thrust its peaty water into the culvert.

A weak sun peered shyly from behind a straggle of lilac clouds, then grew bold and thrust them apart, making the roofs steam and bathing us with a glorious warmth.

The pikes were steaming too. I pushed my hand into one and drew out some hay. It was dry. I capered around the pike, the dogs jumping and barking after me. 'It's dry, it's dry,' I yelled happily.

'Telled yer,' came a deep and triumphant voice.

Vicky bent over the sink giggling as I paced the kitchen floor. 'I'll have him, one day I'll get the clever sod.'

'He was right.'

'I know—it's just the way he says it. Ted hath spoken, hear ye and obey. He never, for one moment, thinks he could be wrong.'

*   *   *

Praying Billy came for the books. He smiled nervously and twisted his hat in his hands. 'The thing is, I've no money till the end of the week—but you will get it.'

I helped him carry them out to his van and watched as he lovingly wrapped them in a car rug and wedged them alongside his wind-up gramophone.

'Who can we trust if not a dedicated evangelist?'

He knelt on the van floor and sorted out his placards. He makes them himself. They are all beautifully signwritten, sombre black on pristine white, just a hint of the gothic in the bold letters. His choice for the day was, 'Thy grace is enough for me'. Dragging it out joyfully he revealed, 'The end is nigh'.

I could not resist pulling his leg a little. 'Billy,' I said in a serious voice, 'can you make sure you pay me before the end does come. I'd like the shop accounts to be settled for Judgement Day.'

'It's our spiritual accounts that have to be in order,' he answered sharply, slamming the van doors and marching across the green, his placard erect, his face zealously aglow with a compulsion to seek out the Devil and do battle.

I cleared the dutch barn, making it ready for the new hay, stacking old straw bales on the weather side and clearing away the toys the children had left there.

'Thought we were having an easy day?' Vicky admonished me as she plonked the coffee mugs on the wall.

'Got to get it ready, best hay in the Dale to come in here.'

'I'm glad we put it in pikes—gives us a breathing space.'

'I'll have to get it up here.'

She shoved the mug into my hand. 'Well, not today; when we've drunk this we'll go sit in the shop and take it easy.'

We were taking it easy when Rabbit burst into the shop waving a cheque. 'Hey, it's come—fifty quid. Can yer cash it for me?'

We couldn't, there was nothing but the float in the till.

'Can't the shop cash it for you?'

Rabbit shook his head. 'I've a bit of a problem there—I owe her more than fifty quid yer see. She'll get paid. Allus does, but after t'shootin' season when I've got me beating money together.'

'Pub?'

'Good thinking.' He slammed the door behind him, making the windows rattle. In ten minutes he was back looking as miserable as only a man in a greasy cap and outsized overcoat can.

'No good?' I asked.

'Naw.' He leaned against the door jamb and kicked at the mat. 'Says he has an agreement wi' the bank. If they won't sell beer, he won't cash cheques.' He took the cheque out of his pocket and stared at it. 'All this brass and I can't get at it.'

I opened the till, causing Rabbit to lurch forward and the gloom to lift from his face. 'Tell yer what,' he said cheerily, 'give us what yer can, and the rest later.'

'I'll see what I've got in the egg money,' Vicky

252

said, hurrying to the kitchen. I robbed the till of the entire float, and Vicky proudly returned, her cupped hands filled with coins.

'There you are Rabbit—thirty-five quid, the best we can do.'

'Good on yer, good on yer,' he grinned as he spread the cheque on the counter and scooped up the money. 'T'other fifteen'll do any time this week.'

Our worries about having no float in the till were unfounded, for we did not have one single customer that day. It was probably our attitude, for we sat slumped in our chairs, answered questions in a polite but desultory way, and showed no enthusiasm whatever. That indefinable something that enables salesmen to turn browsers and enquirers into buyers was missing. Our day of taking it easy gave us no pleasure, for in spite of aching limbs, we felt guilty.

'We're too conditioned to the work ethic,' I told Vicky as we shut the shop, 'we ought to take a leaf out of Rabbit's book.'

'He hasn't got kids to feed,' Vicky yawned.

'Tomorrow, if it's fine, I'm going to start leading that hay home.'

'Well, you're doing it on your own—I still ache all over.' She pulled a stool up to the sink and, resting her forearms over it, began to peel the potatoes.

When I got back from milking the goat she had had a bright idea. 'Borrow Ted's tractor and trailer, two loads and you'll have it.'

'No—it's something I want to do. Besides, if we don't work the pony there's no point in keeping her.'

I tugged the hay ladders out of the cart shed roof, covering myself with dust and cobwebs. I liked to see the coup cart fitted with them—it made it look a real working vehicle. The pikes were bigger than I had anticipated and I was unable to load an entire one on to the cart. Trampling the hay to compact it, I combed the loose strands from the sides, and roped it down.

Topic was a little fractious. Whether she didn't like the front hay ladder jutting out over her rump or whether it was because it was a heavier load than she was accustomed to I didn't know, but she certainly didn't behave well, tossing her head and starting at the least thing.

Twice I lost the entire load as she charged into the lane, bouncing the cart over the deep ruts. Back in the yard, as I forked the third load into the barn, Ted appeared. In a moment of weakness I told him of the spilled loads. His fat hands slapped the cart.

'What yer should be doing is roping it through the leading strouter over the top rave, across yer load to the rear staff, through the trailing strouter and back over.'

'One more load today and that's my lot,' I told him as I flung the pitchfork and ropes into the cart.

The work did Topic good. She went at her oats that night like fury—there was no tossing them about and picking here and there. I always trail a little molasses over them and fill the hayrack when she's been working.

The oats were polished off and she was into the hay before I had finished rubbing her down.

I was tired, and early evening saw me dozing by the fire, but there is a thirst engendered by handling hay that nothing but beer can properly quench.

254

The taproom was full. Rabbit greeted me with a smile.

'I'll get that one,' he called as Charlie pulled me my pint.

Ted was sitting with Billy Potts and Baz. I pulled up a buffet and joined them. 'Now,' Ted beamed, 'I was able to put this young fella straight today. Losing his load he was, but I told him how to rope loose hay on. Did you do as I said?'

'Yes, Ted, I did.'

'Through the leading strouter and over the top rave?'

'Yes.'

'Across and to the rear shaft and back again?'

'Yes.'

He threw himself back against the settle and folded his arms, a smug look on his face.

I gave him a little time to bask in the glow of his self-esteem, and then said in a low but clear voice, 'Aye—but it still bloody fell off.'

CHAPTER TWENTY

'I'm in a bit of bother, guv'nor.' Fiery Frank squatted on the milking stool, looking very, very, dejected. It was a hot day and the back door and the door to the shop were wide open.

Vicky was showing Mrs Smythe-Robinson a pair of ruby lustres. The tingling of the glass drops, the little subdued conversation and the twittering of birds emphasised the quietness of the kitchen as I waited for him to continue.

'Thing is, I did a house clearance—nothing flash,

255

run of the mill stuff. Turned out the bloke didn't own it. He was renting the place furnished—sold me the stuff and did a bunk.'

'So?'

'They're doin' me for receiving.'

'But if you bought it in good faith?'

'I did, I did,' he protested, rising from the stool and pacing the kitchen, his thumbs thrust into the pockets of his scarlet waistcoat. He stopped and stared into the empty firegrate. The little man was normally such a bouncy person, full of life and confidence; it was upsetting to see him like this, hunched up and worried.

'Fiery,' I said slowly, 'we didn't get any of that stuff did we?'

'Naw—tell yer it was nowt flash, household stuff, shipping gear.'

'And it wasn't this chap's to sell?'

'Naw he'd rented the place furnished.'

'Had he been there long?'

'Coupla months.'

'Weren't the neighbours suspicious?'

'Weren't none, place was up on the moors, back of beyond.'

'Can't see why they are doing you.'

I put the kettle on and spooned coffee into two mugs. Fiery was still staring at the empty grate, working his generous mouth and chewing at his lips. I was stirring the coffee when Vicky came in from the shop rubbing her hands and smiling gleefully.

'Who's a brilliant saleswoman?' she quipped, shaking a gloomy Fiery by the shoulders. He gave her a brief smile as he took the coffee from me.

'Fiery has a problem, he's being done for receiving,' I told her.

She put an arm around him, steered him to the table and made him sit. 'Come on, tell us everything,' she commanded.

Twisting his mug in his hands, his head bent, Fiery told us the whole story from the moment he had received the phone call. It was a little more complex than he'd first intimated, because amongst the house contents were a couple of things that the vendor had stolen elsewhere.

'Fiery! He wanted two hundred quid for a brand new cattle trailer that must have cost over a thousand, and you weren't suspicious?'

'Said he was desperate, guv'.'

'He must have been; have they caught him?'

'No.'

'So you're stuck.'

'Aye.' There was a long, pregnant silence. It looked bad for poor old Fiery, but he was a clown, not a criminal. True, there had been that bit of nonsense over the revolver, but that could have happened to any dealer.

Vicky took the empty mug from his hands and grasped his shoulders. 'Is there anything we can do?'

Fiery sat up straight and gave another brief smile.

'There is. Will you two be character witnesses? Me solicitor says it would help.'

'Sure thing Fiery. I'll write a letter now.'

'No. No. Come to court—in person.'

I looked at Vicky, and Fiery, his eyes dark with worry, looked at both of us in turn.

'Course we will,' Vicky said.

A bit of the old Fiery returned. He took out his gold watch, wound it and, thrusting it back into his waistcoat pocket, stood up and grinned. 'Now, guv'. Have you owt in my line? I feel like a bit of honest trade.'

We had little for him. High summer is not the best time of year for shipping goods, and I had spent several days haymaking when I should have been out on the road looking for stock. All we could sell him was a pair of single horned foot beds, and a very mediocre dressing table.

When Fiery had secured them to the van sides with lengths of upholstery tape and draped them in blankets, he started the engine and wound down the window. 'See yer tomorrow, then.'

'Tomorrow?'

'Yep; magistrates' court, Boltburn Town Hall— eleven o'clock.'

It was a problem to get someone to look after the shop at such short notice. Gwen had her mother staying with her, the Martins' eldest daughter was working at the pub and Canary Mary flatly refused. 'Can't sit in a shop all day, I'd go barmy.' We had given up hope of finding anyone and I had resigned myself to going to Fiery's trial alone, when Baz suggested that his wife could do with a little extra cash.

Susan was enthusiastic. 'I know nothing about antiques, but I'd love to do it,' she beamed. She was a quick learner, and soon grasped the dos and don'ts of shopkeeping, mastering the simple code we use for trade prices. Vicky left a cold lunch for the children, and warned them to do as Auntie Susan told them and be good for her.

'We'll be back before tea,' she called to them as they turned into the school gates.

Boltburn is a typical Lancashire mill town. Row

upon row of houses giving on to cobbled streets, vast, stone-built mills—most now devoid of their chimneys—and a superb Town Hall. It was a bustling place; new industries keeping busy the hands that once King Cotton monopolised.

Neither of us like driving in heavy traffic—we are not used to traffic lights, and lane discipline is hard to conform to in a strange town. We had taken the dogs with us, and whether it was the agitation in our voices or the unaccustomed level of noise which upset them I don't know, but they started a loud and excited barking which we could not quell.

The Town Hall was easily found. Its Gothic façade imposing and overawing, it stood, an island of civic worth and pride in a glass and concrete sea of civic madness.

Fiery and Little Petal were waiting for us outside the entrance to the magistrates' court. He greeted us effusively, but Petal merely nodded and reached into a pocket in her caftan for a biscuit. Once inside, his solicitor joined us. He was a jaundiced-looking man with horn-rimmed spectacles and strands of greying hair plastered across a bald pate, his handshake as limp as his grey suit.

He rested his briefcase on a bench and took out a thin beige file. His hands fascinated me—they were so young looking, so beautifully manicured and smooth. There was no hair on them and the nails were buffed and perfectly shaped. He questioned us gently. How long had we known Mr Fox? Had we had extensive dealings with him? A perfect forefinger and thumb pinched a less than perfect nose. It was good of us to come, and it would undoubtedly help Mr Fox.

Fiery Frank Fox had that dejected look again.

259

He leaned on a radiator and whistled noiselessly as he stared at the parquet floor. The corridor we were standing in was busy with comings and goings, heavily panelled swing doors constantly squeaking open and closing lazily with low moans.

A black-gowned usher approached Fiery's solicitor and after a few words smiled and led Fiery away with a friendly 'Come on, son.' Little Petal sobbed, sending sprays of biscuit crumbs scattering over the parquet like fragments of quick-silver.

We sat in the front row of the public seats, Vicky comforting the tearful Petal as the charge was read out.

Fiery stood in the dock, his head slightly bent. When he was asked to plead his voice was clear. 'Not guilty', resounded round the panelled courtroom and brought another loud burst of sobs from Little Petal.

The prosecutor questioned Fiery for ten minutes. 'Didn't you suspect anything? Do you expect the court to believe you were offered such a wealth of goods for so little money? Did you not have any doubts?'

Fiery kept cool. He answered quietly, with a 'yes' or a 'no', but when his solicitor rose and asked him to tell the court in his own words what had happened he waxed lyrical. The three magistrates leaned forward as Fiery stood on his toes, and resting his arms on the dock produced a tattered notebook.

'With yer Honour's permission—I'll just consult me hofficial records.'

There was absolute silence in the court as Fiery tore a rubber band from around the notebook and slipped it on to his wrist.

'Now, yer Honour, I got this phone call on the tenth—no, no, I tell a lie, it was the eleventh. Up I goes on the twelfth, looks the gear over and gives him a price. Seemed a decent bloke.' As he paused and thumbed through his notebook, a tattered page fluttered to the floor, watched by every eye in the courtroom.

Fiery smiled at the clerk. 'Do you mind, guv'?' The errant page was retrieved, and after some shuffling and more thumbing was returned to its place. 'Now, let me tell you this. The stuff in the house was nowt—household stuff. An' don't forget I had to allow for a load to the tip—that takes up time. I gave him a fair price.'

The chairman of the bench, a portly, well-scrubbed man, leaned forward. 'What about the cattle trailer, Mr Fox?'

'Ar' yes yer Worship—comin' to that. This fella just now made a great to-do about that. Just 'cos I gave two hundred quid for it an' he reckons it's worth a thousand or more.' Fiery spread his arms on the dock and sucked at his teeth. 'Thing is, in this trade, sometimes yer gets a little winner—I thought that was my little winner.'

The chairman beamed around the court. 'Bet you did'. The ensuing ripple of laughter obviously pleased him greatly, for he beamed some more and stole sly glances at his fellow magistrates before turning his attention back to Fiery, who continued in a subdued manner.

'He reckoned he was stuck with it, wanted shut at any price, had to get down to Brighton to see his ailing mother—give us a coupla hundred he says. So I did.'

'And you weren't suspicious?'

261

'No, didn't think it was knocked off—would I have stood it in Boltburn cattle market wi' a 'For Sale' sign and me phone number if I had?'

The chairman consulted with his colleagues, a stiff unsmiling woman and a thin washed-out looking man. They nodded their heads in agreement.

Fiery's solicitor tiptoed across to the clerk, who bent his head to the solicitor's whispering; then the clerk stood up and tiptoed to the chairman.

The portly magistrate cleared his throat. 'All the items have been retrieved, we understand.'

Fiery's solicitor sprang to his feet. 'If I may correct you, sir—all but one.'

'And what is that? Not another cheap trailer?' A second ripple of laughter ran around the courtroom.

'No sir, a terracotta garden urn. If I may explain?' The chairman glanced at the courtroom clock, then nodded his approval.

The solicitor pressed his immaculate hands together as if in prayer, and smiled weakly. 'The defendant, sir, in the hurly burly of returning the goods, and the trailer, misplaced the urn. However he approached the owner's agent and has made financial recompense.'

'How much?' the chairman asked bluntly.

'Fifty pounds, sir.'

'So, Fox,' he said, turning to Fiery, 'you're out of pocket.'

'Well an' truly, yer Lordship.'

'No little winner this time—a little loser, in fact.'

'You've said it, yer Honour.'

'This is not the first time you have been before this bench is it?'

262

'Ar' yes, guv'nor. That other was just a bit o' daftness.'

'And are we to consider this a bit of daftness?' Fiery's solicitor was on his feet again, crouching and tiptoeing to the clerk. More whisperings, then they both turned and stared at me. The chairman leaned forward and joined in the inaudible conversation; then he too stared at me.

Little Petal gave out an anguished cry, dropped her head on to Vicky's shoulder, and once more began to sob loudly.

The chairman leaned back, conferred with each of his colleagues then nodded at Fiery's solicitor, who tiptoed across to me.

'Just stand up where you are and tell them about Mr Fox.'

I felt my cheeks flush and the palms of my hands grow moist as I stood up. Vicky took hold of the fingertips of my right hand as I cleared my throat and began in a rather shaky voice:

'Mr Chairman, madam, sir, I've known Mr Fox some years. He is well respected in the trade, and we have had many dealings with him. My wife and I have always found him honest and trustworthy and . . .' My mouth was dry, I could think of nothing else to say. The three magistrates stared down at me, their faces like stone. I glanced at Fiery; the old cheeky grin was back on his face.

'He's a sterling character,' I blurted out and sat down with a thump. There was a deathly silence in the courtroom. It seemed ages before the magistrates stopped staring at me and put their heads together again.

Fiery tidied the pages in his notebook and stroked the rubber band over it.

263

Petal had stopped sobbing. Her head was still laid on Vicky's shoulder, big tears welled from her eyes and ran in jerky arcs around her fat cheeks to plop on to her caftan.

Gradually activity returned to the room, clerks noiselessly glided here and there, solicitors rose and shuffled papers; there was subdued chattering in the public gallery.

The mighty clock in the Gothic tower above us gave one drawn-out dong, the chairman banged his gavel, bringing an instant hush and turned to face Fiery.

'Frank Fox, this court finds you not guilty.'

Vicky let out a squeal of delight and squeezed my hand, Little Petal sat up straight, pulled nervously at her hair, and wiped the tears from her face. She smiled at Fiery who, responding to a wave from the usher, clattered out of the dock and swaggered across to us.

He shook hands with his solicitor and me, kissed Vicky and hugged Little Petal, who once more began to sob.

I slapped Fiery on the back and took the limp and warm hand his solicitor extended.

'Never done anything like this before—was it OK?' I asked. He smiled wanly and snapped his briefcase shut.

Fiery was back to his old buoyant self. He punched me playfully in the chest. 'Sterling character—eh, I like it guv', I like it.'

The usher spread his arms, his black gown hanging from them like bat's wings, and eased us towards the door with a polite, 'Thank you, ladies and gentlemen.'

Outside the Town Hall Fiery broke into a little

dance and hugged Little Petal to him, burying his head in her ample bosom. She bent and kissed him gently, 'Let's go home, Frank.'

'Come on,' the little man laughed, 'all back to our place.' His solicitor declined: pressing business—an appointment that could not be broken. Once more I shook the limpid hand.

We followed Fiery's van through a maze of cobbled back streets. Soot-blackened schools, playgrounds seething with noisy children, boiler-suited men with smudged faces queuing at chip shops and sandwich vans; headscarfed women—one hand thrust into pinny pockets the other dangling a cigarette, sitting on low walls smiling and chatting.

'I've never seen so many people,' Vicky laughed.

Fiery pulled his van up at the end of a terrace of stone-built houses. 'Here we are, guv',' he said, opening the door for Vicky and handing her down.

Alongside the house was a small yard bounded on one side by a mill wall and at the back by a row of disused privies. It was half roofed over with an assortment of rusty, patchily painted, corrugated sheets, and it was piled high with unstripped pine and scrap metal. The big tank he had bought from Long John overflowed with old cookers and washing machines, a ferocious looking Alsatian quivered and yelped at the end of a taut chain.

Hung from the privy doors was an assortment of signs, all painted with Fiery's dashing disregard for uniformity. We were informed that best prices were paid for brass and copper; that rags were bought, also scrap cars and antiques.

The one that made Vicky and me smile was painted in florid pink, its bold characters stretching across the end privy to terminate three stones along the wall. It read, 'We'll buy owt that doesn't eat owt'.

'Come on, he won't touch you,' Fiery shouted encouragingly as he fondled the dog's ears. We followed him through the yard to a small door which gave into a large lean-to greenhouse set against the back wall of the house. 'Here's where I keep the good stuff.'

The glass had been painted white on the inside, to keep out prying eyes we were told, and the concrete floor was swept and clean. There were two mirror-backed sideboards, several washstands and, leaning against the far wall, the brass bed he had bought from us.

'You must have a good turnover, Fiery,' I told him.

'They keep coming, I keep buying. Come on, into the house—a veritable feast awaits us.'

The sitting room was dingy and crowded with furniture. Fiery introduced us to his mother, a small fat woman with straight dull hair and a round expressionless face. 'She's stone deaf,' he explained when she merely smiled at our greeting.

When Vicky hesitantly began signing to her, a grin spread across her face, revealing toothless gums. Her voice was low and husky; she almost hissed her words. 'I've heard of you two,' she said, stabbing a bent index finger towards the floor.

Fiery put his arm around her. 'You're a pearler, what are you?' he mouthed.

She laughed and threw back her head, 'He's a terror.'

'No I'm not, I'm a sterling character—ask him, ask anybody.'

Little Petal shuffled into the room carrying a tray of tea things which she set on a round table that was covered to the floor with a red checked cloth. Then she brought in plates and two enormous stand pies.

Fiery cut the pies carefully. 'These are Entwistle's, best stand pies in the world.'

'Don't let Thievin' Jack hear you,' I warned.

'You've got to come this side o' the Pennines for stand pies and bonny women,' he quipped, pinching Little Petal's cheek. 'How's our little Gunnar?'

'Still asleep,' Petal sighed.

Fiery waved away the proffered cup of tea. 'No, me and guv'nor'll have a drop of stout.'

I've often wondered who first established the pairing of certain foods; fish with chips, egg with bacon, cheese with onion—but one thing I now know, Entwistle's stand pie coupled with milk stout is the equal of any of them. No salt, not a smidgin of mustard is called for; the fragrant meat capped with a thin layer of succulent jelly, the pastry shiny and frangible, kissed to a glowing brown in a coal-fired oven is complemented perfectly by a rich mellow stout.

'Fiery, this is the king of pies.'

'Just the stuff for sterling characters,' he laughed.

His mother lay back in an armchair and smiled at all of us in turn. 'Nice pie,' Vicky signed. The old lady's eyes shone with happiness, and when young Gunnar's gentle, 'La, la,' became a demanding yell and Little Petal brought him downstairs and laid him in his grandmother's arms, she was in heaven.

'Alberta next door comes in and sits with her when we're off—they make a right team.' He squatted at his mother's feet and signed to her.

She laughed out loud and made a clenched fist. Fiery laughed too. 'I'm reminding her about the time they caught a bloke nicking copper out of the yard. That were before I got the dog. Alberta, she's bigger than 'er,' he indicated Little Petal with his eyes, 'sat on him and the old girl here whacked his arse wi' a length o' piping. He was screamin' blue murder when the cops come. "I never heard him," th'owd lass told 'em—well of course, she couldn't, could she?'

His mother was rocking with laughter, and even Little Petal managed a smile as she massaged another biscuit out of her caftan pocket.

Fiery knelt and pushed his face into Gunnar's plump belly and vibrated his lips, causing the child to shriek with laughter and wriggle his arms and legs wildly.

Little Petal cleared away the plates and cups, brushed crumbs on to the tray, and nibbled at a piece of pie crust that Fiery had left.

The room smelled musty; heavy drapes at the window made it dark and it was stifling hot. In need of some air and anticipating a tour of the yard I jumped up and stretched myself and asked Fiery if he had anything in my line. With a sly look he seized the red check table cover and with a flourish and a loud 'Ta—Ra' swept it aside, revealing not a table, but a campana shaped terracotta garden urn.

It was a beauty, early Victorian, with grotesque masks and swags in half relief.

'What do you think guv', is it worth a hundred and a half?'

CHAPTER TWENTY-ONE

Deliveries can be a revelation, and over the years we have learned not to judge by appearances. The well dressed and well spoken couple who bought the dining table do not, as we supposed, live in prim and pampered 1930s mock-tudor, but in a delightfully converted cow byre. The passing coal merchant pauses and sees our Edwardian inlaid display cabinet. Just right for the pigeon racing trophies he's won, he tells us, as he peels the notes on to the counter. 'Can't get it on me wagon—bring it up for us will you?'

He lives not alongside a blackened coalyard in a large seedy house with neglected garden, but in an imposing Georgian mansion. Of modest proportions admittedly, it is a gem of pale cream stone with pillared portico and balustraded terrace, lovingly maintained, surrounded by cosseted gardens enclosed with tightly pleached hedges.

We are instantly on our guard when the long haired youth leans his motorcycle against the shop wall. But he is polite, asks if he may leave his helmet on the duet stool, handles things gently, talks knowledgeably and thanks us as he leaves.

The middle-aged couple arrive in an upmarket foreign car. Their accents are clipped; with studied vowels and careful enunciation they criticise and clunk their way around. We are informed in a loud aside that the tantalus we are so proud of is not a patch on theirs, and when, thankfully, they leave we are a little put out. We feel annoyed as we straighten the cutlery on the table, close the writing

269

slope and put the book back on the shelf.

'What do you think?' Vicky asked, as she helped me load the late seventeenth-century kist into the van.

'Don't know—let me see—converted farmhouse, bit overdone, expensive furniture, couple of Labradors.'

'Yes, I think it will be very Homes and Gardens.'

We both liked Jocelyn Allingham, and we both disliked his wife. He was a surgeon, a heavily built, easy-going man; she, thin, with a peppery temper.

The instructions had been very explicit. Out of Middlethwaite on the moor road, past the limekilns seven tenths of a mile, across the water splash on the left and it's the second house. 'And be there between six and seven, we have some people coming,' she had added in a curt manner. I had given a mocking salute behind her, not realising she could see my reflection in the shop window.

'Did you used to be a chauffeur?' she had asked in an icy voice, turning and fixing me steadily with her cold, expressionless eyes.

The track up from the water splash was bordered with elder trees; white with blossom, their scent lay heavy and musky on the still air. Bees worked over them feverishly, adding to that undertone of insect murmur that accompanies every really hot summer's evening. The track began to rise steeply, and was cut across with deep gullies, making the van lurch and the wheels scatter dust and pebbles as they slipped then bit into the broken surface. At the top the fell side was planted with young conifers and the ruts had recently been filled with quarry waste. We came to the first house, small and stone-built with tin-roofed outhouses. It looked derelict but as we drew in the front of it the door opened and an old woman with wild grey hair threw a sizeable stone at us. As it clattered harmlessly under the wheels, I accelerated away, obscuring her in a cloud of dust.

'The natives aren't friendly,' I said jokingly to an amazed looking Vicky.

The Allinghams' place was, on the face of it, as we had pictured. A long low steading with mullioned windows and a gently undulating stone flag roof, covered with lichen. The garden was set to one side and slightly elevated from the track and it was the scene of a rather gay party. All the men were in dinner jackets and the women in evening gowns; three couples were dancing to a gramophone on a rough lawn, and several more lounged on the stone walls and on the garden seats.

Jocelyn Allingham leaned over the wall and smiled down at us. 'Splendid. Just a tick and I'll nip round and give you a hand.'

He appeared at the gate with a slim, round-shouldered man, who had plastered-down black hair and a round pimply face.

'This is Tarquin, by the way.'

We nodded in response to Tarquin's slight inclination of the head, and when we threw the van doors open he jumped into the van and, drawing the old army blanket aside, he squatted in front of the kist.

'Late eighteenth-century, nice piece—but the feet aren't original,' he said in one of those slightly lisping voices that can be attractive in a woman but never in a man.

'A bit earlier, and we have no reason to doubt that the feet are original,' I replied coldly. His

271

pimply face broke into a patronising smile.

I slid the kist to the back of the van. 'By the way, you've got a hostile neighbour.'

'Oh, no,' Mr Allingham groaned, 'she didn't stone you? I'm sorry, I should have warned you about Maggie.'

'Afraid so—it seemed a half-hearted show.'

'It wasn't yesterday. She landed one right on the bonnet of Tarquin's Porsche.'

'Oh dear—I am sorry to hear that,' I said, turning to fold the blanket and permit myself the tiniest of smiles.

'Yes, stupid old hag, she'll get my boot if it happens again,' Tarquin lisped. I looked down at the little patent leather shoes and remembered the wild looking woman.

She's nothing to fear, I thought.

'Didn't do you any damage?' Mr Allingham asked.

'No, just clattered under the van.'

'She's been doing it for almost two years now, ever since a forestry worker knocked down and killed her cat. She stones indiscriminately I'm afraid—anything on wheels—even bicycles.'

Tarquin insisted on carrying the chest with me.

'Humping', as it's called in the trade, has its techniques. Pick up a chest of drawers with a fellow dealer who knows how to lift and the hands go to the right position, the chest is laid back slightly, and without a word we lift it in unison.

Tarquin had neither technique nor strength. Three times in a dozen strides he grunted and without warning dropped his end. Finally Mr Allingham came to his aid and we got the chest safely into the house.

With her foot Mrs Allingham swept an area of threadbare carpet free of magazines. 'There, just there, under the window, that's where I want it.'

We lowered the kist gently, and I inched it back against the wall.

'No, no,' she cried, 'leave a gap. That wall is filthy damp.'

Filthy was an adjective that could have been fittingly applied to everything else. The floor was filthy, the curtains were filthy, ashes from long dead fires spilled from the hearth and were starred with cigarette butts. The table was littered with empty and half-empty bottles and dirty plates; dirty boots and wellingtons were thrown into the inglenook; cushions had been pulled from a window seat and bore muddy footprints; the sheepskin hearth rug was stained and ripped and half folded under itself.

The immaculately clad guests, glasses in hand, poured into the room to view the chest.

Tarquin held forth. 'It's a transitional piece of furniture, you see the drawers were—'

I caught Mr Allingham's eye.

'We have to be off.'

'You'll have a drink, surely?'

Before I could stop him gin and tonics were thrust into our hands. We went out and sat on the wall. The sun was low over the fells, casting long shadows from the trees and catching ripples on the beck and making them sparkle like fish scales. Behind the farmhouse, wood pigeons clapped their wings as they swooped in to roost. There was that magical stillness the Dale possesses at dawn and in the evenings.

From a hedgebottom came the rusty hinge 'cawk, cawk', of a cock pheasant, and far below us a sparrow hawk wheeled and glided in silent majesty.

A black kitten with a white bib walked slowly along the wall towards us. Vicky held out her hand and clicked her tongue encouragingly. It sniffed her fingers gingerly then dipping gracefully under her arm it climbed on to her knees and, with one paw raised, peered enquiringly into her face.

'You're beautiful, very, very beautiful,' she told it. The kitten gave a plaintive meow, revealing little teeth as white and thin as fishbones.

'You've found our little guest,' Mr Allingham laughed. 'She attached herself to us about a week or so ago. Don't know what to do with her; we're off back to London at the end of the month.'

'Give it to Maggie,' I suggested.

'She wouldn't accept it—won't have anything to do with us.'

'Can I have it?'

'Course you can.'

Vicky gave me a warning look. 'We can't take it—"the most beautiful cat in the world" will go bananas if we take another one home,' she whispered.

'Trust me,' I said, picking up the kitten, 'and you drive.'

It was a good half mile to Maggie's house, so I had plenty of time to explain my plan to Vicky as we bumped down the track.

'Approach the house very, very slowly and stop ten yards from it.'

'What if a stone comes whanging through the windscreen?'

'It won't. She reacts to vehicles speeding past. When one stops she'll be thrown—you'll see.'

I was right. Maggie half opened the door and

274

peered at us. She had a stone in her hand but she did not attempt to throw it.

'So far so good,' I said, as I leaned forward and pulled the bonnet catch. Clutching the kitten to my chest and shielding it from Maggie's gaze I slid from the cab and lifted the bonnet.

'Come on cat,' I hissed, 'let's have a few meows.' But there was not one peep from the little animal. As I fiddled in the engine compartment I could see Maggie from the corner of my eye. She had dropped the stone and was edging along the house wall. I began to meow, quietly at first, then louder.

Vicky's muffled laughter came from the cab, then a forced whisper, 'You're barmy.'

'Shut up and keep smiling,' I whispered back.

When Maggie reached the corner of the house she paused and looked about her. With a great show I pretended to lift the kitten out of the engine compartment and to my relief it began a plaintive and high-pitched meowing.

'Good Lord,' I cried, 'it's a cat. Must have climbed in when we were parked.'

Maggie took two or three hesitant paces towards me. She was crouched forward, her eyes fixed on the kitten.

I turned slowly to face her, holding the kitten out in one hand, feeling its wildly beating heart.

'Hold this for me for a minute, would you?'

Very, very, slowly Maggie reached out her hands and gently took the kitten.

I slammed the bonnet shut and leapt into the van. 'Come on, move,' I yelled.

Vicky grated the gears as we accelerated down the track; the van banged down on the shock absorbers, threw us from side to side, and raised a massive cloud of dust behind us.

We surged through the water splash and out on to the tarmac.

'Do you think she'll keep it?'

'Keep it? You should have seen the way she cupped her hands around that kitten—she lifted it to her chin, closed her eyes and smiled. I tell you woman that moggie's in for a lifetime of TLC.'

'What?'

'Tender, loving care,' I whispered, as I gently nibbled her ear.

*   *   *

The De Selincourts, in spite of their aristocratic name and ways, were very poor. Rabbit once charmingly described them as 'decayed gentlefolk', and this, I believe, was not very far from their own opinion of themselves.

'We were born to be rich,' Piers often told his flamboyant wife. She invariably sighed and agreed with him. They were a colourful and likeable couple, but they had such a cavalier attitude to life, and to creditors in particular. We had been warned about them many times, and the odd occasions they had popped into the shop and proffered a cheque in payment we had had our cover story ready.

'Sorry, we are selling that on behalf of a client. We must have cash—you understand?'

Eventually they understood and turned back to the auction houses, where over the years they accrued some massive debts. Drunken Sam was owed a considerable amount of money.

Now third generation auctioneers, expensively suited and impeccably mannered, have certain ways of calling in debts; and so do blunt, alcoholic ex cattle auctioneers.

Sam would roll up at all hours of the day or night in his battered car, hammer on their doors and windows and bellow through their letter box, 'Oi, when am I goin' to get me brass?'

The De Selincourts, on these occasions, shuddered and retired to the attic of their flat, peeping through a tiny rooflight until the disgruntled Sam called off the attack. For when one's neighbours are the daughter of a genuine baron, a retired naval officer of high rank, and the paramour of a fairly well known television personality, one has to be careful about one's dignity.

Sam, they decided, was not a gentleman, and he was owed the least of all—but he had to be paid. Consequently the next auction he held in the village hall had a little spice in it. The De Selincourts paid off the debt in kind, giving Sam some good but foxed hunting prints, a gold-handled riding crop, and two rather nice watercolours, by a Belgian artist; they were mid-nineteenth century and in very distressed frames, but as Sam pointed out, there was something about them.

The Ring thought so too. They lounged around the doorway laughing and smoking, half an ear cocked to the lot numbers Sam called out in his sonorous voice.

It was a really hot day, and Long John sweated beneath his brown smock as he lugged about bundles of soft goods. I was half interested in the sporting prints, not at all in the riding crop, but really taken with the Belgian nobleman's little pictures. They were coastal scenes depicting boats and fisherfolk, and they had a delightful lightness of touch and sense of depth in them.

They had not been accorded any special place, being stacked on the floor along with old wedding photographs and frameless mirrors. Sam, even though he had been sensitive enough to appreciate the fineness of them, obviously did not value them very highly. Long John's boots chipped bits of gilded plaster from their frames as he bustled backwards and forwards in response to Sam's, 'Keep 'em comin', John.'

Canary Mary sat in her usual seat at one end of the front row, her bags cluttered around her yellow shoes. Long John glared at her as he pushed them aside with his large boots.

'Mind me bags,' Mary exclaimed as he gave the one containing her flask and plastic box of yellow peril a particularly sly kick.

'You want to get them out of the way—you're going to break that glass,' he said, petulantly indicating the pictures. 'Aye, what yer say Sam? Let's get these selled.'

Sam agreed, for it was too hot to do otherwise, and he hadn't had a drink that morning.

'Nice little watercolours. What do you say ladies and gentlemen—a hundred pound?'

Nobody said anything. I very carefully peeped around a filthy kitchen cabinet at the Ring. Elly was well into a good story, flicking the ash from his cigarette as he drew the curvy outline of a woman in the air. The Ring laughed and smoked and lounged with eyes half shut against the sun.

I never start anything off at auction. There are wise owls who sit and watch the dealers, and over the years they learn to read us like a good poker player reads his opponent. So we hide like thieves in the night and convey our bids with a multiplicity of subterfuges.

There was no time for subterfuge. Carefully played I could land these pictures under the noses of the Ring.

I held up a hand of spread fingers and mouthed 'fifty' at Sam.

'Fifty pounds—well, it's a start.'

'Sixty,' came a confident shout from the side of the hall. It was Jocelyn Allingham. I groaned; London values and London money. I had no chance, but he was not going to get them for nothing. 'Seventy.'

Jocelyn turned and smiled at me then shook his head at the auctioneer. Sam sucked his upper lip in as he looked around the room.

'No. Well, I thought they would have made a bit more.' He brought the hammer down heavily. 'Now John, that's a nice mirror you have there. Just the mirror for a bonny woman—give us a pound for it, Mary.'

I tiptoed down the aisle and, with a smile at Long John, pointed at the watercolours.

'Aye—take 'em. Get 'em out of the way.'

The sporting prints were still to be sold, so I had no wish to antagonise the Ring, although I was sorely tempted to do so. I sneaked out of the side door and after a brief gloat put the pictures in the van.

Fatty Batty blew out his cheeks and complained about the heat. 'I'm off in, it's cooler inside.' He sat on a creaking plywood chest of drawers alongside the ugly 1950s kitchen cabinet. 'This thing stinks,' he grumbled as he edged away from it. I slid back one of the reeded glass doors and recoiled slightly. It looked as if it had been used as a medicine cabinet by some farmer, the strong pungent odour of Stockholm tar and sheep dip making me wrinkle my nose.

'And to think somebody's lived with that,' Fatty said, in a deep gravelly voice.

When the sporting prints came up the rest of the Ring trooped into the hall and draped themselves indolently over bits of furniture. 'Where's the watercolours?' Elly asked, a note of concern in his voice.

'They've gone,' one of the wise owls told him.

'Who's got 'em?'

'He did,' she said, pointing at me.

Pleasure in the discomfort of one's enemies: I'm sure the Greeks must have had a word for it—a long, multi-syllable, poetic word that is better than that harsh German one.

But even the descriptive brilliance of the ancient Greek philosophers would have been sorely taxed in any attempt to convey my feeling of euphoria; and when Fatty ground his teeth, kicked the poor little chest and asked me in rasping tones if I would take a profit on them, I nearly burst with happiness as I shook my head and whispered 'No.'

I bid the Aiken prints to dizzy heights, played the fool with the massive monochrome of the Bedale Hunt of 1878 and started the gold handled crop at thirty quid. The Ring glowered and bid me out of everything.

After the sale Jocelyn approached me. 'I liked the water-colours,' he said, 'but I dropped out when I saw it was you. After all, you have a living to make.'

280

I thanked him, and when he asked me if I would do him a favour I readily agreed. He had bought the smelly kitchen cabinet and wanted a lift with it.

When I had securely roped it on to the roofrack of the Volvo I jokingly asked him if he was ready to run the gauntlet.

'Gauntlet?'

'Yes, Maggie—the stone thrower.'

'Do you know,' he said, solemnly inclining his head and holding a jacket lapel in a legal looking way, 'we can't understand it—since that day you came up and delivered the chest she hasn't thrown one single stone.'

CHAPTER TWENTY-TWO

I used to laugh at Canary Mary's superstitions, especially the one about it being bad luck to cut one's nails on a Friday.

Vicky laughed as I stood in dressing gown and slippers in front of a fire banked for the night and with satisfying clicks of the cutters sent the clippings flying.

'To hell with the dark forces—it's a load of codswallop,' I said confidently, but next morning there was a crumpled note pushed through the letter box, big child-like writing in pencil.

'Will you feed my ferits and keep an eye on my place.'

Not, on the face of it, the worst of luck, being asked to help a neighbour: feed two ferrets and watch over his cottage. But when that neighbour is Rabbit and there is no indication of how long you will be required to perform these duties—it is not the best of luck. The simplicity of his lifestyle forces complications into other people's. When he ruthlessly ejects from his life something he considers to be mundane or time wasting it pops up like a cork in a bucket to cause someone else a problem.

He will not keep his poultry in, so the gardeners have to wire and fence. Miss Wells cleans the soiling from his dogs off her lawn and sprinkles pepper dust in vain. Mrs Lewis worries about the amount he owes her and extends his credit grudgingly; and when he is driven by extreme forces to earn a crust other than by poaching or moling, Baz sets him on at a generous rate. The Colonel shakes his head and tells us 'the man is incorrigible', but he still, as Chairman of the Drainage Society, steers all the weed-cutting and drain-clearing jobs his way, knowing full well that Rabbit will only do a token amount before presenting himself on his doorstep cap in one hand, the other outstretched, an ingratiating smile on his face.

'I'm not feeding them that revolting mess of rabbit guts and chicken parts he keeps for them. They'll get tinned dog meat and like it,' I said, as I pulled on my wellingtons. I cannot bring myself to like ferrets. They have a fluidity of movement and that feline grace that all efficient killers seem to possess, and their dedication in pursuit of their prey is remarkable. No one can fail to applaud the bravery of the gill in defence of her young, and if we ignore the coldness of their eyes and the savage look of their tiny mouths they can have a certain beauty; and, I am told, if they are kept meticulously clean they do not have such a rancid odour about them.

My big fear was that they would escape, but I found they were so taken with the dog meat I could have safely left the cages open as long as there was a trace of it left in their bowls. I even ventured to clean them out, removing a four-inch, nose wrinkling layer of bones and muck and urine soaked sawdust.

On the second day, a blisteringly hot one, I walked around the cottage exercising my stewardship, checking windows and trying doors. The door of the back porch was unlocked, and pinned on the game larder was another pencilled note. 'Ferit grub in here. Water the geraniums and feed the hens!'

I had forgotten about the hens. They roosted at the back of his motorbike shed, and by the time I got down to Rabbit's they were off down Mill Lane or searching through the neighbouring gardens.

I applauded Rabbit's sensitivity in foreseeing my reluctance to poke into and portion out that fetid and maggoty mess of innards he usually fed his ferrets on. In the larder were four tins of dog meat, and therein, I felt, lay a clue—a tin a day seemed reasonable. Rabbit would be off for four days. Pleased with my deductive powers I told Baz, who replied dourly, 'I thought he would be—he's gone to sort Joe Sixpence's stuff out.'

'Joe Sixpence?'

'Aye, big mate of Rabbit's, died last week. Queer owd stick he were, bent double.' Baz bent over to show the extent of Joe's deformity. 'Used to peep around the door of the Fighting Cocks and shout, "Hey up lads, me head's here, me arse is coming."' Baz shook his head in laughter then stared over my head at the fell, his eyes twinkling, a broad smile on his face. 'Aye, he'll be missed. Married a gamekeeper's widow up Sedbergh way—a fine, straight living woman. God knows what she saw in Joe, but they were happy enough.'

On the fourth day Rabbit returned; the Watsonian sidecar filled with gamebooks, cartridges, traps, stuffed heads of otter, badger and fox, and on top of it all was a lean looking fell hound, very much alive.

Rabbit pulled his two terriers out of his jerkin and stamped his legs as he slapped his gauntlets on to the motorcycle seat. His flying goggles were high on the black, pudding basin helmet, and were crusted with dead flies. The terriers chased around the garden, and the hound raised its head and started a deep baying.

'Everything all right?' he asked cheerfully.

'Yes—no problems.'

He lifted the hound out of the sidecar and tied it to a leg of a ferret hutch. 'This 'eres Speedwell, a hell of a lish dog. He's lost a bit of muscle whilst owd Joe wor bad, but we'll soon put that right— won't we?'

The hound curled a sickle tail over its back, laid its ears flat and throwing back its head gave voice once more. Rabbit thrust his face to mine, intent mischievous eyes, a mobile mouth. 'Thee and me will make some brass out o' that hound—thee wait an' see.' He lugged a trestle table from under the lean-to and began to unload the sidecar. 'All this stuffs for sale—barring his gun, I'm off to keep his gun. So don't just stand there, give us a hand.'

I looked over the crowded table. There was a bullet mould I liked, a Sykes powder flask just a little split at the seam and a Georgian dog collar, heavily studded and brass mounted. The rest was, in my opinion, unsaleable. All the traps were crusted with rust, the stuffed heads were tattered and moth-eaten and the gamebooks badly waterstained.

'Never mind,' Rabbit grinned, 'somebody will want 'em, 'specially when they know they were Joe's.'

'It took you four days to sort this out?'

'Bless you, no, there were dogs to sell. Allus a big dog man wer' Joe. I've been right up into Cumberland wi' some of his dogs—trail hounds, bred 'em all his life. They kept him, he never struck a bat, lived off them dogs—and women, there was something abart Joe: ugly as a pot dog, but women fair took to him.'

Rabbit took off his jerkin and bent to pat the hound, which had flopped into the shade of the huts. 'Aye, his widow's given me a bit of a problem; she's asked me to marry her.' He took one of the dog's ears in his hand and pulled it gently. 'Bit of a problem. I haven't legally got shut o' the first one yet. Anyway she's coming down to stop for a week or two! She's a grand woman—she's clever with engines—an' she can weld better than a lot of men.' He fixed his eyes on the little stone barn that stands in Ted's bottom land. Heat shimmers lay over its slate roof, like thin ethereal cushions, and from the pine trees behind Jubilee House came the soft cooing of a wood pigeon.

'It'll take a lot of thinking about. She's good with dogs an' she can throw a fair quoit.' He gave me a quick smile, his eyes heavy with irony. 'She's a remarkable cook—aye, you can shoe horses wi' her Yorkshire Puddings—but she looked after Joe well enough: she made him a meat an' tatey pie the very day he died. I tell yer, I'm fair tempted.'

'I'd like to meet this Mrs Sixpence.'

'Mrs Sixpence! Mrs Sixpence! Don't let her hear thee call her that—she'll knock thee flat on thi' back. It wor his nickname, Joe look for Sixpence on account of his being a bit bent like; his right name wor Gardener, that's why all his dogs have flower names. See,' he pointed down at the hound, 'Speedwell, and I've just sold Cranesbill and Periwinkle for his widow—an' that's where thee and me is going to make some brass. I'm offering thee a third share in Speedwell for twenty quid.'

'Very kind, but—'

'Wait until you know all the tale.' He placed a hand on my shoulder and leaned towards me until the pudding basin helmet almost touched my forehead.

'I'm not daft. I've kept the fastest dog, and them lads up there know it.' He shook me gently. 'An' that's how we can make a bob or two. Cos dogs can't allus run as predicted—get it.'

I didn't, but I pretended I did, giving him what I felt was a knowing smile. Rabbit tightened his grip.

'There's dogs that run to form an' them as don't; an' it's them as run to form that make men rich. Now, Speedwell here is a form dog, true as Ripon rowels that animal. Work his guts out for you he will; and he's intelligent. Worth his weight in gold that dog, an' I'm offering thee a third share for twenty quid—an' a pund a week keep money.'

I knew I would do well out of the watercolours I'd bought at Sam's, and if we can't go through life without a reckless decision or two it's best that they are made on a perfect summer's day.

'Go on, I'll have a bit of sport with you.'

'Good man.'

'Who are the other partners?'

'Well, there's me naturally, an' Baz, an'—look.' The hound stood up and yawned. 'See what I mean. Look at that depth o' chest, look at them legs, we can't fail man. We cannot fail.'

The last words were uttered with such feeling, such confidence, my fingers flew to my wallet.

*   *   *

The dog came on beautifully. Every day Rabbit had it out; rain or shine it jumped walls and gates, forded streams, streaked over open ground and breasted through heather until it became a super-fit animal without an ounce of fat on its muscled frame.

It glowed with health. Its eyes were clear, its coat like silk, the ever twitching nose shone like Whitby jet and the pink tongue lolled between glistening white teeth like a piece of choice boiled ham.

Baz and I had to agree that whatever Rabbit's shortcomings were, he certainly knew how to bring on a dog.

It was a Thursday afternoon, when I was digging up the first earlies, that I heard a shouted conversation that caused me some concern.

Thievin' Jack had left his travelling butcher's van on the green, and with a large aluminium bowl full of offal and bones under one arm he had walked down to Rabbit's cottage.

He returned whistling happily, slapping the empty bowl against the calf of his leg, and as he had climbed into the van he shouted out to Ted, 'Just taken some grub down for Speedwell—I've a third share in that dog.'

'So have I,' Ted shouted back.

When I reported this to Baz he groaned, closed his eyes, and let drop his cement bucket. 'The sod, the devious sod; he can't do owt straightforrard.' He leaned back on Miss Wells' gate post and folding his arms stared down at his scuffed boots. 'We'll have to find out how many *third* shares he's sold in this damned dog.'

Ted and Thievin' confirmed they each had a third share, and so did Charlie at the pub. 'We'll have to nail him,' Ted said, half closing his eyes and making his mumpy mouth.

Rabbit sat in the taproom, his terriers under the seat, Speedwell's head on his thigh. 'This is nice,' he said cheerily as we formed a semi-circle around him, 'all pals having a drink together—a bit of a chat.'

Ted drew up a stool and squatted in front of Rabbit, his eyes piercing into those of the old poacher. 'You're a lying, devious old git,' he said slowly and with feeling.

Rabbit pulled his chin in, making the light catch the silver stubble on his neck.

'Now, now, less of the old.'

'How many shares have you sold?' Thievin' asked, jabbing at Rabbit's arm with a rigid, nicotine stained finger.

'You've all got a third share apiece.'

'But there's five of us,' Charlie exclaimed.

'Aye, I know,' Rabbit smiled.

'Just a minute,' I said, leaning towards our dog trainer, 'have you still got a share?'

'Course I have.'

'That's six shares, each of one third—the only explanation is; there must be two dogs.'

Rabbit put his head back until it touched the boards of the old settle, one hand fell to Speedwell's ears, and the other hovered, fingers spread, over the table. 'It's like this—'

We drew nearer, the hovering hand slapped down on to the table making Rabbit's empty beer glass jump.

'It's like this—'

'Go on,' Baz said menacingly.

'It's like this—' Rabbit's head came forward and turned slowly from side to side. 'It's once every Preston Guild you get a dog like this, and my friend here,' Rabbit smiled at me, 'hit the nail on the head. What you've got is virtually two dogs. There's Speedwell here, as he is—and there's his potentials—and don't forget that now.'

'Potentials,' Baz and Ted said together, looking at each other then around the group.

Rabbit breathed deeply and lifted Speedwell on to the settle beside him. 'Joe would have been thrilled to bits wi' the way I've brought this dog on. He was a sporting man, he had trust in his friends. Why he said to me once, "Owt happens to me, Rabbit, take me best dog and you an' your pals have some sport with him." That's why I let you buy shares in him.'

'Potentials,' Charlie said, bending to Rabbit's ear, 'tell us about these potentials.'

Rabbit gave each of us in turn a hurt look before lifting the dog down from the settle, pushing his legs under the table and folding his arms. He wiped a hand around his stubbly chin, raised his cap slightly then tucked the hand firmly back into the crook of his arm. 'Potentials is as important a part of a dog as any, don't you go forgetting that he's an entire animal—what I'm talking of here is his breeding capabilities. Like gets like: I don't have to tell you chaps that, you've made a sound investment—trust me.'

The physicist tells us that light is both a wave and a particle. Rabbit tells us that Speedwell is the best trail hound in the north. We have no alternative; we have to accept these statements as absolute truths, for they are both the products of a mind which is supreme in its own field.

'Are we all satisfied?' I asked.

There was a general mumble of agreement, a broadening of Rabbit's smile that was abruptly reversed when Ted pushed his face up to Rabbit's and in a loud voice said, 'What about this quid a week keep money—are we all paying a quid a week?'

Rabbit pushed his lower lip out, thought awhile then answered in a low and wheedling voice, 'Well, it's a big dog; an' there's paraffin an' aniseed to buy.'

*   *   *

Rabbit pushed his motorbike and sidecar from under the lean-to.

It was a clear morning, with long fiery clouds on the horizon and just a tinge of sharpness in the air.

'Grand day for it, forecast is clear with a light breeze, but I hope you've plenty togs on, for it can be parky up on them fells—even at this time o' the year.'

I had a thick sweater under my waxed jacket,

290

two pairs of socks on my wellingtoned feet, and a deerstalker on my head. Baz was wearing new moleskin trousers, his best donkey jacket, and his workboots sported the dull sheen that is brought on by a good dubbining.

Rabbit had on his leather jerkin, his pudding basin helmet and a pair of mulberry coloured corduroys that had belonged to Joe Sixpence. They were on the short side, but when he brushed down the turnups and folded them into his high laced boots they gave him a racy look and that dash of colour that all sporting men seem fond of.

Baz was to ride pillion and I was to go in the sidecar with Speedwell. The hound was lean and fit; his ribs, showing slightly, were hard under my hands as I pushed him down between my knees. The sidecar stank of oil and grease and kippers. My wellingtons slid on jingling spanners, a grease gun rolled persistently about, and the small brown case Rabbit had stuffed in the front and warned me to keep an eye on, chaffed against my ankle.

Speedwell had come, as a pup, from Cumbria. He was a willing hound—a trier—and he was excited. As we pulled out of Rabbit's yard he threw back his head and bayed loudly, exciting Rabbit's terriers into a frenzy of yapping. They ran back and forth in the window of his cottage, clawing at the glass and tearing holes in the yellowed lace curtains. Ted was coming down to see them at lunchtime and feed the ferrets.

There may be some foolhardy people who have an inborn recklessness, a love of speed, a disregard for life and limb who would actually have enjoyed that heart in the mouth, sweaty palmed, heart thumping terror that I experienced on that journey

291

over the tops.

Left-hand bends with the sidecar wheel spraying grit from the gutter, then bouncing on to the grass verge and losing contact with the ground for many yards, were frightening. Right-hand ones engulfed me in sheer terror; as Rabbit and Baz leaned away from me I clutched the dog closer and thrust myself down into the body of the sidecar, sure that it would be torn adrift and be hurtled into a stone wall, a ravine, a stand of timber, whatever had flashed before my eyes before I pressed them shut and winced.

Rabbit crouched over the handlebars, a grim set to his mouth, whilst Baz clutched at his ample waist, his face white, streams of tears sucked from his eyes. Speedwell whimpered: it was, as Rabbit had told us, an intelligent hound.

I prayed for straight bits of road; a hundred yards brought a moment's sagging relief; that wonderful ecstatic stretch past Stone House gave me all of fifteen seconds to compose myself and thank God I'd left the business and smallholding in a sound state. I pictured Vicky and the children, hugged the dog to me and swore that if I was allowed to live through that day I would never again indulge in any sharp practice: the Ring could get stuffed, I'd never lose my temper with the children, I'd sell my gun and throw away my snares and traps, I'd look after all God's little creatures in Ramsthwaite, and Vicky could have the side garden for flowers.

As we passed Hardraw and I saw winding up the Dale that thin glistening strip of tarmac as sensuous as a snake, I tugged at Rabbit's arm. 'Slow down— for God's sake slow down.'

A big, yellow-toothed grin, his head turned to

me for an alarming length of time. 'Yer alright,' he shouted, 'don't worry—Rabbit's in the saddle.'

'You're upsetting the dog—it's shivering,' I lied. To my certain relief, and to Baz's I'm sure, Rabbit did slow down a little. Sedbergh seemed a nice enough town, its cobbles fair sped under the wheels as I lay back and watched the shop fronts flash by. The woman whose shopping bag we speared on the sidecar light and carried a hundred yards up the road did not seem too perturbed. We missed both cats, and the old chap who flung his sticks away and did an astonishing backwards leap of a good eight feet would have something to talk about in the pub.

I started to grin when I saw the scattering of cars on the hillside catching the pale sunlight. A dip in the road, a slightly worrying narrow bridge and then a lovely slow climb in bottom gear.

Baz got down off the pillion with a long drawn-out 'awe' that was partly relief, partly the pain in his legs, as Rabbit flung his gauntlets on to the saddle in a showy way and unbuckled his helmet.

'Let's have that hound out—he'll be wanting to relieve himself.'

'He's not the only one,' Baz sighed.

Rabbit reached between my legs and took out the small brown case. 'I'll let 'em know we're here an' then I'll get this animal fettled.' He strode off with hound and suitcase shouting a greeting here, a friendly insult there, telling a bent old man he was surprised to see him—he'd thought he was dead.

I climbed out of the sidecar and flopped into the heather alongside Baz. Neither of us spoke. We lay on our backs and stared up at a duck-egg blue sky with brisk moving patches of woolly cloud as white

293

as freshly fallen snow. I had not realised it was such a beautiful day.

There was a general hubbub: men shouting and laughing, hounds barking, whining, yelping. One hound started to bay, the long, drawn-out, deep mournful bay that is music to a fellman's ears. It was joined by others, and from cars and vans and little trailers with grilled doors the rising surge of noise became so dense it was almost tangible before it fell away as quickly as it had risen.

It was an earthy crowd, flat capped and wellingtoned, open neck shirted in the main, with a leavening of thornproof tweeds and polished brogues and deerstalker hats.

They stood in groups, leaning on beautifully dressed sticks; a leaping trout, a hound nose to the scent, a sheepdog crouched and tense; big hands workworn and reddened, sharp eyes set deep in thin faces that smiled a lot.

Hardworking, sound and steady, men from the fells and Dales of Yorkshire and Cumbria out for a day's sport, a bit of a chin wag with an old friend or two, to watch good fit hounds that knew their job and went to it with an eagerness. No bloody and mangled furry bodies at the end of the day, just tired hounds and contented men, an innocent trail of paraffin and aniseed to be blown gently away on the breeze.

Baz prised himself up on one elbow. 'He's a lunatic—I'm not going back with him. I'll walk, hitch a lift. He rides that bloody bike as if it was a seventeen hands hunter. When we came round that corner at Doveghyl, he dug his heels in and pulled back at the handlebars, I was convinced he was going to put it at the hedge—I tell you, he's a lunatic. Where's he off to now?'

Rabbit answered the question by appearing with the hound from a clump of bushes. He shoved the little suitcase to the front of the sidecar and stood with his arms akimbo looking down at us, a quizzical look on his red face.

'Come on, it's nearly time for the first run—you'll have to get down there if you've money to put on, not that they're offering owt worthwhile on Speedwell—word gets around you know. They're sharp buggers, they soon get wind if there's a tickle on.'

'You put owt on?' Baz asked.

'Course I have, every penny I've got—on the nose.'

They were offering evens on Speedwell, and shamed by the big money Baz was wagering on behalf of the villagers and other shareholders, I upped my bet from a fiver to a tenner.

'Might as well hang for a sheep as a lamb.'

'That's it,' Rabbit laughed, 'the easy downhill slope to ruin.'

Three blasts on a hunting horn summoned the hounds to the starting line; a jostling pack, keen to be off, yelping excitedly, straining to be free of their handlers, leggy hounds with no spare flesh, all bone and muscle.

Rabbit pushed Speedwell into the centre of the ragged line, took off the leash and flung it back to us, then crouched over the dog, his two big hands around its deep chest, restraining it as it reared on back legs and bayed and trembled with excitement.

The starter stood twenty yards in front, his white flag raised, a whistle between his lips. One shrill blast, the flag dashed to the ground, and they were

295

off.

The hounds streaked down into the valley in a noisy loose pack, poured over a stone wall then spread out as they climbed the fell. We caught flashes of white amongst the heather as they breasted the hill, then they were gone.

A cry from a distant hill top, a pointing arm and we trained our binoculars on a hurrying clutch of white dots which soon disappeared.

Cigarettes and pipes, flasks and sandwiches were brought out and the little groups re-formed, more idle chatter, 'My Wingnut needs a longer course.'

'He asked how much start I wanted for Damson—I said a fortnight.'

'That big wall at Fleshbeck, owd Gem won't like that.'

Baz and I strolled back to the motorbike. Rabbit was sitting in the sidecar chewing on a piece of cheese, and he offered no protest when Baz took the key from the ignition and gave it to me. 'He's driving us back—right.'

A ten mile course in less than half an hour. I had barely had my sandwiches and got my pipe cracking before the watcher on the hill gave out a long halloo—they were in sight again and on the home stretch.

The handlers hurried to the finishing line with feed buckets and bowls. Baz and I followed them, pressing our binos to our eyes.

Two dogs were well in front of the rest of the pack, a big rangy hound, predominantly white, and Speedwell. The handlers began shouting, blowing whistles and rattling their buckets as the hounds rounded a small knoll and began the steady climb to the finish.

'Speedwell!' I screamed. 'Speedwell! Come on Speedwell!'

Baz pulled me around and nodded intently towards a crouching Rabbit who was banging his knees with his fists and shouting wildly for a hound called Cranesbill.

'Ello!' Baz said grimly but I neither knew nor cared about any Cranesbill, for Speedwell had gained on the other hound and I shrieked his name until he plunged over the finish line a clear six lengths in front.

There was a boiling ferment of hounds and handlers which I pushed my way through to grab Speedwell.

'You're a beauty, you're a beauty,' I said, holding his panting head in my hands then slapping his heaving flank.

'You've a hell of a hound there, Mister.' It was the watcher from the hill. 'He was way behind at The Dubbs, then he went down t'beck, supped an' supped an' supped, sicked up a gert pile o' summat, then he wor off like streaked lightning, caught up wi' Cranesbill, an' held him all the way.'

'Sicked something up?'

'Kippers,' Baz said, appearing at my elbow with a grim look on his face. 'That owd bugger over there,' he jerked his thumb towards Rabbit, who was slumped in the sidecar, 'tried to spike him with kippers, just smell his muzzle. I showed you he was shouting for Cranesbill. The devious underhand ghet.'

'But why?'

'The odds—what else. Speedwell was evens, Cranesbill was three to one, so he spikes Speedwell, puts his brass on Cranesbill—the ghet.'

297

Baz leaned from the pillion and punched Rabbit's shoulder as I kicked the engine into life. 'How much did you have on?'

Rabbit mumbled something and pulled Speedwell's ears.

'How much?' Baz shouted.

'A hundred bloody quid,' Rabbit growled.

'All the share money—every floggin' penny,' Baz laughed, 'an' they say there's no justice in this world.'

I had nearly mastered the gears by the time we got to Sedbergh and luckily there was no errant shopping bag, no panicky cats, just a lone walking stick in the gutter by the bus shelter.

It was a lovely evening and I began to enjoy the ride home. Baz sang lustily, Rabbit slumped in the sidecar a dejected heap, his arms folded tight, the hound between his knees.

We paused on top of the moor road and then with shouts and cheers and the horn blaring we swept down the bank into the village and into the pub yard.

Spend your childhood in a village and you acquire a deep knowledge of the minutiae of its topography. How it is possible to squeeze between the gate and Jubilee House and into the maypole field: you know every nook and cranny formed by buildings that evolved rather than were planned, you know that the telegraph pole in the pub yard is further out from the wall than you would think.

Alas, I had no child's knowledge of Ramsthwaite, I had merely walked its lanes and paths, rambled over its fields and common a thousand times with the half-seeing eyes of an adult.

The sidecar wheel caught the pole. There was

a bang, the bike leapt and juddered under me, a rending of metal as the mudguard was torn away, a hiss of air escaping from the burst tyre, then a wobbly cruise to a halt.

When Baz and I jumped from the machine the sidecar wheel gently collapsed, the hound leapt from Rabbit's grasp as his body was flung sideways and after sniffing at the distorted tyre raised his leg and sent a stream of urine over the sidecar door and on to Rabbit's jerkin.

I waited for the outburst, that beautifully constructed, almost poetic stream of bellowed obscenities that Rabbit is so well known for. Silence. Absolute silence as I apologised, silence as Baz apologised, silence as we offered to lift him free, silence as we castigated Speedwell for his lack of manners, silence as we finally shrugged and walked into the pub, the hound at our heels.

'Shall I take him a drink out?' I asked Baz.

'No—he'll come round; an' don't you worry about that sidecar, you've done a service to mankind there.'

Rabbit did come round. Baz had paid out the winners, and I had sold my share in the hound to Ted, when he threw open the taproom door, stomped up to the fire and draped his wet jerkin to dry. He dropped heavily on to the settle opposite me and Speedwell and stared at me in a most unfriendly way.

'Go on, have a pint with me just to show there's no hard feelings,' I said.

He did not reply, merely taking the offered pint glass and turning it slowly on the table, his eyes following me back to my seat.

Speedwell jumped on to the settle beside me and

pushed a kipper smelling muzzle against my arm. Very slowly Rabbit looked from me to the hound, then back to me. I saw the faintest of smiles twitch at his mouth then his chest began to shake and the smile widened to become a grin then a full blown laugh. His hand went to his face and the fingers scrubbed his stubbly chin in his characteristic way.

'Pillocks—a coupla pillocks. I can manage one in a day—but two; just about puts the cap on any bit o'country business.